NURSES WHO KILL

OCTOBER, 1987
GOOD SAMARITAN HOSPITAL,
RIVERHEAD, NY.

Resting comfortably in his hospital bed, Mr. Cucich noticed a man dressed in hospital whites standing in his room.

After asking Cucich how he was feeling, the man in white produced a syringe and injected the elderly patient's intravenous tube with "something that would make him feel better."

Seconds later, Cucich was fighting for breath, his body racked with cramps and his muscles paralyzed.

He gasped for help, hoping that the nurse on duty would hear him.

But what Cucich didn't understand was that the man in white *was* the nurse on duty.

His name was Richard Angelo, the so-called Angel of Death who stalked the wards for helpless victims just like him.

NURSES WHO KILL

CLIFFORD L. LINEDECKER AND WILLIAM A. BURT

PINNACLE BOOKS
WINDSOR PUBLISHING CORP.

PINNACLE BOOKS

are published by

Windsor Publishing Corp.
475 Park Avenue South
New York, NY 10016

First printing: December, 1990

Printed in the United States of America

To Norma Burt for her picture-perfect support

ACKNOWLEDGMENTS

We are indebted to many individuals and organizations for their contributions to the preparation and accuracy of this book.

Police officers, prosecuting attorneys and members of their staffs, courthouse employees, and journalists have all had a hand in its production from the initial concept to the completed manuscript.

But special thanks are due to to Nan Vaughan, RN, for providing much needed input and criticism from a medical professional; Melanie Faith and Ellen Donahue for help with research; and to our literary agent, Adele Leone, for her faith in us and her hard work in our behalf.

CONTENTS

AUTHOR'S NOTE

The following definitions will help the reader who is not a health professional sort out the degrees of education, experience, and skill of nurses referred to in this book.

LICENSED PRACTICAL NURSE: An individual trained in basic nursing techniques and direct patient care, who must practice under the supervision of a registered nurse. The course of training for a LPN usually lasts one year.

LICENSED VOCATIONAL NURSE: This term is used synonymously with LPN. The term is more commonly used in some states, such as Texas, than in others.

NURSE'S AIDE: A person who is employed to carry out basic nonspecialized tasks such as bathing, feeding, making beds, and transporting patients. Most states now require certification, which requires attendance at a state-approved training class and passing an examination for that state.

REGISTERED NURSE: A professional nurse who has completed studies at a state-certified school of nursing and passed the National Council Licensure Examination. RN licensing is a responsibility of individual states.

PREFACE

No one ever enjoys being whisked off to a hospital. To most patients it means isolation from family and loved ones . . . and the ever-present fear of serious health problems.

One in three Americans, at any given time, are in the hospital or have relatives or friends under health care. That simple statistic highlights a problem which we'll have to consider at one time or another in our lives.

One all-important consolation in cases of life-threatening illness and trauma is that it's the one safe haven where we can get the quality care, technology, and medical supervision to recover.

Or so we think.

As authors Linedecker and Burt graphically reveal, serial murders and vicious assaults in hospitals, nursing homes, and the general area of health care are a sad and frightening, relatively new phenomena.

Even more sickening is that medical experts sadly concede that victim statistics do not accurately reflect the abnormally high incidence of such attacks, which have spread like a cancer in recent years.

The horror stories unfolded for the first time in this book are almost certainly the tip of a deadly iceberg.

Whether we're talking about hospitals, nursing homes, retirement facilities, or home care, each and every patient is and will remain a vulnerable potential victim until radical steps can be taken to eradicate this clear and present danger in our midst.

Of the incidents that have come to light, we have clear-cut cases of health professionals who run amok. Or have been allowed to run amok, sometimes over a period of years.

And the amazing thing about many of these self-styled executioners in white is that, when unmasked, they don't turn out to be the drooling, wild-eyed homicidal maniacs you see in movies or television horror films. Instead, the medical menaces are revealed as unlikely suspects, most of them outwardly gentle, compassionate, respected by their co-workers.

And they tend to have a lot in common, everything from unhappy, sexually-abused childhoods to latent, potentially dangerous personality disorders.

Abject cowardice is another shared trait. Invariably their victims are chosen from the very young, the very old, the helpless, the frail, and the vulnerable. And the crimes are orchestrated carefully and cautiously to defy detection, usually under a cloak of darkness.

Obviously this insidious new epidemic of serial killings presents a myriad of problems when trying to figure out motives and possible solutions.

Severe cutbacks in hospital funding and care for the aged have obviously played some part in the proliferation of this type of crime. This has placed intolerable stresses on overworked health administrators and hospital staffs who can barely get through a normal workday, let alone adequately oversee the competence of supposed "professionals" under their charge.

At the same time, however, there is an alarming inability on the part of health-care administrators to face up to the harsh reality of this horrible plague. Too often, as this book hammers home, a whole slew of suspicious deaths are initially categorized as mere coincidence – and nothing is done about them until it's too late.

The seriousness of the situation cannot be trivialized, not when human life is concerned. Health-care authorities have a sacred trust to preserve these lives, no matter the cost in money, time, or research.

Time and money *must* be set aside to deal with this bizarre crime wave before it destroys the entire fabric and faith in our health-care system.

It intrigues me that airline pilots and bus drivers—both responsible for the safety of large numbers of people—are subject to regular fitness and competence reviews, in some cases as frequently as every six months. It saddens me that health-care workers—who share an equal, if not greater, public-safety responsibility—can work for years without such evaluations, their continuing ability never questioned.

Regular and rigorous reviews of existing staff, plus a strict and careful screening of newcomers, is the obvious place to start in rectifying an already desperate situation.

It is encouraging that the highly efficient U.S. Center for Disease Control, headquartered in Atlanta, Georgia, has come up with a sophisticated computerized system which has proven effective in tracking down and solving hospital problems, pinpointing everything from faulty equipment to human error.

But most important is the system's ability, within a comparatively short period of time, to point a finger at a specific suspect. In two recent cases, in Maryland and Georgia, the CDC's system provided the names of possible culprits after an investigation into a series of suspicious attacks. Both were nurses.

The nurses were brought to trial. Since the new tracing technique cannot ascribe total guilt, one of the nurses was acquitted, and the other found guilty of a lesser charge.

But, in each case, the rash of deaths and assaults at the hospitals was stopped in its tracks.

In light of these encouraging examples, there is a solid argument for *all* hospitals to adopt and adapt their own in-house tracking system to stop this senseless carnage once and for all. The results far outweigh the cost in both dollars and lives.

For the moment, health-care supervisors and administrators all over the country must be shaken from their delusions that hospital homicides are isolated aberrations.

More and more of them are coming to light. They are a harsh

reality which won't go away. This grim but fascinating book underscores the seriousness and urgency of the situation.

Stephen E. Langer, M.D.
General Preventive Medicine
Berkeley, California

14

INTRODUCTION

For most middle-age and older Americans, the first recollection of serial medical homicide probably involved the accusations against a pair of young Filipina nurses who worked at a huge veterans' hospital in Ann Arbor, Michigan.

The dramatic case broke on the public consciousness during the hottest days of the blistering summer of 1975, and before it spluttered to a close that was unsatisfactory to nearly everyone almost three years later, the nurses had undergone an emotionally devastating trial, the First Lady of the Philippines had angrily charged the United States with carrying out a vicious racist plot, and the medical community was rent with deeply bitter divisions.

It all started when patients at the huge VA Hospital in the university city just west of Detroit, Michigan, began suffering episodes of cardio-pulmonary arrest at an alarming rate. In a brief period of about six weeks from early July and into August, thirty-five patients, all on IV's, suffered sudden attacks and were given hasty emergency treatment. Some were stricken more than once. Eleven of the patients died.

On a single terrible day, August 15, seven patients were stricken with cardio-pulmonary failure, including four who died.

Hospital employees at first credited the survival of many of those who lived to the heroic effort of two Filipina nurses, Leonora M.

15

Perez and Filipina B. Narciso. In one emergency after another, it seemed that the young women were the first to rush into the stricken patient's room to begin administering life-saving artificial respiration.

So it was a shock, when, after a year-long investigation by the FBI and local police agencies, the two nurses were arrested and charged with murder in the poisoning of several patients.

The bodies of four of the veterans who died during the quixotic near-epidemic of cardio-pulmonary arrests had been exhumed and autopsied. The autopsies disclosed little that the pathologists didn't already know about the deaths, until tissue samples sent to FBI laboratories in Quantico, Virginia, were analyzed. The laboratory tests disclosed the presence of Pavulon in the tissue of each of the men. The drug is a powerful muscle relaxant sometimes described as a synthetic version of curare, the deadly poison South American Indians use to tip their hunting arrows with. Used improperly, Pavulon can temporarily paralyze—and kill.

But the effects of Pavulon, like its sister drug, succinylcholine—which you will read about elsewhere in this work—disappears quickly and its presence is extremely difficult to detect without sophisticated laboratory tests.

Investigators had also inspected patient charts and learned that one or the other of the two nurses was on duty during each crisis. Both nurses pleaded innocent to the charges.

The dramatic trial was front-page news in both the United States and in the Philippines. More than twelve thousand Filipina nurses were working in the U.S., and supporters in both nations raised more than ninety thousand dollars for the defense of the two beleagured women. The war chest included a large donation from Mrs. Imelda Marcos. And President Ferdinand Marcos's brother, Dr. Pacifico Marcos, headed the international fund drive.

The First Lady of the Philippines was as outspokenly supportive with her words as she was with her money, and publicly charged that the case against the nurses was an extension of an unfair U.S. immigration policy. She claimed the charges against the two women was part of a sinisterly orchestrated scheme to keep Filipina nurses out of the country.

But Mrs. Marcos and her fellow Filipinos weren't the only sup-

16

porters of the defendants. U.S. nurses' groups, feminists, and other liberal activists in this country also rallied to their support.

Some American liberals charged that the FBI was the villain in the case, and that the agency set up the foreign nurses as scapegoats to prove itself after its recent humiliating failure to solve the kidnapping and mysterious disappearance of labor leader Jimmy Hoffa.

Overnight, it seemed, the case had become an international cause celebre. The government of the Philippines announced it was sending an observer to sit in on the trial.

When the trial opened in U.S. District Court in Detroit, prosecutors claimed that the women, without intending to murder, were deliberately creating the emergencies among their helpless patients in efforts to dramatize the need for more nurses. The nurses' defense insisted that they were loyal and dedicated health-care givers and the case against them was purely circumstantial. Midway in the thirteen-week trial, at about the same time Nurse Perez gave birth to a second son, the judge tossed out the murder indictment against her. But he allowed most of the charges of poisoning to remain.

At the conclusion of the trial, and after fifteen days of deliberation, the jury found each of the nurses guilty of three charges of poisoning and conspiracy. But Nurse Narciso was acquitted of the murder charge against her. The defense immediately appealed the convictions.

The nurses remained free pending adjudication of their appeals and returned to the Philippines to heroes' welcomes. Nurse Perez's hometown feted her with a parade.

A few months later, the federal court judge who had presided at the trial set aside the convictions. He blamed "persistent misconduct" on the part of prosecutors for polluting the waters of U.S. justice and said the government's case was entirely circumstantial. No evidence was ever presented to show that either of the nurses had the paralyzing drug Pavulon in their possession, he declared.

Some time after that, prosecutors announced that they would not seek new trials. Both women returned to the United States to live.

But no one, it seemed, won anything from the entire sad affair. Patients did die mysteriously at the hospital. The two nurses had

17

been dragged through an exhausting, and pathetically pernicious ordeal. A serious political rift was torn in relations between two long-time world allies who sincerely needed each other. The FBI had been publicly maligned for doing its job. The medical safety and usefulness of the drug Pavulon had been seriously questioned. And some elements of the medical community were temporarily split into warring camps.

Yet the saddest part of the entire affair was the failure to learn from the experience. The deaths at the veterans' hospital in Ann Arbor occurred fifteen years ago, and no one apparently paid any attention to the clarion call of warning.

Today, as you will see in the chapters to follow, frail, infirm, and helpless patients are still dying mysteriously in hospitals, nursing and retirement homes, and in home health-care at the hands of medical serial killers. Others are being emotionally and physically brutalized, some sexually attacked in their beds by the very people they must trust most.

Hospitals and nursing homes are understaffed, nurses are over-worked, and the pay of health-care professionals is generally low. Patients too often are given the wrong medication, overdoses of medication, or deprived of medication they should be taking.

A shocking poll a few years ago of five thousand hospital nurses by the publishers of a professional magazine disclosed that nearly one out of ten admitted they had deliberately given potentially le-thal narcotics overdoses to dying patients. And many said they would do it again.

There can be no question that more effective screening methods are needed to pinpoint drug and alcohol abusers, brutal, burned out, or sexually abusive individuals in the medical care field.

Although most hospitals follow "quality assurance" guidelines recommended by the Joint Commission on the Accreditation of Healthcare organizations, which represents eighty-five percent of U.S. hospitals, the guidelines are limited when it comes to review-ing suspicious deaths. It is normally left to the chief of a depart-ment to conduct a painstaking investigation of each death—all too often a painfully slow process.

Today senior health officials are advocating that quality assur-ance programs be taken a step further and that hospitals adopt a tracking program. In particular, they suggest that the techniques current in epidemiology research—used routinely to track the spread of infection—could be extended to hospitals. Not only would this supervision discourage people tempted to kill, or expose such cases sooner, but it would also improve the quality of health care, say officials.

Dr. Jeffrey J. Sacks, an investigator in the division of injury control at the Center of Disease Control in Atlanta, says that the common practice in some hospitals is for committees to review patients' deaths. "But in an intensive care unit, when a patient dies, it can always be argued that he was going to die anyway," observed the doctor-investigator. By applying epidemiological research techniques, one could quickly find out if the deaths had a pattern—in relation to personnel, equipment, and drugs, for example.

Said Dr. Sacks: "You tell me how long you would wait before you saw something out of the ordinary using this technique. I say you would not have to wait very long at all. I'm not saying that this can stop these things from happening. But one can certainly pick up on them once you look for them."

In Ann Arbor, the opportunity to seriously determine if we are adequately protecting medical and long-term care patients and assuring them of safe, efficient, professional, and—yes, tender, loving care—was lost when society allowed itself to become sidetracked by other issues that were not the most central to the case.

It is time to heed the warnings.

ONE

Genene Jones Turk
Baby Killer

Genene Jones always cried when babies died!

And babies and small children died often when they were in the care of the dedicated licensed vocational nurse (LVN). Either deliberately disregarding criticism that she was acting unprofessionally, or simply unable to react any differently, the grief-stricken nurse would cradle the mournfully silent bundles in her arms and cry and shake with remorse all the way to the morgue.

It was early in 1981 when the tiny charges first began dying in unusually high numbers in the pediatrics department's intensive care unit, (PICU) at the Bexar County Hospital. Part of a sprawling medical center in San Antonio, Texas, the county hospital specializes in charity cases and care of the poor.

Genene took it especially hard when Christopher Hogeda died. The infant had already spent more than half his ten months of life in the PICU with a series of congenital heart problems when he suffered cardiac arrest a few minutes before 7 P.M., on May 21.

Genene was the three-to-eleven evening-shift nurse assigned to his care, and she was already hovering over the small, inert form in the crib administering CPR when the first doctor arrived in response to the Code Blue emergency alert.

Code Blue is commonly used as an emergency alert that a patient is dying. The choice of a code word was designed so that when it is announced over a hospital's public address system it won't frighten other patients or visitors. When Code Blue booms out, doctors, nurses, and technicians—all part of a trained revival team—rush to the patient's bedside. The code is usually announced after a monitoring machine records a heart or lung failure, or after a nurse or aide notices a patient in extreme distress. Most patients in cardiac or intensive care units are hooked to monitoring machines that alert the nurses' station that something is wrong.

Even as the doctor took charge of the Code Blue team, injecting drugs and trying to restore the heart's normal beat with a defibrillator, Genene refused to take a backseat in the desperate life-saving effort. She tried to tell the doctor what drugs to use, and became increasingly insistent when he ignored her suggestions as he desperately struggled to revive the baby. Finally he snapped at her to shut up.

The frumpy LVN responded as if she were a balloon someone had just pricked with a pin and suddenly let the air out of. She hyperventilated, gasped for breath, and slumped to the floor gagging and sobbing. Two husky aides half carried and half dragged the deadweight of her bulky, helpless form from the cubicle and out of the room.

A few minutes later, after the young doctor and the remaining members of his Code Blue team had tried everything in their bag of medical miracles to restore life without success, they reluctantly accepted the inevitable. Christopher was pronounced dead. It was 7:32 P.M. When Genene later returned to the room, she unhooked the maze of tubes and wires, tenderly washed the little boy's body, wrapped him in a blanket, and sat down with him. Clutching the silent corpse to her body, she crooned and softly talked to him until his frantic parents arrived. When Christopher was buried in San Angelo, some two hundred miles northwest of San Antonio, Genene attended the funeral and cried.

The LVN's theatrical performance wasn't the first time her aggressive take-charge attitude and her unprofessional display of emotion verging on hysteria had drawn unflattering attention to her behavior from colleagues. Although as an LVN she had obtained her license after only one year of training and was near the bottom of nursing's professional roles, she had barely joined the staff in

22

1978 before she began acquiring a reputation for bossiness and interfering with other nurses and doctors.

Nurses do not tell doctors what to do. And they don't come in on their own time to check on patients who are being cared for by colleagues on other shifts. But Genene did both. Fledgling physicians angrily complained that she tried to order them around and recommended medications. She tried to boss other nurses, and at least one LVN refused to share patients with her. She simply wouldn't work with Genene.

But other nurses, and some of the administrators, saw more that was positive than negative in Genene's work performance. Though the former hairdresser was a single mother of two children and had plenty to keep her busy at home, she worked long hours, usually showing up early and willingly filled in on extra shifts when the hospital was short-staffed. And she was also a highly skilled nurse. She was especially appreciated for her unfailing ability to insert needles into the delicate, elusive veins of babies when doctors needed to utilize intravenous lines. It was a skill that eluded some of her nursing colleagues, as well as harried residents. But above all, the domineering nurse gave even some of her most unforgiving critics the grudging impression of a devoted care-giver. The hurt seemed to be terrible, and agonizingly personal whenever one of her tiny patients died.

The very first time a child she was caring for died, Genene huddled miserably on a stool in the room, rocking back and forth for almost a full half hour sobbing and moaning. It was an agony that she repeated many times, especially after Christopher's death.

Three days after the Code Blue team lost their effort to save Christopher's life, another infant died following cardiopulmonary arrest. The death of the five-month-old baby occurred on nurse Jones's shift.

A two-month-old boy died on June 7, after his second cardiac arrest in three days. Genene was his nurse.

A seven-year-old shocked the staff on June 15, by failing to awaken after surgery and dying of cardiac arrest. He was under the care of a registered nurse, but Genene was present when he died.

A toddler died on July 3, after his third successive cardiac arrest in as many days. Genene was his nurse.

A two-month-old who was admitted to the PICU with a high fever after earlier treatment for diarrhea and vomiting, died on August 11 following a terrible ordeal of life-threatening medical emergencies. She suffered cardiac arrests on August 5 and August 6, then on August 7 survived a perplexing spell of runaway bleeding before a third and final cardiac arrest finally took her life. Each crisis occurred during Genene's shift.

Three-month-old Patricia Sambrano died on August 14 after her third cardiac arrest in approximately forty-eight-hours. Genene was on duty as her nurse during each emergency.

Another baby died on September 4, of his second cardiac arrest in two days. A registered nurse was responsible for the care of the ten-month-old boy during both emergencies, but each time, Nurse Jones was on hand to help out as a member of the Code Blue teams.

Genene was good at Code Blue, and except for the time she collapsed during the effort to help Christopher, she was conspicuously efficient. She knew her job and had the ability to anticipate what medications or tools the team leader would call for from the crash cart—the nickname hospital professionals used for the metal cabinet full of equipment and drugs kept handy for Code Blues. The medicine or the tools would usually be prepared and ready when the doctor called for them.

One of the young pediatric residents, Dr. Kathleen Mary Holland, seemed to be especially impressed with Nurse Jones's performance. The daughter of a working-class family in Albany, N.Y., Dr. Holland was nearing the end of her internship when she first worked with Genene on a Code Blue. Dr. Holland didn't overlook the experienced nurse's steady performance and skills during the emergency.

But despite Dr. Holland's self-admitted high regard for Genene, Nurse Jones's "babies" continued to suffer cardiac and pulmonary arrests, bleeding difficulties—and to die with alarming regularity. Other hospital employees began to mutter among themselves about the deadly three-to-eleven shift, and about Genene's curiously coincidental presence at so many of the deaths.

Even Genene began to predict deaths, although she was not always exactly on target. She forecast Christopher's death three or

24

four times before he actually succumbed. She even telephoned his parents once to tell them that he was gone, and the grief-stricken couple raced the two hundred miles to San Antonio to find that Nurse Jones had been wrong. Their baby was still alive. Instead of being angry at her, however, they were relieved and thankful only that their baby hadn't died.

Genene's usual efficiency lapsed another time when she neglected to put Christopher's bed rails back up after she was working with him, and he rolled out of the bed, jerking to a stop several inches from the floor where he dangled from plastic tubing and arm restraints. After the initial shock, the LVN chuckled about the accident while telling the story to her colleagues.

Although the sudden upsurge of Code Blues and Genene's odd, inconsistent behavior had other staff members buzzing with suspicious whispers and conjectures, no one in authority took any firm action to initiate a serious investigation of the curious goings-on. So two other licensed vocational nurses, Pat Alberti, a no-nonsense former U.S. Army medic, and Suzanna Maldonado, a quietly efficient young woman of Mexican-American ancestry, undertook an investigation of their own.

Going over a log book that listed statistics involving every child admitted to PICU, the women observed what they believed to be a disturbing connection between babies who died and Nurse Jones. An inordinate number of the Code Blues and deaths had occurred in recent months either while Genene was on duty as one of the nurses for a sick child or shortly after she had left the youngster. The two women approached Head Nurse Pat Belko with their suspicions, and were advised they shouldn't be spreading dangerous rumors. The head nurse, however, approached her supervisor and passed on her conversation. Ms. Belko and the supervisor inspected the book, checked the deaths, and determined that the death rate wasn't unduly high. No one bothered to file a report with Virginia Mousseau, the director of nursing.

Babies on the three-to-eleven shift continued suffering cardiac arrest, pulmonary arrest, and uncontrolled fits of bleeding. A two-year-old died while under Genene's care on September 16. Five days later a one-month-old died while Genene was present, although she wasn't the assigned nurse.

25

In late September, four-month-old Paul Villarreal underwent elective surgery on his skull and was brought to the PICU to recuperate. But the day after his operation he experienced a seizure and was hooked up to a respirator. Then he began bleeding, and his heart stopped beating. A Code Blue team revived him, but the next night, September 24, he began bleeding again and his heart stopped once more. This time he couldn't be revived. The baby's postoperation emergencies occurred on Nurse Jones's shifts.

Three-month-old Placida Ybarra died a week later, after being admitted to the PICU with a suspected congenital heart problem. Doctors attributed her death to cardiac arrest. Genene had been the baby's nurse.

The suspicious nurses finally went over the heads of their direct supervisors and took their story to PICU Director Dr. James Robothom. He notified his superior, Dr. Robert Franks, acting chairman of the pediatrics department. Franks instructed Robothom to check the records and to advise him of his findings.

Jose Antonio Flores died on October 10. The infant was undergoing a CAT scan when he suffered a cardiorespiratory arrest. He was revived, but suffered another arrest about ninety minutes later and died. Genene was present when both emergencies occurred.

A few days later, Albert Garza, a baby with Down's syndrome, began having troubles with unexplained bleeding—always during the three-to-eleven shifts. The infant's blood wouldn't clot, and a doctor decided that Nurse Jones was overmedicating the patient with heparin, a drug commonly used in hospitals as a blood-thinning agent, or anticoagulant. Genene stubbornly insisted she knew what she was doing, but after checking out his suspicions, the physician learned that she had been administering dangerously high overdoses to the infant.

Little Albert's curious bleeding spasms stopped. The day after the incident with the doctor, Robotham issued a directive, stating that whenever nurses administered heparin on the PICU, the injections had to be witnessed by another staff member.

Despite the fledgling investigation of the mysterious infant deaths, and the directive concerning injections of heparin, another baby died on October 31. A two-month-old girl succumbed to cardiorespiratory arrest. It was her third attack in a few hours.

Genene was her assigned nurse.

Genene took a leave of absence from early in November until near the end of the first week of December after telling her supervisors that she was to undergo some minor abdominal surgery. Although two babies died on the unit in November, both deaths had been expected, for the tots were critically ill when they were admitted. There were no Code Blues on the PICU during the time Genene was away.

The Code Blues started again three days after she returned. On December 10, a male nurse returned from his dinner break to find one of his patients, an eighteen-month-old boy, in terrible shape. The toddler's heart monitor was jumping, and his skin had turned a frightening blue-gray. A Code Blue was sounded, and Genene rushed in with the crash cart, followed moments later by other members of the emergency team. After a desperate forty-five-minute struggle to keep the baby alive, his heart fluttered for the last time and he died. Genene and another nurse had been watching over the child while the male nurse was on lunch break.

Two nights later, eleven-month-old Joshua Sawyer died while under Genene's care. The boy had been brought to the hospital several days earlier, comatose from smoke inhalation suffered in a house fire. Genene flashed a Code Blue when the boy's heart stopped, and the emergency team got the organ functioning again. A short time later, however, he suffered another heart failure, and this time he couldn't be revived.

Robotham's report was inconclusive, but had been forwarded to the hospital's director of pediatrics. The pediatrics chief moved the report on to the hospital director. On December 15, PICU nurses were officially notified by written directive that all deaths on their unit should be reported to Dr. Robotham and to another doctor who was a pediatrics specialist.

Four days later, the first report was sent in. The patient was a four-month-girl who had died of hepatitis. Genene was not involved in the girl's care and there was nothing suspicious about the death. A four-month-old boy, also under the care of another nurse, died the next day after surgery for a congenital intestinal defect.

December 21 was an ugly, rainy winter day in San Antonio, and a little girl was in the PICU struggling for life. Less than a month old, the child had been in the unit fighting a serious infection for six days when, in midafternoon, Nurse Jones flashed a Code Blue. Despite a valiant twenty-minute struggle to save her, the child's heart failed and she died. An autopsy later conducted at the request of her parents disclosed the faintest trace of digoxin in her brain tissue. Digoxin is a heart stimulant, which if used in large doses can cause heart failure, and there was no record on the infant's medical chart of its being administered. It seemed possible that the drug could have been given to her during the commotion that accompanied the final fight to save her life and left off the chart by accident. The death was attributed to cardiopulmonary arrest aggravated by poisons from the infection.

A twenty-month-old toddler died two days later following cardiorespiratory failure. She had been Nurse Jones's patient both during her final illness and during an earlier hospital stay. Genene rocked the dead baby in her arms.

A nine-month-old boy died on Christmas Eve. Genene had been taking care of him since he was admitted to PICU with meningitis. His heart simply stopped beating.

Rolando Santos was barely three weeks old when he was admitted to the PICU on December 27, seriously ill with pneumonia. But the plucky little boy responded well to treatment for two days—until Nurse Jones began helping to care for him. It was then he suffered a heart attack. He survived the heart attack, and through the next few days also lived through frightening bouts of bleeding, mysteriously heavy spells of urination—diuresis—another heart attack, and two seizures. Then on January 6, 1982, after another baffling bout of uncontrollable bleeding, his heart stopped. A hospital employee telephoned his parents in the nearby farm community of Pearsall and told them their baby was dead.

Before Mr. and Mrs. Santos could reach the hospital, the baby was revived. His tiny heart had been bombarded with powerful stimulants and buttressed with prolonged CPR to get the organ beating again. When Rolando's grieving parents arrived at the hospital a few minutes later, they were told that their son was alive after all.

But hospital authorities were shaken by the near tragedy, and determined to get to the bottom of the baby's mysterious brush with

28

death. Laboratory tests disclosed that he had a large amount of heparin within his system, so much so that it could hardly have been injected accidentally. That afternoon, a notice was posted advising nurses that no heparin was to be kept near the bedsides of patients, but instead must be stored properly in bottles in the medication area.

Incredibly, only three days after Rolando's near-miraculous return from the dead, he had another near fatal attack. Blood began oozing from all the holes that had been poked in his little body during his near two-week fight for life in the PICU. One minute he was stable, but a few minutes later it seemed that blood oozed and spurted from everywhere and couldn't be stopped. In a desperate but dangerous move, a doctor injected large amounts of protamine sulfate, a drug that worked as an almost surefire antidote to heparin. But it was also a drug that could be deadly to the child if the bleeding was caused by something other than a heparin overdose. As hospital employees crowded around (and held their breath), the bleeding stopped.

At the doctor's insistence, Rolando was transferred to another ward, and a few days later was released from the hospital. Investigation later disclosed that the baby had been given more than one hundred times the safe dosage of heparin for a child of his size and age.

Morale in the PICU was at rock bottom. The rumor mill was abuzz with stories about Genene and the curious coincidences that seemed to link her to so many dying babies. Nurses chose sides in the whispering campaign. Some critics peevishly groused that Genene seemed to think she was running the three-to-eleven shift, even though she didn't have the credentials for supervisor. But some of her supporters muttered that perhaps she *should* be running the shift, because she was the most experienced. The nurses became bitterly divided, short-tempered and nervous. They snapped at one another, grumbled about the Administration—and quit. Some left for other jobs, and others simply dropped out of the workforce for a while.

The doctor whose desperate dose of protamine had stopped Rolando's near-lethal bleeding demanded that the administration take firm action to clean up the trouble in the pediatrics department's critical-care unit. Word of the trouble was again passed up the hospital chain of command. But the tension that was ripping apart the PICU didn't ease. It got worse, because babies were still suffering mysterious medical crises and dying.

During the 11 P.M.-to-7 A.M. shift an experienced and warmhearted LVN had been caring for four-month-old Patrick Zavala, who was recovering from open-heart surgery. When she ended her shift on January 11, the infant's condition was stable, and he remained that way through the morning and into the early afternoon. Nurse Jones took over his care at 3 P.M., and a few hours later she reported that he was having difficulty breathing and wasn't responding normally to her treatment. Genene wanted to take him to the CAT-scan room for neurological tests, but the doctor in charge rejected her suggestion. She was brooding over the doctor's response when a male nurse called a Code Blue for one of the babies he was caring for.

Although Genene was usually in the forefront during Code Blue emergencies, this time she didn't make a move to join the team rushing to the infant's aid. Instead she approached another doctor and tried again to get an okay to take Patrick for a CAT scan. Unaware of her previous conversation with the other physician, he agreed to her suggestion.

The baby was barely moved into the room before he went into cardiac arrest. Genene immediately called a Code Blue and began giving him CPR. She also yelled for drugs, but they weren't available in that department. It was only moments, however, before doctors and another nurse arrived in the CAT-scan room with cardiac stimulants. They administered the drugs and began moving to the elevator with Patrick to take him to PICU where the emergency equipment they needed was kept.

It was then that Nurse Jones pulled another one of her curious performances. She picked up a saline syringe and swept it in the sign of the cross as she pushed the plunger to squirt the saltwater over the silent, elfine form.

Patrick died a few minutes after he reached the PICU. Genene carried the silent little body around the room in her arms, sobbing as if her heart would break.

The nurse who had been caring for Patrick was horrified and

grief-stricken when she reported for her shift that night and learned that her patient had died. When other nurses told her what had happened, the words erupted in a tortured moan as she asked what Genene Jones had done to him. The words just spilled out. Then, as if she had just realized what she was saying, the heartbroken nurse muttered an embarrassed apology and slipped out of the room.

But the damage had been done. When she reported for her shift the following night, she was advised that she was being transferred to another unit in the hospital. Genene and two other nurses had lodged a complaint against her, alleging that she had accused Nurse Jones of responsibility for Patrick's death. The nurse's forced transfer exacerbated the already tense and troubled atmosphere in the PICU.

The distrust and fears were beginning to manifest in other ways as well. When a pathologist conducted an autopsy on Patrick, three other doctors and three nurses gathered around the flat metal table to observe. However, it was difficult to determine the exact cause of death. Eventually, presumed infection was cited on the infant's death certificate.

Dr. J. Kent Trinkle didn't believe it. He was chief of the cardiothoracic surgery division. He was also considered to be one of the premier chest surgeons in the world, and he knew that the operation on the baby had gone well and that the infant's heart was strong and functioning well when he was transferred to the PICU. Dr. Trinkle was outraged over Patrick's death after the successful operation and demanded immediate action to put a stop to the deadly hijinks in the PICU. If something wasn't done, he threatened, he would begin sending his pediatric patients to the Neonatal Intensive Care Unit after operations.

Dr. Trinkle wasn't a man anyone wanted to cross, and Marvin Dunn, dean of the university's medical school, was subsequently notified of the trouble. He was advised that a review of the morbidity-mortality rate in the PICU was being undertaken.

A memo was sent to Dr. Robotham and to Judy Harris, a nursing supervisor, directing them to launch an investigation. They were advised to be prepared to submit a report to a special committee within eleven days.

Before the meeting, however, a five-month-old boy on the PICU unit began bleeding uncontrollably. The infant lost consciousness, and a short time later, his heart stopped. A blood sample drawn from the baby mysteriously vanished before it could be analyzed. The medical student who drew the blood said later that he had given the vial to a dumpy nurse with brown hair to take to the lab, but it was never delivered.

The baby had been under the nursing care of Genene Jones when he began bleeding. And an infant who suffered a heart attack the next night was also under her care. The emergency team managed to save the child's life, however.

A few days later, top executives representing the hospital and the medical school met to go over the problems in the PICU: the quibbling among staff and the drop in morale, the sudden upsurge in Code Blues, and the baffling deaths. Robotham pointed out that he had attempted to remove a nurse whom he felt was the cause of much of the trouble from the PICU but had been opposed by the Nursing Department. He referred to "burnout" and "mothering dead children."

But the nurse had already threatened to sue if she was fired. There was no hard evidence that she had actually harmed any of the babies. And if she was fired and subsequently sued the hospital, she might win.

Eventually it was decided that another internal investigation should be launched. No decision was made to fire the troublesome nurse. And no one at the meeting took it upon him- or herself to notify law-enforcement agencies, although Texas state statutes clearly stipulated that anyone suspecting incidences of child abuse was required to report the information to police. And infanticide is clearly child abuse.

Months later, a hospital malpractice attorney stated during a press conference that he had advised the concerned health-care professionals at the meeting that there wasn't sufficient evidence at that time to warrant making an official report to police.

A six-member panel of medical experts, doctors and nurses from the U.S. and Canada, was flown to San Antonio to conduct the inquiry and review information gathered. Dr. Alan Conn, an anesthesiologist from Toronto's Hospital for Sick Children, one of the leading pediatric treatment centers in the world, headed the panel. Years earlier, Dr. Conn had been one of the instructors who helped train Dr. Robotham in intensive care.

Ironically, the respected Toronto pediatrics hospital where the committee head was on staff, had been experiencing its own trauma with a series of shocking baby deaths. A cardiac ward nurse there had been charged in the deaths of four babies, then found innocent after a bitter court trial. But the ordeal had created a turmoil within the hospital staff that was eerily similar to the situation in San Antonio.

In a press release, the committee's assignment was announced not as an investigation but as an evaluation of services in the PICU. The release described the event as part of "an ongoing review of patient-care programs that will help assure us and the community that we are delivering the highest quality of patient care." The piece of press flak also talked of future planning.

Hospital staff weren't fooled by the flowery press release. They knew the difference between an inquiry and "an ongoing review of patient-care programs." And they knew the spotlight was on the PICU and sick babies who seemed to be made sicker—or were murdered—after they were admitted to the hospital.

By that time, the PICU resembled a fortress under siege. Pediatric residents stood guard over their tiny patients at night. Some nurses refused to prepare or administer medication without a witness. Distrust spread. And the whispering, gossip, and paranoia in the PICU increased. It was worse than ever before, and Nurse Jones began to confide to trusted colleagues that she thought someone was out to get her.

The committee inspected the PICU and other units, went over memorandums, medical charts and records, and interviewed staff. When Pat Alberti was called before the panel, she bluntly informed them that Nurse Jones was killing babies. That wasn't what they wanted to hear.

And when it came time to evaluate the information, the committee still wasn't ready to accept Alberti's ugly, blunt summation of the problem. They decided they couldn't pinpoint a single major cause of the trouble, although they concluded that the level of supervision and competence needed improvement. They pointed the

33

finger at Dr. Robotham and Nurse Belko for failing to provide the kind of leadership needed to maintain and restore morale and efficiency.

Consequently they suggested appointment of a new head nurse, and placement of the PICU under the overall authority of an interdepartmental committee—meaning that Robotham would lose his position as the unit director. The committee suggested that because of the low number of patients treated, a PICU might not even be justified at the hospital.

The panel also recommended that the hospital get rid of Nurse Jones—and one of the most persistent whistle blowers, Pat Alberti. They pointed out that because both nurses were LVN's, the hospital could get rid of them by upgrading the units and requiring their positions be filled by RN's, nurses with higher training levels. Five other LVN's working in the unit would also have to be sacrificed, but it was agreed that handling the problem in that manner rather than an outright firing might avoid a nasty lawsuit.

Finally, the committee called for another, more inclusive review of the medical charts. It was recommended that the charts of every patient on the PICU for the past year be included in the inquiry to investigate any suspicious incident that occurred, in addition to deaths.

Hospital bigwigs balked at the proposal to close the PICU. And although a new PICU medical director was appointed, Dr. Robotham was retained with the title, Pedi-ICU Co-Director. But he later formally complained that his demotion had damaged his reputation. And Director of Nursing Virginia Mousseau opposed replacement of Pat Belko with such determination that the others eventually agreed to place the head nurse on unofficial probation for six months.

The director of nursing held a staff meeting for the PICU LVN's and informed them of the decision to "upgrade," but promised that jobs would be found elsewhere in the hospital for those who wanted to move. The news shocked the nurses. Some screamed that it wasn't fair. Some cried. Genene shrilled that the hospital was behaving like they were in a Communist country, and offered to leave if all they were looking for was a scapegoat. "We know you just want to get rid of me," she declared.

34

Pat Alberti didn't hear the news until she walked into the PICU that night to begin the graveyard shift. Then she stalked out, and never came back.

A short time later, after she was advised there was nothing available for her on the pediatrics floor, Genene resigned. At last the hospital had rid itself of the two nurses who seemed to be most involved in muddying the troubled waters. And no one filed any lawsuits.

But the troubles weren't over yet. The morning before Genene's resignation took effect, Suzanna Maldonado found a chilling two-word message stuffed into her hospital mailbox. "Your Dead," the note threatened. She showed the note to Pat Belko, who asked Genene if she had written it. Genene denied it was from her.

But Suzanna Maldonado wasn't satisfied with the head nurse's action, and she informed hospital security about the threat. The next night she found another note in her mailbox. The word "Soon" was scrawled on it. This time the nurse turned the frightening note over to hospital security. But after an interview with Suzanna, security dropped the case. Nurse Jones's resignation had taken effect and she was at last gone for good.

Even her name was left out of the Conn Committee's final report on their inquiry. The most significant recommendation in the report, in fact, was a call for the immediate appointment of yet another committee to study the care of patients in the PICU during the previous year. It was six months before the new committee began the next phase of the inquiry.

By that time Nurse Jones had moved on, outfitted with a letter of recommendation signed by her former head nurse, Pat Belko. The letter read in part: "During the time of employment, this employee has been loyal, dependable, and trustworthy.

"Ms. Genene Jones, LVN, has been an asset to the Bexar County Hospital District, and I would recommend continued employment."

And by that time, Dr. Robotham, who had stayed at the hospital despite his unwilling role of scapegoat, had also made one last desperate effort to warn possible future employers about the suspicious nurse.

In a letter to Virginia Mousseau, Dr. Robotham recommended

35

that a notation be made in her work records about what he referred to as "the stresses she experienced, so that she will be properly protected and judiciously supervised at any future place of employment." His plea was apparently ignored.

There was no notation in her records when she skipped through a series of temporary assignments in San Antonio she obtained through a nursing agency. Finally she landed a job at the Santa Rosa Medical Center in downtown San Antonio, and was assigned to the three-to-eleven shift in the surgical intensive care unit. When an administrator there telephoned the Bexar County Hospital to inquire about the LVN's work record, a personnel department clerk responded that she could say only that Nurse Jones was eligible to reapply for employment.

But Genene barely began working at Santa Rosa before her colleagues and supervisors began to suspect there was something wrong with the newly hired LVN. She wasn't performing her duties in a professional manner, and told stories about her personal problems that didn't add up. But before her supervisors had an opportunity to take possible disciplinary measures, Genene advised them that she was quitting.

She had already found a new full-time job working for a young pediatrician she had met at the Bexar County Hospital, Dr. Kathleen Holland. The two women had worked well together while Dr. Holland was completing her residency in San Antonio, and soon after the doctor decided to open a pediatrics practice in Kerrville, she contacted Genene and offered her a job. Dr. Holland was one of the few doctors and residents at San Antonio whose faith in Genene had survived the final dark weeks before the PICU was "upgraded," and the LVN reciprocated the loyalty.

They got along so well, in fact, that when Genene had trouble finding a house in Kerrville that was both within her price range and available to a single woman with pets, a ten-year-old boy, and a five-year-old girl, Dr. Holland bought an investment property to rent to her.

Kerrville is a friendly town of about fourteen thousand people in the rugged Texas hill country some seventy-five miles northwest of San Antonio. It is the kind of rural American community people talk about when they use the phrase, "a nice place to raise kids," and there were plenty of young families there and only one pediatrician. When Dr. Holland decided to begin her professional practice in Kerrville, she was warmly welcomed by the medical community, including the staff at the Sid Peterson Memorial Hospital.

The 116-bed Sid Peterson Memorial was a good hospital, but it was weak in pediatrics, and, in fact, didn't even have a pediatrics ward. The influx of young people into the community was relatively new, and previously the hospital was more likely to be treating grandparents than small children. Consequently, Dr. Holland looked outside Kerrville for an experienced pediatrics nurse, and after talking to a few possible candidates, she settled on Genene. She was well aware of the whispering at the Medical Center Hospital about the LVN. She knew that Genene could be an aggressive, take-over-type individual, but she was capable of coping with that. And she simply didn't believe the other stories: gossip that the nurse had a lot to do with the baffling string of Code Blues and patient deaths in the PICU. And she knew as well that, despite the talk, the hospital had given the LVN a good recommendation for future employers.

Consequently, on August 23, 1982, when Dr. Holland opened the doors to begin practice of pediatrics in a complex of doctors' offices called the Fine Medical Center, about a half mile from Kerrville's downtown business district, Genene was her nurse.

They saw only one patient on the first day they were open. Their second patient, and the first of the second day, was fourteen-month-old Chelsea Ann McClellan. The daughter of Reid McClellan, a utility-line repairman, and his wife, Petti, from rural Gillespie county a few miles outside Kerrville, Chelsea had been a premature baby. She spent her first twenty-one days in the hospital, and when she was ten months old she was hospitalized for most of another week after experiencing breathing problems.

Although the pediatrician and her staff members would later talk about an erratic breathing problem, Chelsea's mother listed a "bad cold" on the patient-information form she filled out when she brought the little girl in to see Dr. Holland.

Dr. Holland was talking alone with the mother in her private office when the pediatrician heard her nurse call to the child,

"Don't go to sleep, baby. Chelsea, wake up!" Moments later, Nurse Jones called for the doctor to come outside. When Dr. Holland reached the treatment room she found Chelsea on the examining table and Genene hurrying to attach an oxygen mask over her face. It was an emergency. The child wasn't breathing.

As Genene pumped oxygen with the respiratory bag, she and the doctor began an IV. Then Chelsea went into seizures. Dr. Holland ordered an anticonvulsant drug, then ran outside the room and called for the Kerr County Emergency Medical Service.

The little girl's mother was unaware of the emergency until Dr. Holland walked back into her office and told her that Chelsea had suffered a seizure. A few minutes later, an ambulance was rushing Chelsea, her mother, Dr. Holland, and Nurse Jones to the hospital emergency room.

Chelsea was breathing again by the time they arrived, and she recovered quickly, although she remained at the hospital ten days. Despite numerous tests, doctors could not determine why the child had experienced the mysterious breathing trouble and the convulsions. But the McClellans were impressed. The new pediatrician and her nurse, it appeared, had saved their daughter's life.

Brandy Lee Benites was also a premature baby. When her teenage parents, Gabriel and Nelda Benites, noticed that she had diarrhea and blood in her stool, they took her to the Sid Peterson Hospital emergency room. Staff members there gave them Dr. Holland's business card and told them to call the town's new pediatrician.

The parents sat in the waiting room while Dr. Holland and her nurse examined the month-old girl. Genene was left alone with Brandy for a few minutes before the doctor returned to the examining room. Suddenly Dr. Holland burst from the examining room and advised the parents that the infant had stopped breathing. An ambulance was called and rushed the baby to Sid Peterson. But after a few minutes, Dr. Holland decided to take the baby to Santa Rosa in San Antonio, and Brandy was again loaded into an ambulance.

Dr. Holland was following in her car and Genene was riding with a paramedic and a respiratory therapist in the back of the ambulance when Brandy's pulse almost disappeared. Genene barked

38

out orders for the ambulance to stop. The LVN and the respiratory therapist were giving her emergency treatment when Dr. Holland joined them, and after examining the baby, determined that her breathing had improved sufficiently to resume the trip.

The other medical professionals were puzzled when Nurse Jones started an IV in the baby's foot, although another IV was already going. But they had no time to ponder her curious behavior, because the baby suddenly turned a nasty gray, and again began struggling to breathe. Nurse Jones and the others helped her breathe until they reached the hospital. Once Brandy was rushed into the emergency room, her recovery was rapid. She was released to her parents after six days. Doctors were unable to determine what had caused her frightening brush with death.

Meanwhile, the relationship between the doctor and the nurse had developed into a close friendship. They shared rides to work and back, coffee, cigarettes, and confidences, as well as their professional relationship. Dr. Holland even stayed at times at Genene's house, which was already home to another nurse, a teenage girl the LVN had taken under her wing, the two children and pets.

Then one of the strangest occurrences that seemed to haunt Genene happened as army paramedics from Fort Sam Houston just outside San Antonio were helping move an infant and a seven-year-old boy by helicopter from Sid Peterson to Santa Rosa. Genene was riding in the back of the chopper with the boys when she began yelling and gesticulating. The paramedics couldn't hear well over the noise, but it seemed that she thought the older child was going into seizures. The paramedics looked at him, and he was stable. Then Genene began shouting that his heartbeat was dangerously irregular. One of the paramedics checked the boy's monitor, and determined that the heartbeat was normal.

But before they could stop her, Genene injected something into his IV line. Almost immediately the boy's monitor began to show heartbeat irregularities. Then he stopped breathing. Genene tried to pump air into the boy with a respiratory bag, but because of severe facial deformities, that didn't work. Finally one of the paramedics gave the child mouth-to-mouth resuscitation.

After the helicopter made an emergency landing in a plowed

field and the paramedics and the nurse tried unsuccessfully to maneuver a breathing tube down the child's throat, they took off again. The medics kept the child alive by administering mouth-to-mouth and massaging his heart until they reached Methodist Hospital in Northwest San Antonio. The boy's condition was quickly stabilized by an emergency-room team.

Genene later said the medicine she administered to the boy inside the helicopter was Neo-Synephrine, a pharmaceutical used to open breathing passages and dry secretions. The child was hospitalized for seven weeks in San Antonio, at Sid Peterson, and finally back at Santa Rosa in San Antonio, where he died.

Dr. Holland's fledgling pediatrics practice had gotten off to quite a sensational start. But the excitement—and tragedy—wasn't ended yet.

Twenty-one-month-old Misty Shayne Reichenau had a narrow escape after she was taken to the new pediatrician with sores inside her mouth. After Dr. Holland began her examination and advised the worried mother, Mrs. Kay Reichenau, that Misty might have meningitis, an IV was started. Then the baby stopped breathing. Both Dr. Holland and Mrs. Reichenau had been out of the room briefly while Genene prepared the medication for the IV. After emergency treatment at Sid Peterson, Misty was transferred to the Medical Center Hospital in San Antonio, and soon recovered. Doctors were unable to discover a cause for her sudden breathing emergency.

But the pressure was beginning to show. Early in September, Nurse Jones showed up at the Sid Peterson emergency room as a patient. She complained of cramps and said she was vomiting blood. Genene remained in the hospital five days, treated for a suspected ulcer. An RN filled in at the clinic while Genene was hospitalized, and helped Dr. Holland with several patients. There were no emergencies.

The trouble resumed on Nurse Jones's first day back at work. And the first patients at the clinic that day were Chelsea McClellan and her brother, Cameron. Mrs. McClellan had asked the doctor to see her son, who had the flu, and the pediatrician suggested that she also bring Chelsea in for a checkup. Dr. Holland recommended to the mother that Chelsea be given two inoculations: one for measles and mumps, and another for diphtheria and tetanus.

Mrs. McClellan was holding the little girl on her lap when Genene injected the first syringe of medicine. Almost immediately Chelsea started having trouble breathing, and her mother screamed for the nurse to stop. She yelled that her baby was having another seizure.

But Nurse Jones replied that the baby was merely reacting to the flicker of pain from the needle, and plunged the second syringe into Chelsea's other thigh. Then the baby turned blue, struggled for breath, and plunged into a seizure. When Chelsea and Nurse Jones arrived at the Sid Peterson emergency room in an ambulance, an IV had already been started and a breathing tube had been inserted in the little girl's throat.

The emergency team, including Dr. Holland and Genene, managed to restore Chelsea's breathing. But Dr. Holland wanted her transferred to San Antonio, and shortly after noon, an ambulance driven by paramedic Steve Brown, with Chelsea, Nurse Jones, and another paramedic, Tommy James, left Kerrville. Dr. Holland followed in her car, and Chelsea's parents trailed behind her in their car.

The ambulance traveled only a few miles before it skidded to a stop. Chelsea was going into cardiac arrest. Dr. Holland leaped into the back of the vehicle, and, while calling for resuscitative drugs, took over the heart massage that had already been started. At her command, the driver drove to the first available hospital, Comfort Community, where Chelsea was rushed into the emergency room. But this time the lively blonde, blue-eyed toddler could not be saved. Dr. Holland gave the stunned parents the tragic news.

When the procession of cars arrived back at Sid Peterson, Genene, with tears streaming down her face, carried the silent bundle through the hospital corridors and downstairs to the basement morgue. At Dr. Holland's request, Chelsea's father signed a form permitting an autopsy. Pending results of the examination, Dr. Holland filled out Chelsea's death certificate listing the cause of the cardiac arrest as a seizure. But the cause of the seizure was listed as undetermined.

Dr. Holland was still at Sid Peterson some three hours after

41

Chelsea died when five-month-old Jacob Evans had a close brush with death that began in her office. Jacob had been crying for weeks, although otherwise he seemed healthy, but his mother, Lydia Evans, wanted the new pediatrician to examine him. Nurse Jones began the examination herself, then shooed the mother from the room so she could start an IV before transferring the baby to Sid Peterson where Dr. Holland could look at him. The nurse explained that the IV would make it easier for doctors to administer medicine in case Jacob suffered seizures while the tests were being run. Mrs. Evans responded that Jacob had never had seizures, but reluctantly joined her parents in the waiting room while the nurse continued working on her son.

They heard Jacob screaming, then suddenly go silent. The receptionist rushed from the examining room and telephoned the hospital that they had an emergency. A doctor and a nurse from adjacent offices hurried in to help Genene, who was administering mouth-to-mouth resuscitation. Jacob was rushed by ambulance to the Sid Peterson emergency room, and normal breathing was eventually restored. Dr. Holland wrote an initial admitting diagnosis on his emergency-room records of "probably meningitis."

Jacob's first cousin, Anthony Winn, was Genene's next emergency patient. New first-time mothers, Lydia Evans and Elizabeth Wynn, were sisters and they both had heard good things about the new baby doctor in town. It was Saturday night and Dr. Holland was spending the weekend with her husband a few miles outside Kerrville after the exhausting first few weeks as a privately practicing pediatrician when Elizabeth and Donald Winn became worried that their baby was sick. They called Genene's house and asked to talk to Dr. Holland. Genene explained that the doctor wasn't there and instructed them to take their son to the clinic.

She met them there, advised that she couldn't reach Dr. Holland, and began examining the baby herself. Little Anthony was lucky to survive. Shortly after Genene began working on Anthony, she pronounced a diagnosis of both a staph infection and low blood sugar, and had him rushed to the hospital emergency room. Dr. Holland had been awakened by her answering service and advised that her nurse was in the clinic with an emergency case. Dr. Holland was stunned to hear that instead of sending the tiny patient directly to the hospital emergency room, Genene had undertaken the examination herself.

Anthony appeared alert and healthy when he appeared in the emergency room. A blood-sugar test revealed no trace of hypoglycemia. And a spinal tap performed by Dr. Holland showed no sign of meningitis. The doctor and her officious nurse exchanged sharp words after the incident. But they continued to work together. And the Monday after Chelsea's death, both attended the little girl's funeral. Genene cried!

In the approximate month since Dr. Holland had opened her practice in Kerrville, far too many sick babies had been rushed to the emergency room. The whispers and talk had started at Sid Peterson, just as they had at Bexar County Hospital in San Antonio. Nurses began to exchange observations about babies that suddenly became deathly ill at the new doctor's clinic, then mysteriously bounced back soon after they arrived at the hospital. And Genene's officious, know-it-all manner around other nurses was difficult to swallow. Most important of all, however, Dr. Duane Packard had become very suspicious of the new pediatrics team that was at the center of the ruckus. Dr. Packard was the hospital's chief of staff, and the dean of Kerrville's medical community.

In late September, he was among a small group of health-care professionals called to a meeting with Sid Peterson Hospital Administrator Tony Hall to talk about the upset among the staff created since the new pediatrician and her nurse had arrived in town and set up business. They agreed that something had to be done, and Hall telephoned Dr. Holland to set up a meeting with him the next day.

Before they could meet, however, the Holland Clinic staff was involved in two more emergencies. Five-month-old Rolinda Ruff was brought to the clinic with diarrhea, and shortly after the doctor and nurse had begun treatment, the baby was stretched out on an examining table with an IV in her hand and an oxygen mask over her face.

Soon there was another Code Blue at the hospital. This time one of the other doctors helping attend the baby thought he detected behavior that indicated the child might have been administered Anectine. Anectine is a trade name for succinylcholine, a powerful muscle relaxant that can become lethal and stop breathing by paralyzing muscles when given to an infant or young child. But the doctor didn't have much time to ponder over his suspicions.

Incredibly, while the Code Blue team was still hovering around Rolinda, another baby was in trouble in the emergency room. And Nurse Jones was right in the middle of the action.

The patient was Chris Parker, a baby who had been waiting with his mother, Mrs. Mary Ann Parker, to be seen at the clinic when Rolinda's breathing attack had caused everyone to rush out and head for the hospital emergency room. As Genene had dashed from the building, she told Chris's mother to bring him to the hospital where Dr. Holland could examine the boy after the emergency.

Rolinda was still being worked on when Genene walked into the hospital waiting room, picked up Chris, and took him to Emergency. She had a brief confrontation with an ER nurse after placing the baby on a bed already prepared for a cardiac patient before she took him to another bed, ordered X rays, and began drawing blood. She had barely moved into the cubicle with the baby, however, before she called out a Code Blue. Chris had suffered a cardiac arrest, she yelled.

Nurses had already cleared his throat of mucus when Dr. Holland rushed in and began ordering drugs. The baby appeared to be breathing normally when someone noticed a half-filled syringe on his bed. Dr. Holland picked it up. It wasn't one of the syringes just used by the nurses at her direction, and she asked what it was. No one seemed to know, so she picked it up and pressed the plunger, emptying the liquid inside. Then she tossed it into the trash.

With both babies stabilized after the Code Blues, Dr. Holland kept her appointment with the hospital administrator. Hall told her that nurses and other members of the hospital staff were fed up with Genene's behavior. Dr. Holland agreed to talk to Genene and try to straighten things out.

But Hall and others, including Dr. Packard, knew by now that the problem was far more serious than a mere, overly bossy nurse. Packard asked a young doctor who had done his residency at the Medical Center Hospital in San Antonio to use his contacts to check out the background and previous performance of Kerrville's troubled new pediatrician.

A couple of hours later, Dr. Packard attended a meeting of the medical staff's executive committee. There, he and Hall went over the problems with the bossy nurse, the rash of Code Blue babies, and the suspicions of the doctor helping attend Rolinda, that she had been administered Anectine. There was nothing on the infant's charts to show that she had been given the drug.

It was decided to wait and see what the young doctor checking into the pediatrician's background came up with, then have another talk with her.

The young doctor learned from a friend in San Antonio that a baffling series of sudden baby deaths had occurred at the Medical Center Hospital – and that Nurse Jones had left under a cloud. At least some of her colleagues had been convinced that she was killing babies. Alarmed at the ominous report, he passed the information on to Packard, and Packard informed the executive committee.

Events moved swiftly after that. Dr. Holland was interviewed by the committee and asked if she could explain the baby deaths. She could. One by one she went over the symptoms and events. The doctors asked if she had ever used succinylcholine. She said she had during her residency, but not yet in private practice, although she had some Anectine at her office.

The doctors asked if she knew about Genene's reputation at the Bexar County Hospital. She confirmed that she did, but she didn't believe the stories. Dr. Packard advised her that he wanted another physician consulted on every patient she treated at the hospital, just her beeper clicked in. There was an emergency with one of her patients.

After Dr. Holland left, the committee agreed to cancel her privileges to admit and treat patients at the hospital, although they didn't immediately decide exactly when to take the action. But they did decide at that time that the problem and their suspicions were too critical to keep among themselves. With the committee's concurrence, Dr. Packard notified the Texas Board of Medical Examiners about the rash of emergencies that had plagued Dr. Holland. And Hall notified authorities in the Austin office of the Texas Board of Vocational Nurse Examiners. The hospital administrator

45

talked with an investigator for the LVN licensing agency, advising him of the suspicious Code Blues and deaths in both Kerrville and San Antonio. He said that he and his colleagues suspected that a baby killer was at work.

As the new investigation was getting underway, Genene confronted her boss and said she had done a stupid thing. She informed the doctor that she had taken a handful of an antianxiety drug prescribed for her ulcers. Dr. Holland yelled at her receptionist to call an ambulance, and rushed to the office of the doctor next door for help.

Paramedics who transported Genene to the hospital said she was semiconscious when they reached her. They administered oxygen in the ambulance, and her stomach was pumped in the emergency room. Doctors admitted her to the hospital.

Dr. Holland had also questioned Genene about the succinycholine, was told a hardly believable story, and finally was given two bottles for examination. One bottle, although it was still filled with liquid, had holes punched in the rubber top as if the drug had been pulled out into a syringe. Dr. Holland's previous unwavering faith in Genene had at last begun to dissolve.

The pediatrician told her story to the young doctor who had checked out her background in San Antonio and showed him the succinycholine bottles. They both agreed that they had to find out more about the drug in a hurry and called an anesthesiologist. Ironically, he was the same doctor who had suspected Anectine was administered to the Ruff child. After he arrived, they telephoned Hall at his home, and he joined them in Dr. Holland's office. Together, the alarmed quartet searched through office records to determine exactly how much of the powerful muscle relaxant had actually been purchased for Dr. Holland's clinic. Invoices indicated three bottles were purchased, and they only had two. Despite another frenzied look around the office, the third bottle could not be located. Hall kept the two bottles which were found to take to the Texas Rangers. When Nurse Jones showed up for work at the clinic the next day in her starched white uniform as if nothing had happened, Dr. Holland fired her. At last, the close relationship between the young pediatrician and the nurse was broken. And the baby killing ended.

Genene moved two hundred miles to the dusty West Texas town of San Angelo just about the time that a Kerr County grand jury was convened to investigate the strange deaths and emergencies that had afflicted children brought to Kerrville's new pediatrician during the frenetic six weeks she had practiced there. In San Angelo, Genene settled in a mobile-home park and returned to work almost immediately, at a state school for mentally retarded adults.

While Genene kept a low profile in San Angelo, the investigation of her connection to dead babies spread from Kerrville to San Antonio. Inevitably, the news media picked up the trail and discovered that a suspected baby killer had been at work in the two Texas towns. As the story spread and was picked up by the national media, the Bexar County grand jury was convened to investigate the baby deaths at the Bexar County Hospital. News reports eventually talked of as many as forty-two possible baby deaths in San Antonio and Kerrville all possibly tied to the same pediatrics nurse.

Unlike Dr. Holland, who pleaded her Fifth Amendment right against self-incrimination and refused to testify before the grand jury in Kerrville, Genene marched through a crowd of reporters to testify. She blamed the troubles at the county hospital on incompetent doctors, and insisted she had done nothing wrong. A few days later she repeated her claims of innocence at a press conference.

And she got married again, to Garron Ray Turk. Her new husband was a nineteen-year-old high-school senior, who met her at a nursing home where he was working as a nurse's aide. The new bride was a matronly thirty-three, and cited her marriage as proof against ugly rumors that had followed her from Kerrville that she was a lesbian. The sudden marriage also provided the internationally notorious Nurse Jones with the relative anonymity of a new identity and name, Genene Turk. But the wedding didn't prevent indictments being returned by grand juries in San Antonio and Kerrville. Genene was arrested and taken to jail on charges of murder.

It was January 15, 1984 nearly two years after she was fired by Dr. Holland, when Genene Jones Turk went on trial in Georgetown on charges of first-degree murder in the death of Chelsea McClellan. The case was venued to the central Texas Williamson

47

county town north of Austin because of heavy publicity. Prosecutors charged that the chunky woman the media was referring to as the "Death Nurse" had sought to portray herself as a hero by saving infants in life-and-death situations. Furthermore, they claimed that she created the emergencies as part of a cruel plan to produce enough dead or seriously ill babies to justify the opening of a pediatrics intensive care unit at the hospital in Kerrville.

Little Chelsea's body had been exhumed, and traces of succinylcholine were found in her tissue. Pathologists used a revolutionary new series of complex tests developed in Sweden to pinpoint the powerful drug in the child's remains.

At the conclusion of the month-long trial, the jury deliberated only three hours before finding Genene guilty of murder. She was sentenced to ninety-nine years in prison.

Nearly a year later, she was convicted in San Antonio at a bench trial, after waiving her right to a jury of injuring Rolando Santos at the Bexar County Hospital by giving him a dangerous overdose of the blood-thinning drug heparin. Nurse Suzanna Maldonado testified at the trial about the death diary she had compiled listing the babies who died on Genene Jones's shift, and she told the court about the death threat she received. A sixty-year sentence was ordered to be served concurrently with the previously imposed prison term.

Despite an exhaustive two-year investigation at the Bexar County Hospital and several resignations, including those of Pat Belko and Virginia Mousseau, no one else was charged, and Genene was named on only the single indictment for her behavior there. A brief flak occurred when hospital executives had thousands of pounds of records shredded early in 1984, and prosecutors in the Genene Jones Turk case obtained a court order to prevent destruction of additional material. But hospital and medical-center authorities claimed they had kept duplicates of important materials and were only engaging in some routine cleaning up.

After an investigation, the Texas Board of Medical Examiners declined to take any action against Dr. Holland. Early in 1986, Genene's nursing license was suspended by the Texas Board of Vocational Nurse Examiners after agreeing that she represented a danger to public health.

Genene Jones Turk is serving her sentence in the Mountain View Unit of the Women's Penitentiary at Gatesville, in Central Texas. With time off for good behavior, she is already eligible to be considered for parole.

TWO

Anthony Joyner
Sex Predator

When most people envision a setting for murder, they are unlikely to think of a location like the Kearsley Home of Christ Church Hospital.

The home is an imposing structure of Gothic stone, sitting in a rapidly changing neighborhood in West Philadelphia, Pennsylvania. It is nearly two hundred years old and was founded as a retirement home for clergymen.

It served a variety of purposes over the years as different owners occupied it, and by the early 1980's it was a retirement home for elderly women. More than sixty residents, whose ages ranged from seventy to ninety-four, lived on the premises in private apartments. A security force patroled the grounds and a physician was on call around the clock.

The residents enjoyed their independent lifestyle, tucked securely away from demanding children, rambunctious grandchildren, and noisy teenagers. Their days were their own to pass watching television soap operas, reading, or reminiscing about everything from past marriages and long-deceased sweethearts to vacations in Europe or the Caribbean. They felt safe and generally content at the Kearsley Home, singularly fortunate to live out their twilight years in such comfortable and genteel surroundings.

The atmosphere at the home was informal. Women formed

friendships, held cookouts, played cards, picnicked, and visited local museums and theatres. Traveling in groups, they were easily recognizable because of their age, their special "Kearsley look," and the fact that they were invariably accompanied by solicitous staff members on their outings.

The staff was high quality, exceptionally well trained, regardless of whether their specialty involved food preparation, carpentry, nursing, or administration. They were good at their jobs, and most of the employees seemed to be genuinely fond of the residents and concerned with their welfare. Administrators were careful about whom they hired, and worked to attract the best qualified people possible. The wages and benefits were generous and compared well with those of competitors in the field.

There had never been any scandal or serious troubles at the home until Anthony Joyner appeared.

Joyner was a polite young black man who made a good impression when he showed up at the home for a job interview. Administrators were impressed with his manners when he replied to their questions with courteous and prompt, "Yes, sirs" and "No, ma'ams." And they were particularly pleased with his apparent affection for older women. He was hired on the kitchen staff as an assistant diet technician. Despite his modest salary and job description, he appeared to be the type of energetic employee who could be expected to work his way up and eventually assume greater responsibilities.

Dr. Gordon W. Webster was on the other end of the job spectrum. He was the house physician, a job he had held for two decades. A graduate of the University of Pennsylvania School of Medicine, he had built up a lucrative medical practice on the Main Line, the string of wealthy communities that lie along the western edge of Philadelphia. But the silver-haired medic genuinely cared for the old women at the home and was devoted to his practice there.

Staff and residents at Kearsley were quick to point out that a rest or residential home is not the same as a nursing home. Nursing homes are for the sick or infirm, while rest homes are precisely what they are called. They are homes where the elderly can retire and spend the remaining years of their lives.

Most of the residents of the Kearsley Home were in good physical condition, except for the normal problems associated with aging. Some, however, required special care and diets, and a number were on medication that was closely monitored by nurses. A few were confined to the home's hospital unit.

Security was an important consideration to the residents, and shortly before Joyner was hired, the administration installed new locks on all the doors.

Margaret Eckard was one of the most popular, as well as oldest, residents. A bubbly ninety-two-year-old who delighted staff members and other residents with her positive attitude, she had lived at Kearsley longer than anyone else. She was vivacious and active, and her fellow residents looked forward to seeing her at meals and social functions. But on the chilly morning of January 21, 1983, she did something unusual. She failed to show up for breakfast.

Concerned about Mrs. Eckard's uncharacteristic absence, Nurse Delores Kirk walked to her apartment to investigate. The door was slightly ajar, and the nurse knocked lightly, then gave it a gentle push. The door swung open, revealing the body of the old woman lying on the floor next to her rumpled bed. The body, clad in a nightgown, was curled in a fetal position, and Mrs. Eckard appeared to be dead.

The nurse called for help and bent over the inert form to check for a pulse. There was no trace of life. Dr. Webster was among the first people to arrive at the room and, after a brief examination, pronounced her dead. Signs of rigor mortis were already beginning to appear.

Although it appeared that the death was natural, a not surprising occurrence for someone of Mrs. Eckard's advanced age, the doctor was disturbed by bruises on her face and smears of blood around her mouth and nose. A later examination also disclosed streaks of blood in her vagina and anus, which was a bit unusual even though the body often loses vital fluids at the time of death.

The unusual presence of blood was curious, and the presence of the bruises was vaguely troubling, but the doctor decided they weren't sufficiently disturbing to warrant making an issue. There seemed to be nothing about the death that was unnatural or unusual enough to warrant a postmortem. A few days later, Mrs. Eckard was sorrowfully buried by her family, and the staff and residents of the Kearsley Home quietly returned to their normal routine.

A month passed, and life in Philadelphia continued as usual. In the core city, chill winds swept papers and trash through the dirty, littered streets, people got drunk, pimps beat up on their whores, and crack and heroin addicts prostituted themselves, stole, robbed, and died from the poison and the violence.

Only a few miles to the west, the women at the Kearsley Home seemed to be thousands of miles from the misery and the violence of the streets. Surrounded by the protective staff and the comfortable surroundings, they continued their lives in the quiet and serenity they had become used to.

Philadelphia and the Delaware Valley had been sprinkled with a few light snows earlier in the winter. But on Saturday, February 12, winter roared in with a vengeance, dropping a smothering, traffic-paralyzing twenty-one inches of snow on the city.

But Katherine A. Maxwell and her fellow residents at the home didn't have to worry about weather-related traffic tie-ups or other problems linked to the winter onslaught. They could appreciate it for its beauty, watching from windows in their snug and secure apartments at the home. Mrs. Maxwell's tidy apartment was on the fourth floor of a new wing of the home. But if her friends were looking forward to a breakfast chat with her about the weather, they were disappointed. She didn't show up.

A nurse was dispatched to her apartment to investigate. Mrs. Maxwell's door was ajar, and after knocking gently, the nurse peered around the edge to look inside. The eighty-five-year-old woman was lying on her bed. Her pajamas were spotted with blood.

Normally, Dr. Webster would have been called to examine the body, but the heavy snow and blizzard conditions had kept him at his home that day. The entire city was immobilized by the monster storm, and although the physician was disturbed at news of another death among the residents, he didn't examine the body.

According to normal practice at Kearsley, when a resident death occurred and Dr. Webster was not available, the body is delivered to nearby Lankenau Hospital where another doctor is called on to officially confirm the death. The death is then reported to the Philadelphia medical examiner, who, in most cases, releases the corpse to an undertaker. That procedure was followed with Mrs. Maxwell's body. Since there was nothing obviously suspicious about the death, there was no autopsy.

Again, Dr. Webster was disturbed at the report of blood on the old woman's pajamas in the area of her genitals, but a pathologist indicated that some bleeding could occur through natural causes at the time of death.

Much later, Dr. Webster would remark that the blizzard might have contributed to preventing a closer probe into the cause of death and a possible criminal investigation after Mrs. Maxwell's death. Without the incapacitating storm, staff members might have been more inclined to suspect that an intruder could have entered the home.

Elizabeth Monroe was in excellent health and spirits when she attended a party with relatives and friends for her eighty-sixth birthday. Despite her advanced age, the party didn't appear to tire her, and she stayed up late celebrating with cake and refreshments until her guests left. She was glowing with good spirits when she finally called it a night and turned in.

The next morning it was Mrs. Monroe who failed to show up for breakfast, and like the other two women before her, her lifeless body was found in her bed by a nurse who was sent to her apartment to investigate. Her face was discolored and there was bleeding in the vaginal area. And again, the door to her apartment was ajar when the nurse arrived.

This time Dr. Webster was out of state, and another physician was filling in for him at the home. The substitute physician didn't know about the earlier deaths, and he followed routine procedure. There didn't appear to be anything unduly suspicious about the old lady's passing, and the body was transported to a local undertaker, where it was embalmed and readied for burial.

Dr. Webster learned of the death when he telephoned his answering service, and he was immediately concerned. The next Monday morning after he returned to the Philadelphia area, he telephoned the director of nursing at the home for more information. She told him about the blood spotting.

Dr. Webster's concern was turning to alarm. The three deaths, coming so close together, were disconcertingly similar, perhaps too similar to be mere chance. The physician was determined to do something about the baffling string of deaths.

He talked with a pathologist friend, who suggested a medical examiners' investigation and autopsy. Unfortunately, the fact that the body had already been embalmed made that difficult. Nevertheless, Dr. Webster contacted the undertaker and ordered him to hold the body.

Then he telephoned the Philadelphia medical examiner, but the health official reportedly didn't appear to be especially impressed with Dr. Webster's suspicions. In fact, he appeared to be more upset about how his telephone number had gotten into the hands of the Kearsley Home physician than about the puzzling string of deaths, Dr. Webster later told the press.

Dr. Webster said that at the ME's suggestion he dialed another number at the medical examiner's office, and was met with a similar reaction. The physician said he was reminded that the women were elderly residents of a retirement home, and a certain number of deaths should be expected. But he was insistent, and the case was finally accepted for investigation. A short time later, the ME ruled that Mrs. Webster's death had been due to natural causes. A notation was included with the finding that embalming had made it "difficult" to conduct a proper examination of the body. No formal autopsy was conducted because an examination of the exterior of the body had not disclosed any significant injuries.

Lillie T. Amlie was a flamboyant, longtime resident of the home who acted younger than her true age of eighty-nine. Other residents enjoyed her colorful and offbeat personality, although there was occasional carping among some of the women about her ability to continue attracting men, including some much younger than she. But Lillie didn't mind the gossip, and she never slowed down in her determination to continue living life to the fullest.

She had a boyfriend near her own age who lived in another area rest home and visited her regularly. And she was carrying on a spirited correspondence with a lonesome young man in prison, as well. She simply enjoyed male companionship. If there was any potentially dangerous aspect to her unbridled zest for life and trusting nature, it was her habit of allowing people into her room. Lillie

Amlie was not very security conscious, and just about anyone was welcome to walk into her room at just about any time, even when she was taking a bath.

A nurse discovered the body of the aging bon-vivant on the floor in her room on June 1, after she had failed to appear in the dining room for dinner. The incident broke the pattern set by the other deaths. She had been seen by staff members only a few hours earlier that afternoon before going to her apartment for a nap. The midafternoon respite had become a habit which she dearly loved, and after a couple of hours of rest and privacy, she usually showed up in the recreation and dining areas refreshed and eagerly anticipating the evening activities.

Mrs. Amlie's body wasn't lying on the floor, or on a rumpled bed, as the others' had been. *Her* body was discovered immersed facedown in a few inches of lukewarm water in her bathtub. Despite the water, when nurses moved Mrs. Amlie's body onto her bed, they noticed traces of blood around her mouth, nose, vagina, and rectum, as there had been with the other three women who had died recently. And curiously, for someone who might have been either beginning a bath or about to leave the tub, she was wearing hose and jewelry.

But the fun-loving woman had recently suffered a cardiac arrest and it seemed possible that she could have had an attack and toppled into the tub as she was dressing or undressing.

Dr. Webster was concerned about the presence of the blood. It was becoming increasingly difficult to accept coincidence as an explanation, as one resident after another was found dead at the home in perplexingly similar circumstances. But the doctor had just returned to Philadelphia from a trip to France and was due to attend his daughter's graduation from his alma mater, Brown University, in Providence, Rhode Island in a few days.

Again, struggling to keep up with the demands at Kearsley and his private practice, while also making time for his family and personal life, he decided against asking doctors at Lankenau to perform an autopsy as a courtesy. It was simply impossible to perform an autopsy after every sudden death.

On July 5, the day after residents had enjoyed a local fireworks display during the annual Independence Day celebration, seventy-

56

five-year-old Abbie Mortimer died of what seemed to be natural causes. Her private physician was called to the home, and Dr. Webster was not asked for assistance.

The women at the Kearsley Home were enjoying a full schedule of summer activities. Summers in the Delaware Valley are hot and moist, and the weather was perfect for picnics on the tree-shaded lawns. The women also enjoyed cookouts on the patio with family and friends, munching on sizzling hamburgers, potato salads, and punch or iced tea whipped up in the kitchen by the cooks and their assistants, who included the pleasant dietitian's aide from West Philadelphia, Anthony Joyner. The women also traveled away from the home to movies, museums, and art shows. Philadelphia is a city with myriad attractions for just about any taste, ranging from some of the nation's finest art museums and galleries to the famed Philadelphia Zoo, professional baseball, football and basketball teams, and such quaint institutions as the outdoor Italian produce market on the South Side.

Ninety-year-old Eugenia Borda hardly had a chance to begin taking advantage of some of the tours and outings before she was found dead in her second-floor apartment at the home. She had moved into Kearsley less than a month earlier because she could no longer keep up with her housework and the other demands of independent living. A religious woman who never married, just two days before her death she had ridden to church with her minister and his family. Her pastor would later remember her as a fine woman who was full of life.

Like so many other women who died at Kearsley before her, Miss Borda's body was speckled with blood around her mouth, nose, vagina, and rectum when she was found dead in her bed. She was pronounced dead by her personal physician. But this time, Dr. Webster realized that the perplexing string of deaths simply could not be attributed to coincidence or the fact that the women were elderly. Something sinister was going on.

During his near two decades of medical practice, the doctor hadn't knowingly examined homicide or rape victims previously. But he suspected that the women dying at Kearsley Home might have changed all that. He decided he would refuse to sign a death certificate for Miss Borda, in order to force the medical examiner to accept the case as a suspicious death. It was to quickly become even more suspicious.

Only a few hours after Miss Borda's death, Webster was caring for private patients at his office in suburban Havertown when he received a telephone call from Eleanore Matuskowitz. The Kearsley Home administrator was shaken, and fighting to remain calm while she passed on the shocking news. Seventy-two-year-old Mildred Alston had just been found dead in her apartment across the hall from Miss Borda's rooms. The body was in almost exactly the same condition as that of Miss Borda. There were the same smears of blood in the same body orifices. A pair of the old woman's panties were found discarded on the floor next to her body. Webster telephoned the news to the medical examiner.

Three days later, the medical examiner ruled that both women were victims of homicide. An autopsy had disclosed that Miss Borda died of strangulation. Another autopsy had indicated that Mrs. Alston was suffocated, apparently with a pillow from her bed.

A team of detectives from the homicide and rape units in West Philadelphia had already been busy interviewing residents and staff members at the home. The information they were coming up with was chilling. They learned that Mrs. Alston and her neighbor were only the latest of several elderly women who had died suddenly at Kearsley under mysterious circumstances.

And, except for the normal ailments and complaints of old age, most of the women had been in reasonably good health. The health of some had been excellent, in fact. A granddaughter of Mrs. Alston said the old woman's health was exceptional. And the young woman added an ominous observation about her grandmother: "I think she was murdered," she said. "She always locked her apartment door."

Whether or not Mrs. Alston was murdered, there was evidence to indicate that she *had* been robbed, either before or after her death. A diamond ring, wedding band, and a change purse were missing from her body and her room. The elderly widow would not have willingly parted with any of the objects, especially the rings.

Detectives quickly decided that the killer was probably someone who either worked at the home or who was known to residents or staff there. Very possibly, because the earlier suspected victims died during the evening or early predawn hours, the killer was a night employee or someone who had access to the home during those time periods. They theorized that the killer was someone who knew the routine of the home and the hours and habits of the security guards. It almost had to be someone who could move about the building without drawing attention.

But the employees were devastated by the deaths. To many, perhaps most of them, the elderly women whom they shared their working hours with were like family. Some of them broke down in tears when they were questioned. One of the employees had cared enough to attend the funerals of the women who died. Anthony Joyner was especially conspicuous at Mrs. Alston's funeral. Grieving relatives of the elderly woman watched as he approached the open casket twice, to peer mournfully inside. As they watched him, a granddaughter leaned toward her sister and muttered suspiciously, "That's probably the fellow who killed Granny."

Police investigating the most recent deaths checked out deliverymen, repairmen, painters, plumbers, and carpenters—anyone who had reason to visit the home on a regular, even irregular, basis. It was plodding, painstaking work, but the homicide detectives knew their jobs and carried out interviews and background checks in a patient, exacting, and professional manner. The detectives and their superiors were especially anxious to track down the suspected killer, or killers, because of the community outrage over the crime. Only a monster, it seemed, would attack, sexually abuse, and murder helpless old women. And the public, through newspapers, radio, television, and on the street, was demanding that he be stopped and brought to justice.

The Kearsley Home employed more than forty people, and one by one they were questioned, sometimes requestioned. Their backgrounds were checked, and they were cleared—or kept in mind for future investigation. Anthony Joyner was one of those who very quickly in the investigation began to receive special attention.

A resident of the Overbrook section of West Philadelphia, Joyner was described by his friends as a "cool dude," who was pleasant and "had it all together." Some of the young men on the street grinned, and joked about the special affection he had for old women. In Joyner's neighborhood, and among his friends, that coupled with his slight build made him a natural subject of jokes and accusations that he was weird or homosexual. Joyner didn't like the jokes, but he grudgingly accepted them. Almost everyone who knew him and talked with police agreed, however, that he was a fine, industrious individual who wasn't a troublemaker.

One of his fellow employees at the Kearsley Home described him to police as "a very nice fellow." Then she followed the comment with the half-quizzical observation that he seemed to like older women.

Only one of Joyner's acquaintances had anything negative to say about him during the initial spate of interviews conducted by the homicide detectives. The friend told police that Joyner had bragged about raping an elderly woman who lived in the neighborhood and stealing her jewelry after forcing his way into her home.

"He says this was his job," the informant told officers. But he quickly added: "Maybe he's just kidding. Maybe he just wanted to show us he's a man, not a faggot."

A quick check with the Sex Crimes detail in West Philadelphia turned up an unsolved case of a sixty-eight-year-old woman who was recently robbed and beaten by an intruder who forced his way into her home. A pair of detectives drove to the Kearsley Home, walked into the kitchen, and took Joyner into custody.

Transported to the city's main police headquarters, which among Philadelphians is known as "The Roundhouse" because of its circular construction, Joyner was whisked into an interrogation room and set down for a serious talk. Finding himself in a Roundhouse interrogation room was a shock to the slightly built, soft-spoken youth. He was barely twenty-two and had never been in trouble with police before. He was no match for his experienced interrogators.

Although he was reluctant at first to talk and replied to questions in monosyllabic denials, the detectives were persistent. He became confused, and his denials became increasingly weak and desperate. Finally, he blurted out what his interrogators were waiting to hear:

60

"Okay . . . okay," he whined. "I killed them all."

Once he had made the initial breakthrough, the words came easier. Joyner said he had raped and killed the helpless old women to prove that he was a man. Sex wasn't the motive, he said. He said he abused and murdered the women after fighting with his girlfriend. Then he peered up at the stern-faced officers and pleaded: "I'm in desperate need of help to have somebody make me stop doing this. I want the truth out . . . it's tearing me apart."

Responding to continued prodding by the detectives, Joyner went over the sexual assaults and murders one by one. The homicide officers had plenty of time to listen.

Joyner said some of the women had smothered after he pressed pillows over their faces in efforts to "put them to sleep."

Recounting the Eckard murder, Joyner said it was his night off when he forced his way into the cellar of the home and made his way to the old woman's apartment. He said he slipped up to her bed and pressed a pillow over her face so she couldn't recognize him. Then he raped her. As he was getting up to leave, he said the old woman grabbed him. "I pulled away and heard a thump, and ran out," he said.

Masking his cynicism, one of the detectives asked if he had hit the old woman. Joyner recoiled as if he had been insulted. "I wouldn't hit any of the old ladies," he protested, his features twisting in disgust.

The kitchen worker said he used a key to let himself into Mrs. Maxwell's apartment and covered her face with a pillow to put her to sleep and keep her from screaming. After raping her, he continued, he slipped out of the room on tiptoes so that he wouldn't disturb her slumber.

He said he again used a pillow when he attacked Mrs. Alston, pressing it over her face in case she woke up. Then he pulled up her nightgown and raped her. He said that when he noticed there was no longer any movement under the pillow, he thought that the old woman had fallen asleep.

Miss Borda was smothered with a rag Joyner jammed into her mouth. He said that he grabbed her after sneaking into the apartment and used the rag to stop her from screaming. Then he raped her.

Joyner said most of the assaults occurred during his evenings off work, and that he entered the building through the cellar. He also told the officers that he had no particular system for selecting his victims, and there was no special like or dislike for most of the women he attacked. With one exception, he said, he chose his victims at random. Mrs. Amlie was the exception.

The suspect said he didn't like her because she had accused him of stealing from her. Asked if it was true that he had stolen from her, he conceded that it was. He said he waited for the dinner hour and slipped into her apartment to loot it again when he was surprised to find her perched on her bed wearing only her stockings. She was undressing to take a bath.

Joyner said he grabbed her and threw her onto her back and raped her. Then he pressed a pillow to her face in an effort to suffocate her. After the woman stopped struggling, he got to his feet and riffled her purse, taking thirty dollars he found inside. He said he was getting ready to leave when the woman struggled up from the bed and lurched into the bathroom, apparently trying to get away from him. But he leaped after her and pushed her down, shoving her head into the water and holding it there until she drowned.

A few days later, he changed his story about the Amlie murder and claimed the old woman had invited him to her room for sherry. He said that she answered the door wearing only her stockings and a garter and that they chatted calmly for a few minutes until she told him to leave. It was then, he said, that he threw her down on the bed, held the pillow over her face, and raped her. After the rape he followed her to the bathroom and held her head underwater until she drowned.

Joyner was charged with multiple counts of murder, rape, assault, and robbery after his initial confession to the crimes at the Kearsley Home. He had admitted the brutal rape and murder of six elderly residents of the home. The murder counts carried a possible maximum penalty of execution in Pennsylvania's electric chair. He was also charged with rape, robbery, and burglary in the attack of the West Philadelphia woman in her home. Police transported him to the Philadelphia Detention Center, where he was locked up and held without bail.

When the assistant dietition's photograph was printed in Philadelphia newspapers the next day, it brought a shock of recognition from a granddaughter of Mildred Alston. She realized that he was the Kearsley employee who had attended her grandmother's funeral services.

"Like an arsonist who returns to the scene of the fire to see the results of his work, he probably came back to see what Granny looked like," the horrified woman observed.

Joyner said that he couldn't afford to hire a lawyer, so Common Pleas Court Judge Edwin Malmel appointed an attorney to represent him.

Autopsies previously passed over for the Eckard, Maxwell, Monroe, and Amlie women, were finally performed by pathologists for the medical examiner's office. The frozen remains of Mrs. Maxwell had been donated to medical science and were being kept at the University of Pennsylvania Medical School since her death nearly six months earlier. The body was returned to the medical examiner's office for autopsy. Philadelphia district attorneys' officers obtained a court order for the exhumation of the other three bodies. The belated autopsies confirmed that each of the women had been sexually assaulted and murdered.

An assistant medical examiner who conducted the autopsy on Miss Borda, one of the two women killed in the terrible twenty-four hours at the home, said there was evidence of forcible intercourse immediately before her death by strangulation. "I believe she was a virgin up until the time she was assaulted," he said of the ninety-year-old spinster.

Once he had legal representation, Joyner attempted to retract his signed confession.

He denied that he had made the statements voluntarily and charged that he was intimidated and tricked into the confession. He insisted that he was unaware that he was going to be charged with murder and was told that he would be free to go home if he would merely sign some release papers. He said he was advised that he was being taken to get a sandwich when he was escorted in handcuffs before a municipal judge. He insisted that he wasn't paying attention because he was thinking of going home and didn't hear the judge advise him he was being charged with murder.

63

He admitted, however, that no one had made any effort to stop him from reading any of the papers he signed.

Joyner failed in his effort to have the confession ruled inadmissible, and it was a key element in the prosecution's case against him when the trial opened before Judge Malmel in April 1984.

But the court did forbid any discussion during the trial of police suspicions that the six women named as victims in the indictments might not have been the only ones murdered at the home. A records check disclosed that seventeen women died at Kearsley in the twenty-two months that Joyner worked there. Even though some of the women were in the home's hospital unit and under close twenty-four-hour observation, it was a startling number when one considered that it represented more than one quarter of the population of residents at any given time.

The formerly clean-shaven Joyner had grown a neat goatee and mustache for the trial. Slicked up with his new facial hair and a business suit, he listened intently to the testimony as the trial progressed, scribbling occasionally on a yellow notepad and whispering with his attorneys.

His former girlfriend, twenty-three-year-old Vicki Marie Davis, was one of the key prosecution witnesses against him. She testified that Joyner had bragged to her two days before his arrest that the next time she would hear from him he would be famous. "He told me to watch the news," she said.

She told the court that Joyner had previously refused to permit her to go to the Kearsley Home, explaining that police wouldn't let her past the gate "because there had been a lot of murders."

Homicide Detective Phil Checcia also contributed damaging testimony when he retraced the interrogation session and confession police obtained from the defendant at the Round House. He said Joyner told him and his colleagues that he was drunk the night of the double murder of Mrs. Alston and Miss Borda. Joyner explained that he was angry because his friends had been teasing him and called him a "faggot," so he worked off his pique in the orgy of rape and murder.

Checchia said Joyner told him that he was admitting the slayings "to get it off my conscience so I can sleep at night again." The detective said that when the defendant first admitted the crimes, tears welled up in his eyes. "But then he seemed to act calm."

Sex Crimes Unit Officer Carol Keenan also testified that he voluntarily confessed to raping Miss Borda, Mrs. Alston, and others while holding pillows over their faces to keep them from recognizing him or crying out. She echoed Checchia's testimony that the confessions were given knowingly after Joyner was advised of his constitutional rights, and voluntarily waived his privilege of remaining silent.

Alice McGhee, activities coordinator at Kearsley, provided confirmation of his admission that he had been caught stealing from Mrs. Amlie. The witness said Mrs. Amlie told her that Joyner was visiting her in her room and had complimented her on her appearance when she excused herself to use the bathroom. After she returned, she discovered twenty dollars missing from her purse and she reported the theft to the activities coordinator.

Joyner testified in his own defense, a voluntary act which murder suspects usually decline in order to avoid cross-examination by prosecutors. But as the neatly dressed defendant seated himself in the witness chair, he appeared to be at ease and gave every appearance of a man who was eager to tell his story and clear himself of terrible accusations.

Repeating his denials that he had confessed voluntarily, he attempted to discredit Checchia's damaging testimony by indicating that he was unduly intimidated by the detective's behavior. He pointed out that he had never been arrested before and complained that the husky six-foot two-inch Checchia pushed him around and frightened him. "It seemed like fire was in his eyes. He was pointing at my face, saying I was lying about something," Joyner said. At one point he refused to repeat a statement he blamed on Checchia, primly explaining that "I don't use four-letter words."

He also denied telling his girlfriend that when she heard from him next he would be famous. "Those words never entered my mind. Unless I did something pretty good—that would be famous," he said. "This is not famous."

The jury of six men and six women deliberated ten hours after conclusion of the testimony and closing statements before returning with a verdict. Joyner stood impassively with his hands clasped in front of him as the jury reported finding him guilty on five counts of first-degree murder, one count of second-degree murder in the death of Mrs. Eckard, and several lesser charges. One woman juror was so emotionally upset that she couldn't stand when the jury was polled on their vote, and she was permitted to remain seated.

But in its deliberations at the conclusion of the penalty phase of the trial, the jury deadlocked over a recommendation of death by execution or life in prison. Consequently, Judge Malmed sentenced Jordan to the mandatory term of life in prison.

Nattily dressed in a dark suit with a red handkerchief in his breast pocket, the handcuffed Joyner greeted the news of the jury deadlock and the sentence with a broad smile. He had beaten the death penalty. "He was very happy about it," Defense Attorney Arthur James later told the press. "As a matter of fact, when I told him, it was the first smile I'd seen in a couple of days."

THREE

Richard Angelo
Angel of Death

Dedicated Nurse Lauren Ball kept trying to convince herself that her immediate boss and colleague, Richard Angelo, was a regular guy.

The heavyset, bearded male nurse who worked two night shifts a week with her at Good Samaritan Hospital in West Islip on New York's Long Island had never given his colleagues any reason to distrust him.

In fact, he would go out of his way to ensure everyone liked him. He desperately wanted their respect.

But Nurse Ball just couldn't shake off an uneasy feeling that the quiet-spoken, super-efficient Angelo could be linked to the alarming increase in the death rate in the hospital's intensive care unit.

It could be put down to women's intuition, but patient Nancy Falabella shared Nurse Ball's nagging suspicions about Angelo, her night-shift supervisor. "Keep that nurse with the beard away from me," sixty-seven-year old Mrs. Nancy Falabella, a retired teacher's aide from Brooklyn, told her son Sam shortly before her untimely death in the chilly dawn hours of October 11, 1987.

Deaths at Good Sam—the hospital's nickname—were like a miniepidemic: One minute elderly patients were stable and doing well when night nurses made their bed checks; a few seconds later they would be turning blue in the face, gasping for air, fighting for

67

life.

Doctors and nurses alike were baffled and horrified over this macabre sequence of events.

Twenty-five patients had died over a six-week period, all in similar circumstances and all while Angelo was on duty. Suspicion of foul play, with Angelo the logical suspect, was so rife that authorities decided that as many as thirty-three bodies of patients who had died over a period of several months should be exhumed for autopsies.

Incredibly, Angelo still had many admiring, still-unsuspecting colleagues and friends who were convinced that the awful death toll in the compact twenty-four-bed intensive care and cardiac units could have been higher if it hadn't been for the heroic efforts of the twenty-five-year-old who was the night-shift supervisor and had a king-size reputation for saving lives. They were among the ones who never failed to marvel at the dedication and professionalism of the eager beaver former Eagle Scout and altar boy Angelo. Richard was always first on the scene when a patient crisis call— known as a "Code Blue" in hospital jargon—went out.

Members of the night-shift Code Blue team at Good Sam were consistently impressed that the first member of the revival team to reach the dying patient was invariably Nurse Angelo. Admiring co-workers would nudge one another and nod with approval. They could barely conceal their respect and admiration at the way the stocky, genial but shy New Yorker efficiently sized up the situation and invariably elected to be the one who administered CPR to patients in seizures while they were desperately gasping for their lives.

There were other nurses, however, who developed nagging doubts. Maybe this guy was just too good to be true. Wasn't it strange that most Code Blue emergencies seemed to happen only on the nights Richard worked.

October 11, 1987, was like D-Day for deaths on the night shift. It was the day Angelo got caught in his own warped web of deceit and murder. The first to die early that fateful morning was patient Joseph Mirabella who was in excellent condition minutes before Nurse Angelo checked up on him; then came a near-fatal assault on a Yugoslavian patient Gerolamo Cucich, who was saved in the nick of time by Nurse Ball's alertness. Angelo's final victim was

68

probably sixty-seven-year-old Mrs. Falabella.

Despite Angelo's outwardly caring and amiable demeanor, he somehow managed to project a strange, menacing aura. Many patients—including the late Mrs. Falabella—had become so scared of the burly, bespectacled night nurse that they begged to be tended by "anyone but the nurse with the beard."

The spine-chilling story behind Angelo's transformation from a hospital's Angel of Mercy to an Angel of Death only came to light in those grim evening and early-morning hours when two patients inexplicably developed seizures less than four hours apart. Mr. Mirabella died; Nurse Ball saved Mr. Cucich. Angelo's 11 P.M.-to-7 A.M. night shift of horrors culminated with the 6 A.M. death of the suspicious but vulnerable Mrs. Falabella.

Seventy-one-year-old Joseph Mirabella had been operated on for an intestinal disorder and, to everyone's surprise, including doctors and nurses, he was in great spirits shortly after he came to in the recovery room. Joe Mirabella was one tough cookie. The president of a Deer Park, N.Y., aluminum-door company, Mirabella had pulled through his operation marvelously. He looked so good and was in such fine fettle that his loving wife Jenny and the entire family shed tears of joy and pride as Dad gave them the thumbs-up sign as they left his room in the intensive care unit. His cocky parting gesture reassured them he was on the road to a normal life again.

The Mirabella family had barely walked into their home when the telephone rang. It was an urgent message from the hospital for Mrs. Mirabella. Nervously, she picked up the phone. She couldn't believe what she was hearing. She was in a state of collapse—her husband Joe had just died of a massive, unexpected heart attack at 1:30 A.M., less than an hour after the family had left him in hale and hearty condition.

The grieving Mirabella family returned to the hospital. Solicitous and caring, Nurse Angelo escorted them to the morgue where they viewed the corpse of the brave husband and father they had said a cheery good-bye to earlier that evening.

Angelo, devoutly religious, comforted them in their grief as he led them from the morgue to the hospital exit.

Less than an hour later, another Code Blue was signaled. But this time the spunky victim survived to accuse Angelo as his would-be assassin.

Brave Nurse Ball, responding to the sound of an alarm buzzer in the room of seventy-three-year-old Gerolamo Cucich, heard him struggling, gasping for breath, fighting for life, as she called the emergency code. Immediate resuscitation snatched Mr. Cucich from near death.

In brief, halting sentences, he was able to tell Nurse Ball a chilling story that immediately confirmed all those nagging suspicions she had had about Angelo.

Mr. Cucich, a Yugoslav who took ill while visiting relatives in Long Island, New York, was in pretty good shape for his age and was only in the hospital for a routine operation. He recalled dozing in the early hours of the morning when a heavyset male nurse with a beard and wearing a white coat came into his room. "I'm going to give you something to make you feel better," whispered the male nurse as he injected a liquid into Cucich's intravenous feeding tube. Immediately, the elderly patient felt frightening changes in his body and was unable to breathe. Only Nurse Ball's timely intervention saved his life.

Angelo's lust for adulation and glory had not been satisfied that night. Mrs. Falabella was still to die.

Mrs. Falabella, a sixty-seven-year-old retired teacher's aide from Brooklyn, N.Y., had successfully undergone her operation to have a cancerous spleen removed but was moved into an intensive care unit—under Angelo's jurisdiction—after internal complications set in. But from day one she never liked Angelo, recalled daughter-in-law Jean Falabella.

It was shortly after her transfer to Angelo's territory, the intensive care unit, that the Falabella family noticed that their mother began to experience difficulty in breathing. "I'll never forget my husband telling her, 'I swear on my four kids, Mom . . . you're going to be fine. I wouldn't lie to you,' " Jean remembered tearfully. But her condition during her short stay in the ICU deteriorated rapidly. "The next day she was lying limply across the mattress on her bed, as if she had had a stroke. The difference in her condition was like night and day." Jean remembered how her mother-in-law's eyes were glassy and how, when she tried to lift her limp arm, it felt like a deadweight. "It has been a nightmare. This man had no right to play God and do what he did to her!"

What made Mrs. Falabella's death an especially hard blow to her devoted family was that she had not wanted to be treated in Good Samaritan Hospital in the first place. But because of the hospital's good reputation, Sam and Jean, her caring son and daughter-in-law, insisted that Good Sam was the best hospital for her to go to to have her cancerous spleen removed. It was a fatal decision—and, sadly, it has burdened a loving family with a guilt they will carry for the rest of their lives.

Jean Falabella confirmed her mother-in-law's strange premonition about Angelo. "She used to say to me, 'Keep that male nurse away from me.' At first we thought she was embarrassed about being seen in bed by a male stranger. But now we suspect she had a gut instinct there was something wrong about Angelo."

The same gut instinct applied to Nurse Ball. But at that stage she was still shaken from the near-death of Mr. Cucich. He was so convinced Angelo was responsible that Nurse Ball had no choice but to confront Angelo with the sinister accusation. An indignant Angelo denied ever having been in the patient's room.

Unconvinced, Nurse Ball persevered, passing on her information and suspicions to higher authorities the following day. Because of Angelo's impeccable credentials, Nurse Ball was advised to keep her suspicions to herself until a preliminary investigation was made.

As a result, Mr. Cucich was examined extensively and traces of the powerful, paralyzing muscle relaxant Pavulon were found in his blood and urine and in his intravenous tube. Fortunately, the hardy Mr. Cucich survived his ordeal and was able to testify against his would-be killer almost three years later when he returned from his native Yugoslavia as a key witness at Angelo's trial.

Pavulon is the same drug used in massive doses to execute death-row murderers in Texas. In small doses it is used as a muscle relaxant during operations or to relax patients while life-saving breathing tubes are inserted down their throat. In many respects it resembles curare, the deadly poison South American Indians use to tip their arrows. In small doses and in adulterated forms it can be a valuable medicine. In the wrong hands and in large doses, it can only offer death by slow torture, suffocating its victim slowly.

Two of the drugs found in Angelo's possession, Pavulon and po-

71

tassium chloride, are used routinely on the Texas death row, along with another drug called sodium thiopental. The sodium thiopental knocks out a condemned man in less than twenty seconds, explained a Texas Department of Corrections spokesman. Moments later, the other drugs kick in. Pavulon freezes the victim's breathing apparatus, causing suffocation, while the sodium chloride shuts down the heart. At least twenty-six murderers have died that way since Texas reinstated the death penalty ten years ago.

To get further insight into the potency of Pavulon and its effects on humans, one must be aware that its initial effect is to paralyze the lungs. Then the victim's tongue curls back in the mouth, facial muscles freeze, and there is a terrifying choking sensation. Within eight to ten minutes the victim stops breathing completely.

What makes death even more horrible is that the victim becomes fully awake after being injected with the relaxants, Pavulon and Anectine. They are acutely aware of what is happening to them, as the drugs do not impair the ability to think, hear, or feel pain. They can actually feel every terrifying emotion as they suffocate to death.

"It feels like instant death. It's like somebody has grabbed hold of your throat. Then it's just a matter of how long you can hold your breath . . . thirty, maybe sixty seconds? After that you can feel your whole body going numb," described one Pavulon injection victim who went through the awful experience but was resuscitated at a veteran's administration hospital in Detroit in 1975. In that case a nurse was the alleged attacker and was convicted on six counts of illegally administering poison to patients, but the convictions were overturned.

After October 11, Angelo was not allowed to put any more of his helpless charges through that hellish torture. He was immediately suspended from duty pending further investigation.

Suffolk County Medical Examiner Dr. Charles Hirsch immediately called for an in-depth review of the charts of thirty-seven patients who died or experienced life-threatening medical problems while Angelo was on night-shift duty.

Dr. Hirsch went all out to build a watertight case against Angelo. Although he had confessed, there was little physical evidence against him. It was known that he had used Pavulon. It was also suspected that Angelo had paralyzed other victims with the other drug, Anectine. Dr. Hirsch even recruited the assistance of a sophisticated research laboratory in Stockholm, Sweden, to analyze body tissues for traces of Anectine.

Early in November, authorities began the grim task of resurrecting bodies from the cold winter soil for examination. The first two possible victims were sixty-seven-year-old Nancy Falabella, and sixty-year-old Frederick LaGois. Mrs. Falabella's son, Sam, signed the waiver authorizing the exhumation of his mother's corpse from Calvary Cemetery, in Queens, N.Y. Lillian LaGois also signed a waiver allowing the district attorney's office to exhume her father's body from Calverton National Cemetery in Long Island. The D.A.'s office had to get additional permission from the graves registry in Washington, D.C., to exhume Mr. LaGois, because Calverton is a national cemetery.

Friday the thirteenth of November 1987, was an unlucky day for Angelo. Police searched his locker and turned up hypodermic needles and a vial of potassium chloride, a drug which can cause fatal heart rhythms when used improperly. These drugs are normally kept under lock and key in the hospital dispensary and are not what you would expect to find in a nurse's personal locker. A search of the cardiac care unit's refrigerator revealed that a quantity of Pavulon was missing.

As the case against Angelo mounted, the police couldn't keep a lid on the magnitude of the horror anymore. They heard that the mass-circulation New York City and Long Island daily newspaper, *Newsday,* was planning to publish details about the case. Detectives decided it was time to take him into custody. On Saturday, November 14, police swooped down on Angelo's Lindenhurst apartment. He wasn't there, but they discovered further evidence – unmarked vials of Pavulon and Anectine.

Now the anxious detectives were asking themselves: Had the so-called Angel of Death decided that the game was up and flown the coop?

He wasn't at his home, he was still under suspension at the hospital, he wasn't visiting his parents in Florida, he wasn't at the volunteer firemen's headquarters. All leads seemed fruitless. Then Detectives Stephen Cleary and Kenneth McBride learned there was a three-day convention of medical technicians, hosted by the New York State Emergency Medical Services Council, at the state

73

capital in Albany.

Working a hunch the detectives decided to pay the convention a visit. That's where they found Angelo, a dedicated student of his chosen profession of nursing right to the end. The name of the conference was Vital Signs '87. The detectives had no difficulty in tracking down Angelo from the seven-hundred-fifty other names registered for this particular state seminar. He agreed to accompany them to police headquarters at Yaphank, Long Island, without a whimper.

Although distraught and emotional, Angelo waived his right to have a lawyer present and was quick to admit guilt. In four separate, sobbing, emotional statements, he told police that he had injected Mr. Cucich with the poison, and that on other occasions he had injected Pavulon and other dangerous paralyzing drugs into "dozens" of patients.

One of the most bizarre pieces of news to emerge from Angelo's confession was that he had conducted extensive research—or rehearsals—for his cold-blooded hospital killings on field mice!

He boasted to police that he became expert in the use of the drug Pavulon by trying it out on the little mice that he caught in a field bordering his Lindenhurst, New York home. Ghoulishly, he told detectives that he had stolen Pavulon from the hospital "so I could take it home to experiment with on my mice." In a macabre vein, Angelo admitted that "more than a couple" of mice had died while he was perfecting his skills. He hunted the mice himself, in a field—Firemen's Memorial Field—adjacent to his lodgings in Lindenhurst.

News that Angelo had been arrested and was in police custody washed over Nurse Lauren Ball in a wave of relief. She was the first to expose Angelo, a man she personally liked but about whom she always had the sneaking suspicion that he wasn't always the saint he would have liked people to believe. For more than a month, Nurse Ball knew intense investigations were going on, that she was a key witness, and that Angelo—the man nurses had nicknamed "The Kiss of Death" and the "Angel of Death" was on the loose. She had been instructed to keep her mouth shut about the case. At the same time she feared for her own life. Angelo knew that he had buffaloed a lot of people in the medical profession. But the killer was aware that Nurse Ball was not one of them. She had damning evidence that could put him away for a long time.

"It was tough going to work. I tried to keep to myself. I was told to cooperate, but keep quiet," said a relieved Nurse Ball. At home, she prayed. She cried a lot and had difficulty sleeping. She carried a burden of fear until Angelo's arrest.

As for blowing the whistle on the callous killer, Nurse Ball had no regrets. "I know it was the right thing to do," she told reporters. "I am happy now that I reported him because it may have saved a lot of people from harm."

"I'll still pray for him," she added. "I feel sorry for him. I had mistakenly thought he was a nice guy."

Investigators were still a long way from amassing sufficient physical evidence—exhumation and autopsies of alleged victims—to bring their first charge of murder against Angelo. Initially, the authorities were only able to pin the assault of Mr. Cucich on Angelo. Forensic and pathology experts warned there was going to be problems finding significant traces of deadly Pavulon in many of the other exhumed bodies because of elapsed time, decomposition, and the embalming process. Nevertheless, investigators from the district attorney's office proceeded doggedly and methodically digging up corpses and testing them for Pavulon.

"The fact that we found traces in one body increased the chance that it could be found in others," explained Assistant District Attorney Richard Lazio.

A Suffolk County grand jury eventually handed down its first murder indictment against Angelo on January 13, 1988. As autopsies continued, Angelo was charged in the slaying of sixty-year-old Frederick LaGois, a retired restaurant-supply manager and father of three, of West Babylon, New York.

Mr. LaGois had entered Good Sam at the end of September 1987, for a prostate operation. Like many other Angelo victims, he was in good health otherwise. To completely make sure he was fit for surgery, he was placed in the intensive care unit for preoperative heart testing. He was found to be in tip-top condition, and his prostate operation was set for Friday, October 9. But only hours before the scheduled operation, doctors phoned his wife at the family home in West Babylon, New York. He had gone into cardiac arrest at 3:30 A.M., and then into a coma. "That was it . . . he had another heart attack and passed away," said a relative.

A month later, when his body was exhumed, it was found he, too, had been injected with Pavulon.

Ironically, according to Angelo's videotaped confession, LaGois was the only one of his many victims who the beefy nurse could recall by name—a minor fact, but very significant when one considers the callous indifference Angelo felt for his helpless victims.

Allegations against the Angel of Death accelerated when Medical Examiner Hirsch revealed that yet another patient, seventy-five-year-old Milton Poultney, who died on September 16, 1987, after successful gall bladder surgery, was found to have poison in his corpse. Angelo and the drug Pavulon had been at work together again.

The Death Angel case took a dramatic turn as news of Angelo's monstrosities made lurid national headlines. Angelo had been desperate to be released from jail on bail since he was taken into custody in November. Suffolk County Judge Alfred Tisch granted his wishes in December—fifty thousand dollars cash bail or a hundred-thousand-dollar bond. Judge Tisch's decision to give Angelo the opportunity to go free came as a shock to the district attorney's office and to relatives of victims.

Richard Lazio, spokesman for District Attorney Patrick Henry declared: "Angelo is the ultimate bail risk. He is facing homicide charges, and will be quick to flee." Dorothy LaGois, widow of one of Angelo's victims, made the plea: "I'm sure he murdered my husband. I don't think he should be released after what he did."

But as things turned out, there was no need for any kind of public outcry.

Angelo's original intention was to seek release on bail so he could spend Christmas with his parents, but one of the bail conditions forbade him to travel to Sun City, Florida, where his parents lived. But in a weird turnaround, Angelo opted to stay in jail because he thought it was safer for him behind bars!

After a chat with his attorney, Eric Naiburg, and his devoted parents, Joseph and Alice Angelo, who had traveled from their retirement home in the Sunshine State to be with their beloved son every step of the way, the self-confessed killer reached the conclusion that things might be too dangerous for him beyond the prison walls. Explained lawyer Naiburg: "My client has decided not to come out because of the question of his safety."

76

Angelo had been receiving numerous threats on his life while sitting in jail and was afraid. It took his lawyer only forty five minutes to explain to his frightened client why he would be better off staying put. Lawyer Naiburg then told a group of reporters waiting outside Suffolk County Jail: "My client will not be coming out today or in the near future."

Asked why, Naiburg said he had advised his client to wait until the public furor had died down before taking advantage of the bail offer. "Angelo can't just walk into a local supermarket and buy a can of tuna fish. People will get emotional on him. People will yell things at him."

Angelo's reaction to his lawyer's stay-in-jail advice? "I've had better Christmases." Naiburg then revealed to reporters Angelo's bizarre but appropriate taste in literature. Over the holiday period, Angelo was reading *Say You Love Satan*, a book about the 1985 trial of Satan-worshipper James Troiano who was acquitted of murdering a teenager, even though he had confessed to the crime. Naiburg was also Troiano's attorney

Coincidental with Angelo's depressing pre-Christmas news, West Islip's Good Samaritan Hospital also came in for its share of criticism. The New York State health department accused the authorities at Good Sam of missing signals that should have alerted them that patients there were dying "for no clear reason." The department also faulted the hospital for sloppy record-keeping and shortcomings in patient care. In January 1989, Good Samaritan was fined fourteen thousand dollars, with five thousand suspended, for violations of state regulations that were uncovered during the investigation of the Angelo case. The health department had charged the hospital with fourteen violations of state health law.

One really damaging flaw in the general administration of the hospital was that a "mortality review committee" did not meet that summer, or during the period when a great number of unexpected deaths had occurred. "The hospital lost an opportunity to find and correct a problem faster," observed Wayne Osten, a top state health department official.

Top brass at Good Sam had already conducted their own investigation as to why Angelo hadn't been uncovered as a homicidal saboteur. The reason, they decided, was probably a combination of four factors. First, Angelo had both excellent references and substantial experience when he was hired in April, 1987. Second, he didn't really want to kill his victims. According to police he just wanted to make them sicker so he could rush in and save them. Those who get sicker don't get as much scrutiny as those who die. Third, Angelo's victims were old and sick. Thus, in many cases, heart or respiratory emergencies among these patients would not be out of the ordinary. And last, Pavulon and Anectine, the drugs Angelo used, were readily available to nurses in Good Samaritan's intensive care-coronary care unit.

As the hospital was put under an investigative spotlight, Good Sam president, Daniel P. Walsh, conceded that the institution had been besieged by calls from people who wanted to know if their loved ones had been among Angelo's victims.

At the same time, President Walsh displayed staunch loyalty to his shattered employees when he sent a letter "to everyone in our Good Samaritan family," thanking them for their courage and support "while our hospital's reputation has been under siege."

There was no doubt that Walsh and his staff were reeling under heavy buffeting and blame from the press, the public, and outraged relatives of the Death Angel's victims. Chief coronary care nurse and director of cardiac care nursing at the West Islip hospital, Barbara Rouleau, admitted her staff was "completely devastated" as the news of their colleague's activities slowly emerged. "My staff is so completely shocked, so horrified, they're beside themselves," said Chief Nurse Rouleau. "These are good people, excellent nurses, but somehow this man betrayed all of us. I think about the victims' families every day. Those poor people . . ."

Why did no one turn Angelo in any sooner?

Said Nurse Rouleau: "There was absolutely no way that anyone could have suspected it. Richard was their teacher, their helpmate. He was intelligent . . . involved . . . a natural leader. His assessment of patients, nurses' notes, and care plans were so thorough."

The problem, she said, was basically "he knew what he was doing and no one else did." A month after the official investigations began, Nurse Lauren Ball, who had originally fingered Angelo as a killer, resigned from her post. Nurse Ball emphasized that her resignation had nothing to do with any unhappiness over the way Good Samaritan officials handled the investigation. "I feel very bad about what has happened to the reputation of Good Samaritan. It's a wonderful institution," said the nurse.

Ironically, as the Falabella family had observed, the Long Island not-for-profit hospital had enjoyed a first-class reputation for its facilities and care since its opening on May 18, 1959. It had been built thanks to community donations. It is equally ironic that one of the services Good Sam prided itself on was its selfless, dedicated, and efficient employees. The hospital described them as among their "greatest assets." "The hospital has a reputation for delivering very high standards of care. It has a range of services," said Robert Ward, director of the Nassau-Suffolk Hospital Council, whose members include Good Samaritan.

The 415-bed facility treated almost 19,000 patients in 1986, posting a busy 94.2 percent occupancy rate. The statistics indicate a heavy demand for its services, showing how well the hospital is regarded by patients. "Our biggest strength is our people. We have extremely dedicated employees who have a reputation for being extremely caring and are always ready with a smile," commented hospital spokesman Ted Shieble.

Meantime, the man who had done most to sully the fine reputation that had taken Good Sam four decades to build, Richard Angelo, was sitting in prison ruminating his fate. He was no longer upset about missing the opportunity to spend Christmas in Florida with his parents. Angelo, thanks to the wide publicity his monstrous activities had generated across the U.S., was still receiving countless death threats from inside and outside the prison walls. He was now quite happy to stay where he was—under a twenty-four-hour suicide and security watch.

He was allowed out of prison once before his trial . . . to go on a field trip to the scene of his crimes to help lawyer Naiburg prepare his defense. In handcuffs and leg shackles, surrounded and shielded by jail, hospital, prosecution and defense representatives, Angelo was whisked from the prison in Riverside to Good Samaritan Hospital where, for one hour, he showed authorities the special care and cardiac units where he was formerly employed. The whirlwind tour was made in the utmost secrecy because Judge Alfred Tisch, who authorized the midnight visitation, didn't want Angelo's presence to needlessly alarm or harm the critically ill patients still in the hospital.

Originally, the hospital had opposed any such visit, claiming that Angelo's presence there would create "a circuslike atmosphere," according to hospital spokesman Ted Shiebler, who initially offered to supply the lawyers and other officers of the court, including jurors, with videotapes of the units in question. But defender Naiburg successfully argued that it was essential that all those concerned view the hospital units firsthand to ensure Angelo a fair trial. Thus, the surreptitious midnight visit.

One of the most chilling observations to be made in this whole horrifying tale was Angelo's cold-blooded approach to his crimes. In fact, one victim injected by Angelo died slowly and painfully as Angelo looked on, dispassionately, totally devoid of human emotion. Another Good Sam night nurse, Laurie Sutherland, vividly described how seventy-five-year-old patient John Stanley Fisher stopped breathing at 2:45 A.M. on September 8, 1987. She heard a cardiac arrest alarm in Fisher's room go off while she was writing notes in the nurses' station. It only rang for a few seconds, and Angelo told her he had turned it off. It was a false alarm. But when it went off again, she and Angelo went into Mr. Fisher's room together.

"Mr. Fisher was blue. He wasn't breathing and his pulse rate was in the thirties, so we called a Code Blue," said Nurse Sutherland.

For about twenty minutes, Sutherland, Angelo, and other medical personnel worked on Mr. Fisher "but he did not respond."

After investigations revealed that traces of Pavulon were found in Mr. Fisher's corpse, his physician, neuropathologist Dr. Norman Chernik said he would never consider using Pavulon on a patient in Mr. Fisher's condition. Hospitalized with stroke symptoms, Mr. Fisher's cardiac and respiratory condition had stabilized and the patient was in good shape when Dr. Chernik saw him the day before his surprise death.

The Fisher case was one of several instances where Angelo's warped plans for self-glory backfired. Basically, the callous hospital killer's motive was to make himself look like a hero. As his elderly patients lay defenseless in their beds, some hanging on to life by a thread, they could do little to protect themselves from drug overdoses induced by the suspect, Angelo would return to their rooms, recognize the problem right away, and save his victim's life. Tragically, in many cases he had overdosed some patients with his lethal injections so that they were beyond help.

Apart from the intuitive suspicions by a few colleagues and a patient at Good Sam, Angelo was the type of man who could easily get lost in a crowd. Overweight, short-sighted, balding, Angelo was a loser from the word go. An only child of doting parents, he had low self-esteem and the only way he could live with himself was to be the best and most respected in all his endeavors. He always needed to be the white knight riding to the rescue in the nick of time. Certainly Angelo's timing left much to be desired. Of thirty-seven Code Blue emergencies reported in the hospital units under his care over a six-week period, twenty-five of the patients died!

He told detectives himself that he was pretty much like those guys who go around setting off fires so they can perform some kind of heroic rescue or perform a noble public service by putting out the fire.

Not only did Angelo fit into that category, he was, in fact, a highly respected volunteer fireman in his hometown of Lindenhurst. He kept to himself most of the time and was never seen going out with girls. Notwithstanding, Angelo saw himself as a pillar of the community. He even volunteered to dress up in an elf's costume for the volunteer fire department's Christmas parade one year. Friends and neighbors knew him as a kindly, gentle soul. Among his favorite outdoor activities was mowing the lawns or lending a hand filling oxygen tanks at the volunteer fire department headquarters.

His former next-door neighbor in Lindenhurst, a tidy and comfortable little town of twenty-nine thousand people on Long Island's South Shore, Mrs. Frances Maher, was stunned when told that the man she had known all his life as "little Ricky" had been playing God with peoples' lives. "I think the kid must have been crying out for attention," she said. Even the town's assistant fire chief Alfred Drouin, who had difficulty believing there was a dark, murderous side to his young friend, said: "I wish I had twenty more just like him. He was always very gentle when people were injured or sick. He and I have cut people out of cars together . . . I would never in a million years think this man could do anything to hurt somebody. When I heard the news I thought first of all that he must have a brother."

81

A God-fearing Roman Catholic and former angel-faced altar boy, Angelo had no dark secrets in his domestic or social life. His parents were schoolteachers. They were model citizens, a close-knit family who kept pretty much to themselves. They lived together in a comfortable Cape Cod home in the suburbs of Long Island. The Angelos lived the ultimate middle-class American dream. Richard was one of the do-gooders. He could have stepped out of a television sitcom depicting the perfect, well-scrubbed, moral and ethical U.S. family.

Growing up, young Ricky wasn't the type of boy you had to tell twice to mow the lawn, rake up leaves, or do other tiresome chores for his parents and neighbors. He was always on the plump side, so he did not shine when it came to Little League baseball and other sports. But Ricky never stopped trying to be the best he could ever be. He proved this in the Boy Scouts when he was awarded the much-coveted Eagle Scout badge.

As a boy, Ricky loved going hunting and fishing with his proud and caring father. And he adored visiting his warm Italian grandma who used to bake delicious Italian pastries especially for her only grandson, her pride and joy.

"He was always helping his father," observed Muriel Mavelli, who lives across from Angelo's childhood home. "But he seemed to be a solitary person. I never saw him with too many friends."

Because of his parents' background, Angelo was a studious kid. His dad, Joe, was a junior high school guidance counselor and his mom, Alice, a substitute home economics teacher. As a result, he got the best Catholic education in the area; the Perpetual Help Elementary School and then St. John the Baptist High School.

At the same time, he was cultivating a religious lifestyle that was to stay with him all his life. Like his parents, he never missed a Sunday Mass. An early influence in his life was an uncle, a priest in Pennsylvania. Ricky was proud of his role as altar boy at the Our Lady of Perpetual Health Church. His face shone with delight and he basked in the attention as he assisted at Mass, carefully carrying the silver communion plate, conscientiously following the priest down the aisle to the chapel's grand altar.

In fact, as he matured, he seemed almost too perfect for some people. "He never drank, he never smoked, he never went out with girls," said a neighbor.

After high school graduation in 1980, Angelo took a two-year nursing degree from the State Agricultural and Technical College in Farmingdale, New York. This led to a job in the burn unit of Nassau County Medical Center. But he did seem to be able to handle things well. "He was competent, but no more than that. He had trouble with his fellow employees," said medical center spokesman Edward Smith. "The reason he was always in trouble was because he was always calling in sick." He moved on to another job at Brunswick Hospital in Amityville, New York. For some reason this wasn't to his liking, so he quit in January 1987 to visit with his parents now retired permanently in Florida. As his Good Sam activities came to light, extensive investigations were made, but authorities are pretty certain that Angelo did not involve himself in any similar kind of activities in his first two jobs.

With his parents' retirement, Angelo was on his own for the first time in his life. This meant he had to take a room in a private home on another quiet street in his hometown of Lindenhurst. That's where he was living when he returned from Florida after four months to take his responsible job at Good Sam.

Even today, Ricky's loyal neighbors in Lindenhurst prefer to close their ears to any criticism of Angelo. Friend and neighbor Fran Peragine sang his praises: "He was just a normal kid. He was in the Boy Scouts, Little League, and he won the highest award, Eagle Scout. I remember him asking me to come along when he was presented with his award. He was a volunteer fireman, even as a kid . . . he volunteered as young as they would take him. You won't get anything bad about him out of me. He was a good boy."

All grown up and ostensibly working happily at Good Sam, holding down a responsible, supervisory position, Richard kept a low profile, conservative and proper. When he wasn't at work, he liked nothing better than labeling his cherished rock collection — which was very valuable and so unique it had been put on display in public libraries — or voraciously reading encyclopedias, particularly the medical sections, continually satisfying his thirst for knowledge and self-improvement.

Neighbors at his new address in Lindenhurst knew little of the quiet young man who lived on the top floor of Mrs. Jean Scarigliano's home. "I am shocked. I just can't believe it," said landlady Mrs. Scarigliano, who lived downstairs. She described him as a good tenant who always paid his rent on time. But, like others on the same street, she was unable to throw much light on what he was like as a person, other than he worked all night, slept during the day, and drove a nondescript black four-wheeled vehicle.

After his initial sobbing confessions to the police, Angelo kept the same low profile throughout subsequent investigations and his marathon trial. The accused and his attorney insisted every step of the way that no one was supposed to die, and submitted Angelo's inadequacies and low self-esteem as important ingredients of his defense. But it was Angelo who said in one of his many voluntary statements: "I did do it intentionally. I wanted to prove myself to the staff." Then, in a pathetic afterthought, he whined: "I look silly now . . . and I'm sorry."

Frail but fiesty Mr. Cucich was the only patient who lived to talk about his ordeal. He did not waver when at last he got the chance to have his day in court—even though it meant jetting halfway round the world to help bring Angelo to justice. In the witness box, he did not hesitate, and it was almost with relish that he raised his hand to point the accusing finger and positively identify the portly, bespectacled accused as his Angel of Death.

Angelo did not raise his head or look at the witness as the old Yugoslavian, a retired hotel worker, unwavering in his testimony, damned him with that outstretched hand and pointed finger. He had no doubt that the defendant was the man in the white coat who had callously and painfully taken him to the brink of death. Cucich had been visiting the U.S. with friends in Long Island when he was admitted suddenly to Good Samaritan hospital on October 1987 for observation after suffering chest pains. He had no hesitation in remembering how Angelo had entered his room and in a calm, soft voice had offered to give him something to make him feel better. After Angelo administered the injection, Cucich, in halting English, attempted to describe the torture that swept throughout his aging body. "I was jumping, moving. I couldn't breathe. I called out for anyone I could ever remember. Father! Mother! Anybody! I remember thinking about my family and how they would think I had died of a heart attack," said Mr. Cucich emotionally. The courtroom was hushed as he delivered his moving evidence. Relatives of Angelo's victims and relatives of many more suspected victims who had not survived that kind of barbaric torture had tears in their eyes as they sat silently in the spectators' gallery.

Prior to the deadly injection, Mr. Cucich was aware that there was a man in his room that fateful night of October 11, 1987, but he thought it was only a doctor doing the rounds. He remembered the man asking how he was feeling, and that he had replied "Not bad." It was then that the man offered to give him something "to make [him] feel much better." He then produced a needle, which the patient thought at first was a fountain pen, and injected Cucich's intravenous tube. In seconds, the helpless patient couldn't breathe, and a kind of cramp and paralysis gripped him like a vise as he gasped for help. "When he stuck me, I felt cold liquid in my body. My muscles couldn't move. Everything was going dead," Cucich added.

Fortunately, it was his regular nurse, Nurse Ball, who responded to his cries. Nurse Ball and other medical personnel fought to resuscitate. Weeping, she pleaded for Cucich to open his eyes. He began to get some movement back in his arms and remembered how to put his hand over his eyes, trying desperately to force his eyelids open. When he did and started to breathe again, he suddenly became aware of the man in the white coat in the room. It was Richard Angelo, Cucich leveled his finger at Angelo, and told Nurse Ball, "He did it!" When Nurse Ball asked Angelo what he had been up to, he replied, "Nothing." Mr. Cucich, who was more alert than Angelo gave him credit for, instantly identified Angelo's voice as the same reassuring voice that had asked him how he felt just minutes previously.

Angelo was a lethal Walter Mitty. In police interviews, he gave the remarkable confession: "The reason I injected Mr. Cucich was the unit had been terribly busy, and I felt very inadequate in general. I felt I had to prove myself to the staff and to myself. The staff were asking me questions and using me as a resource person. I knew what I was doing and did it intentionally. I knew it would cause a respiratory distress and I knew we would have to intervene." Angelo gave similar analyses of himself in other confessions, describing himself as an 'inadequate person' who wanted to come across as a medical hero in the eyes of the doctors and nurses with whom he worked.

He was equally devious in the way he administered the lethal injections of Pavulon and Anectine. Assistant District Attorney

Edward Jablomski, who attended one of the accused's confession sessions, told how Angelo took great pains to prevent being discovered.

He would take doses of the lethal drugs home with him where he would mix the Pavulon and Anectine with saline solutions. The saline solution was commonly used by nurses to help clear patients' intravenous feeding tubes. It was particularly effective in clearing clogging blood. That way, if anyone caught him giving a lethal injection, he could always shrug it off by claiming he was just clearing their IV with saline solution. "He thought he could always bring them back to life. And he knows now that in some cases he didn't," added prosecutor Jablomski.

Meantime, inquiries into suspicious deaths, seizures, and other emergencies during Angelo's shifts at the hospital continued. Experts exhumed many bodies searching for traces of Pavulon, Anectine, and potassium chloride—all thought to be used by Angelo during his killing spree.

At one stage, there was evidence that Angelo could have killed anywhere from ten to twenty-five patients of the thirty-three bodies exhumed. How many other killings that were aborted because patients were successfully resuscitated are not known.

In any event, thanks to the miracle of modern forensic medicine, Medical Examiner Dr. Charles Hirsch found traces of the deadly drug Pavulon in six of the thirty-three exhumed bodies. In four of the cases, there was enough Pavulon found in the body to cause death. In the other two, there was insufficient evidence to establish that the drug had directly contributed to their deaths.

After an eight-week-long trial, including seven long days of jury deliberations, Angelo, now turned twenty-seven, was convicted on December 14, 1989, of second-degree murder and manslaughter by fatally injecting four patients with a deadly, paralyzing drug.

Throughout the trial, his attorney, Eric Naiburg, conceded that Angelo had administered the injections but had not intended to kill the patients. But the prosecution was not only successful in linking Angelo to the dangerous drug through confessions on both videotape and written admissions but provided other damning evidence, such as the syringe containing telltale traces of Pavulon found in Angelo's apartment the day before he was arrested.

The defense had also attempted to prove that Angelo was mentally ill, and therefore not legally responsible for the carnage at the Good Sam hospital that summer and fall of 1987 — a defense ploy that just didn't play in the light of the damning evidence and what Angelo had stated in his confessions.

The jury retired with the final words of the prosecutor, Suffolk County Assistant District Attorney John Collins, ringing in their ears. Prosecutor Collins dismissed the defense assertions that there were any deep-rooted psychological excuses or mental illness behind Angelo's barbarous behavior. "The defendant had a brilliant medical career going for him. He was an emergency medical technician of advanced status and a registered nurse who worked in elite units."

Earlier in the trial, Assistant DA Collins didn't mince words in his assessment of Angelo: "He is the embodiment of your worst nightmare . . . where you're being buried alive and can't do anything about it because you can't scream or catch your breath."

"He conducted uncontrolled experiments on unknowing and totally vulnerable human beings for his stated purpose of improving his image and his reputation," Collins added. "He was not content to stop — even after he experimented on mice and let them die."

Demanding the maximum sentence, District Attorney Collins said that Angelo's excuse that he had acted out of feelings of inadequacy might be true to a certain extent but that the defendant's key motivation all along was his deep-rooted contempt for authority. "Angelo truly was a monster," he added. "He violated the childlike trust that hospital patients must have in a hospital staff charged with their care." Collins asked the court to treat Angelo with the same compassion that he had shown his victims.

It took the seven-men and five-women Riverhead, New York, jury, who had been chosen from a huge pool of prospective jurors — Suffolk County's largest ever, almost eight days to reach their verdicts. This was because the variables in the case were so complex and the motives so obscure that the jury, in fairness to the accused, decided to take its time to ensure a fair verdict. As juror Allen Teplitzky said later: "We had to figure out what was going on in this man's mind. There was yelling and screaming by every one of us." Jury foreman Michael Loquercio summed up how he felt about his eight weeks of listening, deliberating, and coming up with a verdict in a case of such horror and complexity: "It was a fair sentence after a fair trial. Angelo knew what he did and now he knows the consequences of his acts."

The jury, after deliberation, accepted the prosecution's assertion that Angelo was "a monster in nurse's whites" who dreamed up diabolical schemes to win acclaim as a hero by bringing back dying patients from the brink of death.

On January 17, 1990, Angelo was sent to prison for fifty years to life for the slayings. Imposing the maximum sentence allowed by state law, Judge Alfred Tisch told Angelo: "You had no right to usurp God's function. Each of those patients had a right to enjoy, in their own way, every day that was available to them." The judge's maximum sentences in all the counts against Angelo actually totaled a sixty-one-and-a-half-year sentence but state law dictated a fifty-year limit.

His shoulders hunched, Angelo, smartly dressed in a gray sports coat and navy-blue slacks, didn't as much as sneak a glance at the jury during the reading of the verdicts. Occasionally he was seen biting his lip as he was found guilty of second-degree murder in the deaths of patients Milton Poultney, 75, a retired teacher, and Anthony Greene, 57; guilty of second-degree manslaughter in the death of John Fisher, 75; and guilty of criminally negligent homicide in the death of Frederick LaGois, 60.

He was also found guilty of second- and third-degree assault for injecting a drug into seventy-five-year-old Geralmo Cucich, the patient who survived and was able to provide investigators with the only firsthand description of his attacker.

Angelo was also found guilty of assault in the deaths of Poultney, Fisher, and Green. He was found not guilty of other charges of assault by injection in the cases of fifty-three-year-old Joan Hayes, and John O'Neill, two other fortunate patients who survived.

Even defense lawyer Naiburg—who had tried to convince the jury that, while Angelo had administered his victims with lethal doses of muscle relaxants, he had not intended to kill them—stoically accepted the sentence with the observation: "This is probably a fair verdict. Obviously I'm disappointed he was convicted on two murder counts, but I believe there was substantial evidence to support these counts. I feel sorry for anyone who will spend the rest of his life behind the four walls of a jail," he added. "I don't think that Richard Angelo will be a survivor for very long." But he did comment that there probably would be an appeal.

Judge Tisch made no attempt to conceal his contempt or his horror at the "cruel and inhumane" behaviour of the accused as he sentenced Angelo. "During my nineteen years on the bench, I've heard many stories of horror, but this one is at the top of the list.

"The course of conduct taken by this defendant gives new meaning to the concept of depraved indifference."

In a more sympathetic vein, Judge Tisch briefly addressed Angelo's parents, Joseph and Alice Angelo, both retired schoolteachers, who had sat quietly behind their son, Joe with his arm around his wife, showing little or no emotion during sentencing. Throughout the trial Angelo avoided making eye contact with his mom or dad. "It is likely that during the remainder of your natural life, your son will be incarcerated," the judge told the Angelos.

Angelo's parents, decent, intelligent retirees, were numb with shock as they sat through the trial and listened to the macabre and grotesque behaviour of their beloved son. In one of the few statements he made about his son, Joe Angelo commented: "We are very close. We used to talk to each other twice a week." The accused would speak about his work at the hospital. Remembered his saddened father: "I can almost recall my son's words exactly. He told me: 'I don't want to be just involved in examining the patient and writing the prescription. I want to get involved in the day-to-day treatment of patients.' "

Asked what he thought of the verdict, Mr. Angelo Senior stiffened and his face grew red. "I'm disappointed. I know Richard was not aware he had caused the death of anyone. He would not have been able to live with himself if he had," said his saddened father.

As Mr. Angelo spoke, there was an outburst in court as Angelo was being led, handcuffed, to the cells below to begin his sentence. "Enjoy life in jail, fat boy," cried out Kiernan Greene, whose father Anthony, a seventy-nine-year-old prominent Long Island lawyer and a former Suffolk County assistant district attorney, was a victim. Outside the court, young Greene said that he "didn't have a minute's worth of sympathy for Mr. Angelo . . . What he did to all of those people is beyond words."

Had justice prevailed?

The Angelo case had left many loose threads hanging, many unanswered questions. Although thirty-three bodies had been exhumed, the prosecution had decided—and rightly so—to bring only the charges with the strongest toxicological evidence. Angelo was cunning in that respect. The drugs he had used vanished quickly from corpses after interment. So for a few heartbroken families—among them the Mirabellas, the Falabellas, and Gardeneers, the O'Neills, and the Seiders—the case of the Death Angel and what he did to their loved ones will never truly be over.

It's a tragic legacy to bear. But at least they had the satisfaction of seeing Angelo removed from society for a long, long time.

Seventy-five-year-old retired illustrator and mailman Fred Gardineer will never know for sure that the evil Angel murdered Ruth, his beloved wife of forty-nine years. He still asks plaintively: "Her heart was good. Why did she have to die?" He still pores over his diary—the scribbled notes he made on pieces of paper during his wife's hospitalization because of a badly infected hip during that fateful October 1987. Here are a few excerpts:

"Oct. 5—heart stopped . . . they told me she had a bad night. Why would she have cardiac arrest when they checked her heart and it was all right?"

"Oct. 10—Nurse told me her heart was good."

"Oct. 12—High sugar! I don't understand. Is it affecting her brain? No case like it, doctor said."

Oct. 14—Noon—no positive signs. Called me at 9—she died!"

Mrs. Margaret O'Neill of West Islip is another person who can only think the worst. Her attorney husband Joseph went to Good Sam with a suspected heart attack on September 21, 1987. But when she left him in the intensive care unit, he was in good spirits.

"Don't forget to bring the newspapers tomorrow," he called to his wife as she left him sitting up in bed, bright and lively. Mrs. O'Neill arrived home to a telephone message that her husband had had a heart attack. Ten minutes later, there was another call. He was dead.

Another suspected victim of the killer nurse was millionaire movie theater mogul Joseph Seider, whose body was exhumed and examined in November 1987. There was little hope of finding any incriminating drugs in his corpse as he had been buried since June of that year.

Mr. Seider's exhumation made the headlines because of his career in the movie industry. At one time he was chief executive officer of Prudential Theaters, a chain of eighty movie houses that were sold to United Artists in 1968. He was involved in the motion picture productions of *South Pacific* and *Oklahoma* and had connections with the Will Rogers Institute in White Plains, New York.

Seider entered Good Samaritan early in June 1987, suffering from dehydration, and died three weeks later after a respiratory stoppage. "I'm terribly distressed about this whole thing," said his son Daniel, referring to the exhumation. He added that he had no inkling at all that his father's death was suspicious. His father was "very sick and the hospital was extremely good to him."

Angelo is behind bars, but he has cast a dark shadow of pain over many decent people. Outside the courtroom, after the sentencing, Kieran Greene and other victims' relatives, many of whom who had attended the eight-week trial every single day, shared mixed feelings about the sentence as they consoled and comforted one another.

Greene made no apology for his outburst in court and said that Angelo should have gotten the death penalty. "You have to get on with your life, but you can never forget," said Greene. Tears in her eyes, Carole Scollo, daughter of another murder victim, Milton Poultney, echoed Greene's sentiments when she said vehemently: "I'll be happy if he never sees the light of day again. I just wish there was a death penalty." Earlier in the investigation, Mrs. Scollo was deeply shocked when it was first suggested that her father was a possible murder victim. "It was really traumatic," she said. "My father died, and you think that's the end of it. Then you learn he's got to be dug up again. So we've had to relive his death all over again. It's like a murder mystery you watch on TV—but you never dream it's going to happen to you.

Sam Falabella, of Deer Park, Long Island, son of victim Nancy, a grandmother who was "full of life," will always feel partly responsible for his mother's death and subsequent exhumation. "It's tearing me apart that she died in that hospital," he grieved. "I was the one who wanted her there. I don't know how I can go through life knowing she was murdered and that I put her in that position."

LaGois's widow, Dorothy, is seeking further justice. Shortly after her husband's body was exhumed in November 1988 and the cause of his death established, her attorney, Stephen Siben, filed two ten-million-dollar suits against Good Samaritan Hospital, one for "inflicting conscious pain and suffering" upon Mr. LaGois, and the other for causing his wrongful death.

Exactly how many patients Angelo fatally injected or put through a torturous ordeal, may never be truly known. Pavulon only stays in the body for a limited period of time. The authorities saddled him with the assault and deaths of patients around whom they could build the strongest case. But at the height of the investigation and exhumations trial, Judge Hirsch did observe: "We may be dealing with the largest series of murders in the whole history of this country." Giving Angelo the benefit of the doubt in dozens of other possible murders, he still comes across as one of the most callous, indifferent hospital serial killers on record. Would he have continued his uncontrollable killings if New York State had reinstated the death penalty?

Death penalty or not, it would be futile to argue that fear of execution would have changed the course of Richard Angelo's almost incomprehensible behavior. Cases like Angelo's have been examined up and down by experts.

Dr. Martin Orne, professor of psychiatry at the University of Pennsylvania, believes Angelo may have been drawn into his killing spree by accident. "Perhaps he actually saved a patient's life one day. Having been praised for that, he could have gone on to 'save' someone who wasn't really dying. And at some point he could have stepped over the line," says Dr. Orne.

Psychiatry professor Elissa Benedeck of the University of Michigan provides the only known common thread linking medical serial killers: "After the first, it gets easier and easier."

The closest explanation anyone could come to concerning a motive for Angelo's crimes was the one put forward by Professor Charles Bahn of New York's John Jay College of Criminal Justice. "Through a sense of personal inadequacy, medical serial murderers begin to experiment with life and death. It's a little bit like playing God. They decide they have a justification in interfering with the medical destiny of patients."

Professor Bahn, who has worked closely with the FBI in the study of such murders, was not surprised that Angelo's modus operandi involved the use of the drug Pavulon. "It seems to be used a lot in these cases," said the professor. "It is a drug readily available in emergency units and other wards." Nor was the expert surprised that Angelo preferred working night shifts. "Serial murderers often work on a late shift when there's less supervision and more opportunity to do what you want."

To add horror to horror, there is nothing to prevent another Angelo from going on a killing spree. Although West Islip's Good Sam hospital has tightened many of its procedures since the New York State Health Commission reprimands, the frightening possibility of another nursing monster emerging is a harsh fact of life.

Good Sam spokesman Ted Shiebler sums it up: "There's no way to stop a person who really wants to do a thing like this. We deal in trust."

FOUR

Bobbie Sue Dudley Terrell
Psycho Murderess

Whenever Bobbie Sue Dudley was on duty at a Florida nursing home, old people died.

But the short, overweight night nurse worked in a nursing home where many of the patients were either very sick or very old, some in their eighties and nineties. In fact, one patient had topped the century mark at 101 and death in bed under those circumstances is rarely suspicious.

It seemed that unhappiness and tragedy had stalked Bobbie Sue almost all her life. From the time of her birth as Bobbie Sue Robertson in a trailer in little Woodlawn, Illinois, a flyspeck hamlet of about five hundred people near the state's southern tip some sixty miles east of St. Louis, she appeared to have been born under an unlucky star.

Overweight, myopic and shy, she wasn't an especially popular girl in school. She wasn't the type in either appearance or temperament who would even try out for the cheerleading squad, and she did little in school to distinguish herself. She made few close friends, and in fact it was doubtful if more than a handful of her classmates could remember much more about her today than what seat she sat in. The few friends she did make during her school years, however, would later recall her as loving and trusting.

The classroom performance of the quiet, studious girl was above average. She earned good grades, and was even chosen to sing in the high school chorus, although she made no secret that she preferred to lend her vocal talents to praising Jesus and the wonders of heaven.

She found that opportunity at church. Bobbie Sue came from religious forebears, and, like them, churchgoing was an important part of her life. She was a devoted Bible reader, who could recite chapters and verses from the Good Book for just about any occasion and situation.

And she hung on to every word of the fiery, hellfire and damnation sermons of the preacher—the vivid descriptions of heaven and hell, the fervent warnings about Satan's temptations, and the eternal dangers of leading a sinful life.

Perhaps most of all, however, she loved the music. Each Sunday, and often during the week, she played hymns on a double-keyboard organ, bedazzling the pastor and congregation with her ability on the instrument, as well as with her high, sweet voice. Bobbie Sue wholeheartedly joined in the hymn singing, and when the congregation clapped their hands and raised their voices in melodious praise to God, her own normally timid voice took on a rich, confident timbre that was present at no other time.

Despite the exemplary Christian life she was leading and her faith in God and in goodness, tragedy was already stalking the family. One of seven children, she had five brothers, and four of them had muscular dystrophy. Two of the boys died of the slow, crippling disease before Bobbie reached her mid-thirties. Sympathetic neighbors would eventually remember that they felt almost as sorry for Bobbie as they did for the boys. The poor girl just couldn't seem to stop crying when her brothers died.

By 1973, with high school behind her, Bobbie Sue chose her lifelong profession and began studying to become a nurse. She was especially anxious to move into the field of geriatrics where she could help the old and infirm. She decided that while continuing her fervent devotion to the teachings of Christ, she would become a Guardian Angel to the aged.

Graduating from nursing school in 1976 with a degree as a registered nurse, she passed her National Council Licensing examination and went to work near her home in the slightly larger towns of Centralia and Mount Vernon. If the economically deprived area she grew up in is noted for anything, it is probably for the sympathy it exhibited for the South during the Civil War, for the moonshining that occurred there during the early years of the century, and for a terrible midcentury coal-mining disaster in Centralia that drew national attention and concern.

But it was home to Bobbie Sue, and she was beginning what were to be some of the happiest years of her life. She married Danny Lynn Dudley, and soon the couple adopted a little boy. Then, with unexpected swiftness, her son was hospitalized and the marriage collapsed.

Her husband eventually filed legal documents accusing her of feeding so many tranquilizers prescribed to help treat her schizophrenia to their seven-year-old son that he became seriously ill. Doctors rushed the boy nearly seventy miles to Children's Hospital in St. Louis, where he was admitted to the intensive care unit. He eventually recovered, but the marriage was irrevocably damaged.

Bobbie Sue's husband told authorities that the boy suffered from drug overdoses on at least three different occasions. Juvenile authorities threatened to place him in a foster home unless the court awarded custody to the adopted father.

In rapid succession, Bobbie Sue lost her husband and her son. And it was merely the beginning of a devastating series of personal tragedies for the previously happy, churchgoing RN. Her health had also begun to fail.

On five different occasions, the young divorcée was rushed to the hospital, where surgeons operated to remove fibroid tumors from her stomach or performed other abdominal surgery.

She underwent a hysterectomy and removal of her ovaries. Then she broke her arm, and it failed to heal properly, subjecting her to more surgery. A serious gallbladder operation followed that. She was treated for ulcers, and for pneumonia.

It seemed that if God was testing her faith, he was having a field day. Bobbie Sue was becoming a modern-day Job.

Loss of her husband and her son, coupled with her debilitating physical problems played havoc with her emotional health. Bobbie knew she had to have professional help. She voluntarily checked herself into a state mental hospital. She was there more than a year, undergoing psychiatric therapy. By the time she was finally released, she seemed to sincerely believe that she was healthy and ready to return to work.

She went through a series of short-term nursing jobs, until July 1983, when she was hired at Hillview Manor in Greenville, Illinois. Almost immediately, a series of bizarre events began occurring that were linked to Bobbie Sue and soon had other nurses whispering to one another about her mental state.

Bobbie Sue began fainting on duty. But when doctors examined her, they could find nothing wrong. Some of the other RN's, as well as nursing aides and supervisors, were convinced that she was staging the fainting spells to gain attention and sympathy. They said she "fake fainted."

Then Bobbie Sue picked up a pair of scissors and slashed herself in the vagina. She performed the self-mutilation twice. One of the injuries was so deep that she was rushed to Barnes Hospital in St. Louis to undergo emergency surgery.

Asked why she had done such a terrible thing to herself, she broke down in tears and sobbed that it was because she couldn't bear children. Her infertility made her feel inadequate.

Bobbie Sue's erratic behavior had become so dangerous that it was impossible for officials at the nursing home to tolerate or ignore. They were concerned about the danger she posed to herself, as well as potential danger to the residents. After reviewing her records and interviewing her, they terminated her employment and advised her to seek psychiatric care.

Details of the strange nurse's behavior were forwarded to the Illinois state nursing regulatory agency, which began reviewing her fitness to continue practicing as an RN. When asked about her suspicious injuries and hospitalizations, she conceded to investigators that she had intentionally hurt herself to get attention.

But Bobbie Sue had already begun planning to move south, and she applied for a nursing license from the State of Florida. Conveniently, she said nothing on her application about her mental problems, her firing from Hillview Manor, or the investigation by the Illinois licensing agency. When an investigator from Illinois tracked her down and asked her during a telephone conversation if she had informed officials in Florida about her previous troubles, she admitted that she hadn't. She explained she merely wanted to obtain a Florida license and begin her new life. She told the investigator that she couldn't afford a psychiatrist.

Bobbie Sue moved to St. Petersburg to start over. Located on Florida's Gulf Coast, St. Petersburg, like much of the state, is a mecca for retirees, and the experienced RN had no difficulty finding work. Her references were excellent. At first glance there was no reason for her prospective employers in Florida to question the glowing recommendations. It was obvious Bobbie Sue knew her business and was good at it.

The RN from Illinois moved around for a while, flitting from one job to another in the Tampa Bay area, staying at one nursing home for a week or two, then shifting to another and staying anywhere from a few weeks to three or four months. Most of the time when she left a job, she cited health problems. For a short time she worked at the Jacaranda Manor Nursing Home in an unincorporated area of Pinellas county north of St. Petersburg. When she left Jacaranda she signed up with a nursing pool agency. One of the facilities they sent her to most frequently was the Seminole Nursing Pavilion, also in rural Pinellas County. Her performance there was so impressive that she was offered a full-time job, but she had to turn it down because she became sick.

Bobbie Sue didn't have much of a social life in Florida until she found a church and began attending regularly. She needed the spiritual comfort, and the companionship provided by the congregation. She was still lonely, and the physical problems that had followed her to Florida were dogging her mercilessly.

When she suddenly and mysteriously began bleeding from the rectum, she underwent an emergency colostomy. But she recovered, and in October 1984, her life seemed to take a temporary turn for the better when she was hired as a shift supervisor at the North Horizon Health Care Center. Bobbie Sue took over the 11 P.M.-to 7-A.M. shift. The fifty-bed nursing home owned by Unicare Health Facilities was regarded by health-care authorities and experts, as well as knowledgeable members of the public, as one of the cheeriest and best in Saint Petersburg. North Horizon is located just across the street from a huge, meticulously tended rose garden in a large, well-lighted, white-frame building surrounded by palm trees. The nursing home was staffed by professionals respected for their competence and experience.

Most of the patients had regular visitors, and those who were well enough could choose from a full schedule of activities that included card games, television, Bingo parties, and other events. But the home was not involved in solely custodial care. RN's under Bobbie's supervision cared for patients who were in reasonably good health despite advanced age, and others suffering from a variety of ailments, including cancer and heart disease. As professionals, the occasional death of patients was a fact of life they had reluctantly learned to live with.

Aggie May Marsh, a ninety-seven-year-old great-grandmother died in her room on November 13, 1984, only a few weeks after Bobbie Sue began work at North Horizon. Mrs. Marsh died on Bobbie Sue's shift. Despite the fact that the old woman had seemed to be in relatively good health, her advanced age helped dispel any suspicion that her death might have been anything but natural. The body of Mrs. Marsh, who was survived by three daughters, was claimed by her family, and she was taken to Spur, Texas, for burial.

Bobbie Sue was also working the night shift a few days later when ninety-four-year-old Anna Larson went into shock from an overdose of insulin. At Bobbie Sue's insistence, the frail old woman was rushed to the nearby Edward W. White III Memorial Hospital for emergency treatment. Doctors described the old woman as being in serious condition when she arrived, and although she was close to death, she survived. When she died two months later, doctors said the cause of death was not related to the insulin injection.

But Mrs. Larson was not a diabetic, and should never have been given insulin. And as night nursing supervisor, Bobbie Sue was the only person working at that time with access to the locked medicine cabinet where insulin, needles, and other pharmaceuticals were kept. Only two other employees worked at the home during that shift, and both were under Bobbie's supervision.

On November 23, Leathy McKnight died of insulin shock. It was later determined that the eighty-five-year-old woman had to have been injected with the medication between the hours of 11 P.M. and 7 A.M. That was Bobbie Sue's shift.

Ominously, the same night that Mrs. McKnight died, a fire was discovered in a linen closet. It was extinguished before it had a chance to spread, and there was no serious damage. But the mere fact that it had ignited at all was frightening, and the potential for a major disaster was distressing.

Three days after Mrs. McKnight's death, two patients who had each seemingly been in relatively good health, died under mysterious circumstances – seventy-nine-year-old Mary Rae Carter and eighty-five-year-old Stella Bradham.

Other patients were dying at North Horizon, but some residents of the home were already terminally ill when they arrived there. Bobbie Sue meticulously recorded all the deaths in an account book she kept. Writing in her small, neat scribble, she noted about one man who died: "Patient was wide awake, alert and talking. He even pinched my rear that morning." At 1 P.M., the rambunctious old man was transferred to a nearby hospital, however. Eight hours later he was dead.

Bobbie wrote of a woman who suffered from terminal cancer, that she had told her: "I am dying and I don't want to be alone." Bobbie wrote at 4 A.M. that the patient was "alert." By 6 A.M., however, she was dead.

With regular employment again, her financial condition had improved and Bobbie Sue was visiting a psychiatrist. During one session, she told him that she was upset because thirteen people at the nursing home had died of overdoses of insulin.

Although the statement was apparently untrue, the sudden and quixotic upsurge in patient deaths was becoming increasingly troubling. But there were other worrisome occurrences as well that were disturbing the tranquility of the sunny nursing home. Things were happening that staff members just couldn't explain. Occurrences like the strange fire the night Mrs. McKnight died, which Fire Department investigators listed as suspected arson. And the mysterious telephone call to the switchboard operator from a woman who whispered that five patients had been murdered by arson.

Someone also smashed a window in a patient's private room. And a few days later someone smashed open a fuse box and knocked out the electricity at North Horizon.

Then, on Monday, November 26, the date that some staff members later referred to as the night of the Holocaust, five patients died – one after another. And as if that wasn't terrible enough, early the next morning Bobbie Sue Dudley, the quiet, efficient overnight supervisor, was stabbed in the ribs. Before she was rushed to the hospital, the RN moaned that she had been working alone in a darkened closet just off the dayroom when she was attacked by a prowler.

Police checked doors and windows around the building and were unable to find any signs of forced entry. And talks with other employees failed to turn up anyone who could remember seeing a stranger in the area near the time of the perplexing attack.

The situation at the nursing home appeared to be flaring out of control. No one had a ready explanation for the weird goings on: the stabbing of the RNs', the unusual number of deaths in recent weeks, and the other inexplicable occurrences.

In a single terrible thirteen-day period near Thanksgiving Day 1984, twelve patients died at North Horizon. And the other baffling incidents that had occurred were making North Horizon more like a madhouse than a nursing home. In late November, officials at the nursing home notified state authorities that something was terribly wrong. Quietly, an inquiry was launched.

Within a month, for reasons they didn't publicly reveal, North Horizon administrators fired the overnight supervisor. Pressed for more information, a spokesman later added only the cryptic observation that the dismissal was for the good of the facility.

Bobbie Sue responded to her firing by filing a twenty-two-thousand dollar claim for workmen's compensation, citing the attack she said she had suffered while on duty. Unicare Health Facilities opposed the claim, and a Tampa psychiatrist hired by the firm's insurance company eventually provided a letter to lawyers describing her as a "borderline schizophrenic" who suffered from a mental illness that caused her to fabricate physical ills.

The psychiatrist reported that after interviewing the woman, he had concluded she suffered from Munchausen's syndrome and "most likely" stabbed herself.

Munchausen's syndrome is a strange condition that is little known outside the medical and psychiatric professions. First identified and described by a British physician in 1977, it is a disorder that may afflict somewhere from four thousand to twelve thousand people around the world, and causes victims to invent illnesses to obtain the medical attention they crave. The name derives from Baron von Munchausen who lived in Germany from 1820 to 1897 and told outrageous lies and fanciful tales of battlefield exploits to get attention.

Some victims actually injure themselves with knives or razors, and swallow poison or overdoses of medicine in order to get themselves hospitalized, where they will obtain the attention they so desperately need. Some mothers who intentionally sicken or injure their children so they can share in the child's attention or earn praise for their own loving care to the youngster have been identified as suffering from "Munchausen's Syndrome by Proxy."

A judge with the Florida Division of Workers' Compensation told Unicare Health Facilities to provide additional information to substantiate the claim that Bobbie Sue stabbed herself, and scheduled the case for a later ruling. The claim was eventually rejected.

But the life and emotional state of the RN were unraveling fast, even before the psychiatrist's report was submitted to the Workers' Compensation judge. The pressures were getting to her, and she was beginning to tell acquaintances that the whole world hated her. She had to have help. On January 31, she was admitted to Horizon Hospital in Pinellas county for medical and psychiatric treatment.

During this time, the homicide division of the St. Petersburg Police Department was quietly launching an official investigation into the tragic string of deaths at the North Horizon Health Care Center.

Detectives quickly learned that a large supply of insulin was reported missing from the locked medications cabinet at North Horizon at about the time that Anna Larson was mysteriously injected with the overdose that sent her into shock. Investigators interviewed staff and asked for records to pinpoint exactly who had access to the locked medications cabinet. Only Bobbie Sue had possession of the key to the cabinet during the late-night shifts. The key was passed between supervisors at shift changes.

Detectives also painstakingly reconstructed and retraced the rounds of North Shore employees to determine who had access to patients on the nights or mornings they died. The officers were provided with a floor plan of the nursing home and spent an entire twenty-four-hour period following employees on their rounds in an effort to retrace the steps taken by the workers and by Bobbie Sue, in particular, on the nights the suspicious deaths occurred.

The investigation was focusing increasingly on the troubled RN, and detectives examined the records she had kept. Nurses at the home were required to note the exact time of day when medication was administered and when they responded to patients' calls. Detectives found that Bobbie Sue had altered information and failed to record certain data on the medical records of some patients.

The probe was meticulous, and time-consuming. Homicide officers with the Pinellas County Sheriff's Department joined the inquiry when it was learned that the RN had worked at Jacaranda Manor and at the Seminole Nursing Pavilion. Investigators reviewed patient records and talked with employees, but failed to turn up any evidence that Bobbie Sue might have been responsible for deaths in either of the facilities.

One difficulty for the investigators was the amount of time that had already elapsed since patient deaths. Some of the patients whose deaths were considered suspicious had already been dead for months. Insulin breaks up quickly in a body, and is extremely difficult to detect unless autopsies are conducted soon after death. And some of the remains had been cremated, eliminating any possibility of autopsy.

Nevertheless, exhumation orders were obtained for the remains of nine of the elderly patients who died at North Horizon while Bobbie Sue was working there. Backhoes were used to disinter bodies from family burial plots in Florida, Wisconsin, Texas, and Pennsylvania.

And Homicide officers contacted authorities in Illinois to fill in background on Dudley. They wanted answers to questions about why she had been threatened with revocation of her Illinois nursing license, why she was fired from the nursing home in Greenville, and about her relationship with patients in the Midwest state.

While raising eyebrows and getting herself fired because of her bizarre behavior in Florida, she hadn't been forgotten in Illinois. Officials had begun an investigation there in August 1983, after receiving a letter from Bobbie Sue's former supervisor, Cathy Greenslate.

Then director of nursing at Hillview Manor, Mrs. Greenslate wrote that Bobbie Sue was fired because of mental instability after she was hospitalized for a self-inflicted stab wound. Mrs. Greenslate reported that Bobbie Sue had been advised not to return to work before obtaining psychiatric treatment. The director warned that instead of seeking help, however, Bobbie Sue had moved to

Florida and was attempting to obtain a license there to continue work as an RN.

Bobbie Sue applied for her Florida license in July, and received it on August 8, four days before her former supervisor wrote the letter.

Mrs. Greenslate said in the letter that as a director of nurses she didn't feel comfortable having Bobbie Sue work with patients, because of the nurse's obvious mental problems. She also noted that the physician for the facility had been concerned about Bobbie Sue's mental competency after giving her a preemployment physical examination. But he didn't follow up on his fears because he reportedly was afraid of a possible lawsuit.

The nursing home administrator told the investigator that she hired Bobbie Sue because skilled-care facilities such as nursing homes were required to have registered nurses in order to comply with certain public health regulations. And in small towns like Greenville, it was difficult to find available RN's.

It took fourteen months before the investigation of Bobbie Sue's distressing behavior in Illinois made its ponderous, bureaucratic way through the system, but the state regulatory board finally suspended her nursing license on grounds of mental instability and self-abuse. Bobbie Sue was contacted in Florida by investigators and asked to return to Illinois to attend her license hearing, but she said she couldn't afford to pay for the trip.

No one in Illinois had bothered to notify authorities in Florida that the troubled nurse was attempting to obtain a license there and return to work. Months later, Michael Mervis, a spokesman for North Horizon, would remark to reporters that "it is unfortunate that Illinois did not communicate with Florida." But in other observations he used the term "flat-out outrage" to describe his response to the lack of communication. "This is dealing with human beings," he declared. "This is a licensed medical professional."

Bobbie Sue didn't remain in the Florida hospital long after her self-imposed commitment. She later said that after spending twenty thousand dollars for treatment, she simply ran out of money. Events in her life, however, continued to move swiftly for her, both while she was hospitalized and after.

One February 12, while she was still hospitalized, the Florida State Department of Professional Regulation, issued an emergency order temporarily suspending her license and asked the Florida Board of Nursing to take it away permanently. In the order, the DPR claimed that it was believed the RN would be an "immediate, serious danger to the public health, safety, and welfare, and to herself, if she were allowed to continue nursing." The DPR cited mental problems that had led her to stab herself while working in Illinois.

Bobbie Sue didn't contest the allegations about her difficulties in Illinois, but she requested a hearing from the nine-member Board of Nursing, the final authority in the state on licensing and professional discipline, before a binding decision was made on her case.

In the meantime, newspaper, radio, and television reporters had learned of the nursing home probe, the sinister string of deaths, and the queer RN whose name kept cropping up so prominently. Dudley suddenly became big news on Florida's populous West Coast.

People who didn't even know Bobbie Sue began telephoning and writing to her. Many of the writers were religious fanatics who wrote of sin, salvation, and hell — subjects Bobbie Sue had already heard much about. But one of the correspondents was Ron Terrell, a lonely thirty-eight-year-old itinerant plumber. He was sympathetic and appeared to be genuinely concerned about her. When he suddenly asked her to marry him, she agreed.

The happy couple moved into a two-hundred-dollar-per-month one-bedroom furnished apartment near Interstate 275 in downtown Tampa. Ron didn't even complain when his bride insisted on stuffing her huge organ and her collection of religious music books inside. Then she put up crucifixes and a framed color picture of Baby Jesus in the manger. Bobbie's lifelong spirituality and love for Christ had never wavered.

Bobbie Sue made a friend of her eighteen-year-old landlady. The teenager was drawn to the pathetic RN, and later told a newspaper reporter, "She was my buddy. I liked her. She was real sweet." The time soon came, nevertheless, when the woebegone nurse, beset by investigators from nearly a half-dozen agencies, sensational newspaper stories, and a shortage of cash was asked to leave the apartment.

She was being smothered by troubles. Shortly after moving in to the modest apartment, Bobby Sue went to a local dog pound and, after paying fifteen dollars, adopted a four-month-old mutt. She named it Mandy. It wasn't long before she decided the dog needed worm medicine, and the puppy overdosed. Bobbie Sue rushed Mandy to an emergency animal hospital and a veterinarian pumped its stomach. The dog lived, but the veterinarian charged Bobbie Sue forty-five dollars for saving its life.

Bobbie Sue was also again committed to a psychiatric hospital for treatment, this time against her wishes. She was still a patient there when she received her hearing before the State Board of Nursing. The board met in a crowded meeting room at the Marriott Hotel at the Tampa Airport, and Bobbie Sue appeared before the solemn agency members who would decide her professional future wearing a red-and-white-striped shirt and red slacks.

She told the board that she talked with a psychiatrist in 1979 after her divorce and was advised that she would never become truly independent unless she left Illinois. She said that although she didn't want to move so far from her son, she realized the advice was good, and consequently applied for a Florida nursing license.

"The problems I have mentally . . . I need to work on," she conceded. But she added that she was "not harmful to myself or to anyone else."

Bobbie Sue said that the floodtide of publicity surrounding her employment at North Horizon had convinced her that she didn't want to continue working at that time as an RN. But she said she was doing well, expected to be released from the hospital shortly, and pleaded with the board to merely suspend her license for no more than one to four years. No one on the board asked her any questions before a five-year license suspension was announced. The suspension order noted that the psychiatrist treating the RN believed she would need long-term treatment in a confined treatment program. And a board spokesman advised her that she would not be reinstated until she proved she could practice her profession safely.

Notification of the suspension was forwarded to the National Council of State Boards of Nursing in Chicago. The National Council functions as a clearinghouse that mails monthly bulletins to the nursing boards in all states notifying them about disciplinary cases.

If the St. Petersburg police and the Pinellas county prosecutor agreed with the landlady's assessment of Bobbie Sue as "real sweet," they had also reached the conclusion that she had a chilling dark side to her personality. They were convinced she was a killer. On March 17, she was charged with the attempted first-degree murder of Anna Larson.

Bobbie Sue had been released from the hospital, and arresting officers found her living in a tent with her husband on the Tampa side of the Gandy Bridge where she had been eking out a hand-to-mouth existence after losing the apartment. Dressed in a pair of athletic shorts, sneakers, and a blue T-shirt imprinted on the front with the words "Armstrong County YMCA 20-K," she was taken in handcuffs to the Pinellas County Jail in Clearwater. Bail was set at seventy-five thousand dollars, but Bobbie Sue was broke and remained behind bars.

She appeared to be more upset over Mandy's fate, however, than her own. Police took the dog into custody when Bobbie Sue was arrested, and she was later told that her pet was missing. She told a friend that she was thinking of filing a complaint against police, charging them with cruelty to animals.

St. Petersburg police were more concerned with a possible serial murder case than an animal abuse suit. And they publicly revealed that they suspected at least two of the twelve patients who died at North Horizon during the terrible thirteen days in November were murdered. The startling disclosure was made in a sworn statement by Detective Robert Engelke as part of their application to a Hillsboro county judge for a search warrant to enter the Tampa apartment Bobbie Sue and her husband had rented.

In his sworn statement, Engelke said that Pinellas-Pasco Medical Examiner Joan Wood had performed autopsies on two of the twelve patients and determined the "cause of death in those two individuals was homicidal and not as a result of natural causes." The identity of the suspected homicide victims was not disclosed.

But the detective also noted in the deposition that the deaths at North Shore had begun shortly after Bobbie Sue began working there "and ended when she quit working." The search warrant was granted, and officers seized two boxes and two envelopes. It was eventually disclosed that police had found the handwritten record the RN had compiled while her patients were dying.

Two weeks after the apartment was searched, a Pinellas-Pasco grand jury returned a formal indictment that was devastating for Bobbie Sue. The indictment charged her with four counts of first-degree murder, as well as with the attempted murder of Mrs. Larson. Bobbie Sue was led to court in handcuffs wearing the same athletic shorts, T-shirt, and sneakers she had on when she was jailed to hear a description of the charges against her.

According to the indictments and affidavits filed by Engelke, she was accused of strangling or asphyxiating Aggie Marsh, injecting Leathy McKnight with a fatal dose of medicine, which caused her to go into insulin shock, injecting Mrs. Cartwright with a fatal dose of insulin, killing Mrs. Bradham either by injecting her with an unknown substance or by strangling or asphyxiating her, and attempting to kill Anna Larson with an overdose of insulin. Bobbie Sue was ordered to be returned to the county jail and held without bail, pending trial.

The suspended RN insisted that she was innocent and hadn't done anything to hurt anyone. She had been talking about her innocence to anyone who would listen, and described the puzzling string of deaths at the nursing home as a "wonderment." Before her imprisonment she told a reporter for the St. Petersburg *Times,* "The Lord will do what he wants. If the Lord is not ready to take them home, no matter what happens, they're not going to go home."

But Bobbie Sue remained silent at a circuit court hearing, as a public defender entered the expected plea of innocent for her. A deputy prosecutor, however, told the court that he would prove at the trial that the RN murdered the victims by asphyxiation, insulin injection that fatally shocked their systems, strangulation, or a combination of all three. A trial date was set for October 20, and Bobbie Sue was led from the courtroom, smiling wanly at spectators.

A trial was never held. Bobbie Sue's public defender attorneys and Assistant State Attorney Bruce Bartlett hammered out a plea bargain, agreed to by the suspect. According to the agreement, the first-degree murder charges against the former RN were reduced to second-degree murder. The attempted murder charge was unchanged. The plea bargain eliminated any chance that Bobbie Sue could be sentenced to die in Florida's electric chair.

In late February 1988, nearly two years after Bobbie Sue's arrest and more than three years after nearly one-quarter of the residents at St. Petersburg's North Horizon Health Care Center died over a brief thirteen-day span, the former RN appeared in court for sentencing. Judge James R. Case ordered a total combined term of sixty-five years in prison.

Deputy state's attorney Doug Crowe told reporters that, considering the nature of her crimes, the prosecution would have liked a more stringent sentence. "But with the difficulty of the case, I think everyone would consider this a good resolution."

Bartlett added that the prosecution had agreed to the plea reduction in part because of the RN's history of mental problems and because many of the witnesses were elderly patients, who were frail or incapacitated.

After sentencing, Bobbie Sue was returned to the Pinellas County Jail, and later transferred to a state prison for women in Lowell, Florida.

But the fallout in the case was far-reaching and frightening. In Illinois, Marion County Coroner Daniel Fischer told reporters he planned to launch an investigation of deaths at nursing homes in that state where the homicidal RN was previously employed. "I haven't had anything that would make me suspicious, but we thought we'd better take a look at it," he told reporters.

But despite the coroner's trepidation, no evidence was turned up to indicate that Bobbie Sue had begun her murderous rampage in Illinois.

FIVE

Anthony George Shook:
Intensive Care Monster

Compassionate mercy killer, calculating, cold-blooded murderer
. . . or a dangerous, emotional loose cannon with homicidal tendencies?

Anthony George Shook, a thirty-six-year-old nurse at a North
Carolina hospital, was labeled all of these before being convicted of
first-degree murder by withholding life-saving medication from a
comatose young woman.

The jury preferred to think of the slender, emotional intensive-
care-unit professional as a compassionate mercy killer, although
that mitigating factor didn't stand in the way of Shook being sent to
prison for a mandatory life sentence.

In the eyes of the prosecution and the dead woman's devoted husband, Shook was a calculating killer who had earmarked the ailing
woman for death, and appointed himself as executioner.

Other health-care investigators saw him as a demented, dangerous young man who had nothing but contempt for his co-workers,
doctors, and fellow nurses. Killing was his way of thumbing his
nose at their perceived lack of professional knowledge.

No one may ever know the illogical reasoning that motivated
Shook to withhold the vital drugs from thirty-five-year-old mother
of two Peggy Lou Epley as she lay near death in Winston-Salem,
North Carolina's Baptist Hospital in the fall of 1986.

Shook entered the Navy in 1969 and was selected to attend a nuclear propulsion school in Great Lakes, Illinois. The school is only open to those with the highest aptitude scores. For four years, he was a nuclear technician on the USS *Lafayette*, a submarine carrying ballistic missiles.

In the late 1970's, after leaving the Navy, Shook worked as a paramedic for an ambulance service in the Durham, North Carolina area. He enrolled in the nursing program at the University of North Carolina at Chapel Hill and graduated with a bachelor's degree in 1981.

Shook later worked as a nurse in Fort Lauderdale, Brandon, and Tampa, Florida, and at Pitt Memorial Hospital in Greenville, North Carolina, before applying successfully for the post at Baptist Hospital.

Sadly, it was the dead woman's anguished husband who, for seven months, kept a round-the-clock vigil at his young wife's bedside, who, with an almost sixth sense, first suspected that the ultra-efficient Shook was a man with a dark side . . . a man out to do harm to his beloved wife.

Gerald Epley sensed that Shook had given up on his wife and wanted her dead. Soft-spoken Gerald Epley was later to tell a court: "I told him I would never give up on her. She was a good wife and a good mother—and she wanted to live!"

Every time Mrs. Epley was under the care of Shook, she became ill. Her husband beseeched the hospital to keep him away from her, but the persistent male nurse had Mrs. Epley placed under his care one more time . . . for her, the last time.

There was never any dispute that Peggy Lou Epley, a furniture inspector from Lexington, Davidson County, North Carolina, was in bad shape before she even came under the care of Shook. She was sent to Baptist Hospital's intensive care unit on April 18, 1986, when her blood pressure dropped and her kidneys failed after intestinal surgery at Lexington Memorial Hospital to remove a blockage. She remained in Baptist in critical shape until her death on October 9 that year.

Co-workers at the hospital, already alerted about Shook, strongly suspected that the dark-haired male nurse had something to do with Mrs. Epley's death. A dedicated nursing supervisor ordered all equipment and drugs in the intensive care unit that could be instrumental in linking Shook to Mrs. Epley's death be placed under wraps for subsequent police investigation.

Every intensive-care staff member was queried about Shook and his behavior, and pertinent records were removed and studied. Shook was suspended from duty that same day.

Why this early flurry of activity, with all fingers pointing toward Shook as a potential murderer in their midst?

Hospital spokesman Roger Rollman would only make the initial, cautious statement: "While comatose patients in critical condition are not expected to survive, Mrs. Epley's death was considered untimely. That raised suspicions among hospital personnel. We acted immediately on these suspicions by suspending Mr. Shook and calling the police."

It was the following day, October 10, that hospital authorities handed all details of the Shook-Epley case over to the Winston-Salem Police department, which, in turn, called in specialized investigators from the State Bureau of Investigations.

Later, R.J. Bulla of the State Bureau of Investigation's drug division confirmed that Shook was the one and only SBI suspect during the course of the ensuing long and exhaustive investigation.

The tide of suspicion against Shook turned almost a year later in September 1987, when the acting state medical examiner, Dr. John D. Butts, issued a new death certificate for Mrs. Epley alleging murder. It corrected earlier certificates that indicated she had died from natural causes brought on by heart and kidney failure.

The reason for the dramatic turnaround, said SBI Chief Investigator David Barnes, was that life-saving drugs—Levophed and Epinephrine, called "pressors" and used to increase blood pressure—were not present in Mrs. Epley's intravenous feeding solution at the time of her death.

Agent Barnes was able to state categorically: "This was done deliberately." The medical and scientific evidence proved overwhelmingly that to deprive Mrs. Epley of her pressors was tantamount to sentencing her to death.

Shook, a 1981 graduate of the University of North Carolina at Chapel Hill, had no prior record of disciplinary problems in North Carolina, or in Florida, where he was licensed and had worked before returning to Winston-Salem to work at Baptist Hospital in December 1985. He had resigned from the hospital four days after being told he was the prime and only suspect in Mrs. Epley's death.

With the evidence against him mounting slowly but surely, Shook surrendered quietly to the authorities early in September 1987, and was held in custody, without bond, charged with first-degree murder.

Although investigators claimed Shook had initially admitted his guilt, he was to recant that statement, protesting his innocence to the end, although at one stage it was thought he might plead to a lesser charge than first degree murder. But the plea-bargaining negotiations broke down and John H. Boddie, Shook's attorney, took the case to trial. The Forsyth County district attorney said he would not seek the death penalty for Shook.

Coincidental with Shook's voluntary surrender to police, the husband of the murder victim, Mr. Gerald Howard Epley, reinforced the growing suspicions about the alleged killer when he revealed how he had never felt comfortable with his wife under Shook's care.

And he added another choice tidbit for the prosecution when he revealed how he had tried to keep Shook away from his wife after another unexplained, near-fatal drop in blood pressure during September 1986 – a month before Mrs. Epley died.

Mr. Epley, a devoted husband and now a single father to two schoolchildren, checked in to see his wife every day of her long illness. He said Shook was not responsible for his wife's care after the September incident until October 9 – the day she died!

"They have never given me an explanation why he was her nurse again. It shouldn't have happened," Mr. Epley complained bitterly. Baptist Hospital declined comment, although hospital spokesman Rollman, speaking in general terms, said hospital regulations ensured there was one nurse assigned to one, sometimes two, patients in the intensive care unit at all times. He confirmed earlier statements that the hospital considered Mrs. Epley a comatose patient not expected to live.

Mr. Epley's comments, dropped just as the SBI's eleven-month investigation reached completion, included the complaint that Baptist Hospital doctors never indicated to him at any time that his sick wife didn't have a chance of recovering.

In fact, on the day before her death, she wasn't in a coma, argued Mr. Epley.

He vividly recalled the first incident when low blood pressure almost took his wife's life. Hospital officials had called him and the two children in and told him Mrs. Epley wasn't going to survive. He noted that Shook was the attending nurse just before this relapse. But after a day and a half, she rallied and pulled through. "They said they could not explain that; it was just like a miracle," said Mr. Epley.

His optimism for his wife's continued survival shrunk a month later when he heard from the hospital by telephone early on October 9 before he went to work and discovered that Shook was again his wife's nurse. Upset, he drove immediately to Baptist Hospital with his son.

When he got there, Shook's shift had ended, said Mr. Epley, and a duty nurse told him his wife appeared to be all right. He fell asleep on a couch in the waiting room . . . waiting until visiting hours began at ten thirty A.M.

But he never did get the chance to see his wife alive again. Before the start of visiting hours, a nurse called him up to his wife's room to tell him she was dead.

Mr. Epley was to repeat his story and his strong suspicions when he got a chance to face Shook again . . . across a courtroom.

It was true, Mr. Epley told the court, that he had never trusted Anthony Shook. Every time the nurse was around his wife, bad things happened to her, primarily the life-threatening drop in blood pressure. He didn't like the way Shook continually went out of his way to remind him how grave his wife's condition was and how she could go at any minute.

"His attitude was like he was giving up on her," Mr. Epley told the court in a hushed voice.

As Mr. Epley's emotional but nonetheless incriminating evidence unfolded, Shook, dressed in a black pin-striped suit, sat between his attorneys taking notes, sharing information with his wife Kathy, also a former intensive care nurse at Baptist Hospital, who was seated immediately behind him, and nervously eating antacid tablets.

"To me, it seemed like Shook wanted me to give up on her," Epley stated. "I told him I would never give up, that she was a good wife and mother and that she wanted to live."

For six months, the faithful husband kept a round-the-clock vigil. It became apparent to him that every time Shook was his wife's nurse, "her blood pressure was always down." And she did not seem

114

to respond to the blood-pressure medicines administered by Shook.

Epley said his wife's blood pressure always rebounded quickly to normal when other nurses were attending her.

The night before his wife died, said Mr. Epley, he had visited her in the ICU, and she seemed in stable condition. Then at 6:30 the following morning, he called the intensive care unit and, to his surprise, Shook answered, sounding hysterical, to tell him his wife had just come through a bad night.

"I asked him how many drips of blood pressure medicine she was receiving," said Mr. Epley. "Shook told me, 'It doesn't matter.' I said, 'I want to know. I can tell.' He finally told me – in cc's, not drips like the other nurses would tell me."

Prosecutor Sparrow prevented Mr. Epley from answering one terse question from Shook's co-counsel: "Isn't it true that Tony Shook was the only nurse honest with you about the condition of your wife?" The thrust of that question was no doubt to infer that staffers at Baptist Hospital had not been as open as they should have been about Mrs. Epley's condition.

But Mrs. Epley's medical records left no one in any doubt as to the seriousness of her condition. If anything, Mr. Epley displayed more optimism and hope than anyone else – an admirable and natural trait for an anxiety-ridden husband.

No one was to challenge the fact that, before her death, Mrs. Epley had been mainly comatose, kept alive by a ventilator, a kidney dialysis machine, and regular intravenous drips to increase her blood pressure.

Head of Baptist Hospital's critical care section, Dr. Donald Prough, said he believed withholding the blood pressure medications could have caused Mrs. Epley's death. But he also felt that, in the long haul, her chances for a recovery were slim.

The fact remained that Shook took more than a professional or passing interest in Mrs. Epley's plight. Four nurse co-workers testified how Shook was continually saying things like "One of these days her blood pressure is going to drop and she's not coming back" and "It's sad we're putting her through all this."

One of the ICU nurses, Dawn Scott, who handed over Mrs. Epley to Shook's care the evening before she died, shared Mr. Epley's concern that "bad things" happened to the helpless woman when Shook was her nurse. It was Nurse Scott who alerted other nurses on the same shift as Shook to keep an eye on him.

All of his former nursing colleagues who were to testify against him at his trial expressed surprise that Shook had put in a request that he be allowed to care for Mrs. Epley during his eight-hour shift the night immediately preceding her death.

"Tony told me at 6 A.M. on October 9 that he told Mrs. Epley that it was all right for her to go home," said ICU assistant head nurse Jill Turner. "In my opinion, that means it's OK to give up and die."

Shook's fellow nurses took careful note of his care of Mrs. Epley on that final night shift. They checked her blood pressure every fifteen minutes, checked her charts to make sure she was getting the prescribed medication . . . and everything checked out fine. Shook was playing things by the book, they thought. Reassured, they were not to suspect as the night wore on that Shook was deliberately withholding the vital, life-saving medicine from her support tubes.

ICU nurse Carole Bryant, who took over the care of Mrs. Epley as Shook was finishing his shift, said he'd told her he had prepared two new intravenous blood pressure medications for the patient: Levophed, which Mrs. Epley was receiving constantly, and Epinephrine, which was an emergency back-up if the first drug failed.

Shook had quit his shift and left the hospital by 8:30 A.M. when Mrs. Epley's blood pressure began to drop dramatically. The duty nurses knew they were losing her when she didn't respond to increased dosages of either Levophed or Epinephrine. She died shortly afterward at 10:15 A.M.

But the medications Shook said he had prepared were later found to be absent from the solution he was supposed to have mixed them in. Since they are clear-colored, their absence went undetected at the time. In effect, Mrs. Epley was being fed plain sugar water to save her life.

Defense co-counsels John Boddie and William Durham did not try to paint Shook's culpability as a mercy killing. Instead, they argued to the jury of eight men and four women that Mrs. Epley's death could have been the result of an unintentional mistake by Shook when he prepared the blood pressure medications.

But his co-workers dismissed this as unlikely. By and large, Shook was a skillful and diligent nurse.

The defense claimed that the patient was far too gone to respond to blood pressure medication because of her continuing weakened condition and that later FBI laboratory analyses suggesting the life-saving drugs were never there to begin with were "scientifically unreliable."

The defense argued for more than thirty minutes that the evidence by FBI chemist Drew Richardson be ruled inadmissible, but Superior Court Judge Judson D. DeRamus Jr. disagreed. Richardson was given the go-ahead to deliver his damning testimony.

Richardson said tests of the solutions prepared by Shook contained no Levophed whatsoever, and the test of the solution containing Epinephrine established that it contained only one-tenth of the amount indicated on the bottle label, which was prepared and notarized by Shook.

North Carolina chief medical examiner, Dr. John Butts, said that although he had originally attributed the cause of Mrs. Epley's death to heart failure, induced by lung and kidney failure, he changed his mind after reviewing additional evidence. "In my opinion, the immediate cause of death was the removal of pharmacological support to her blood pressure," Dr. Butts testified.

District Attorney Sparrow was succeeding in painting a picture of Shook as a man who thought he was smarter than his co-nurses and doctors, a man more captivated with the excitement of critical care nursing than the compassion required for such a position.

Nurse Scott's opinion of Shook was unshaken, despite barbed suggestions that she didn't approve of male nurses and resented the fact that Tony Shook was known to criticize doctors.

The nurse's recollections of Shook's attitude toward Mrs. Epley remained unshaken. She was so disturbed about his comments that she felt no guilt whatsoever about reporting them to the night-shift staff. "He made other remarks, like it was a shame we were putting Mrs. Epley through all this . . . and things like that. Putting it all together, it just added to everything else. It was a gut feeling on my part . . . enough to go tell someone about it." She relayed her suspicions to night-shift supervisor Jill Turner.

Like all her colleagues called to testify against Shook, Nurse Scott appeared in the witness box in her nurse's whites. The sea of white in the crowded courtroom, almost like a demonstration of solidarity in defense of Baptist Hospital's dedicated ICU staff, seemed to unsettle the defense.

Dr. G. Robert Greene, the attending intern at the time of Mrs.

Epley's death, agreed that Shook had called him twice during his shift to inquire about medical treatment for the patient.

Defense Attorney Durham challenged Dr. Greene: "Doesn't it strike you odd, as the prosecution contends, that a man planning to kill this woman would call you twice, then administer Lidocaine for her heart and bi-carb to reduce her blood acid? That doesn't sound like he was trying to murder her." But Dr. Greene was unwavering in his testimony that Mrs. Epley's death was most likely due to the absence of her life-saving medications. Dr. Greene, who was one of an emergency team of physicians and nurses who fought valiantly but unsuccessfully for forty-five agonizing minutes to bring Mrs. Epley back from death's door, told a hushed courtroom:

"If there was no medication in those bottles, it was evident from past experience that Mrs. Epley would not have an adequate blood pressure to maintain life . . . She would die."

Glowering at Dr. Greene from across the room, the defendant shook his head angrily and reacted impatiently as the doctor spoke. He showed his displeasure at Dr. Greene's testimony by removing his glasses and tossing them on the defense table in exasperation.

He grimaced as Dr. Greene told how Shook had neglected to tell him that fatal night that Mrs. Epley was running an unusually high fever of 104 degrees—a condition potentially life-threatening by itself. But it wasn't that fever that killed her.

Ann Moore, supervisor of the intensive care unit, was aware of the dark clouds of suspicion hanging over Shook's head. And that was why, on the morning of Mrs. Epley's death, she instructed nurses to save everything in the room for use in an investigation against Shook.

At last, Tony Shook was given his day in court. And, as expected, his own testimony sketched a self-serving picture of a dedicated young man who did everything in his power to save and prolong the life of Mrs. Epley. In a low, steady voice, Shook said he had worked diligently on Mrs. Epley in the hours before she expired. He reduced her fever and her blood acid levels so that her medication would work better.

"As sick as she was, it seemed that no matter what we did for her, things were rapidly drawing to an end," said Shook. "I don't like it when patients die."

Asked why, with particular reference to Mrs. Epley, Shook replied: "Because of her age. Because of her husband. Because she had children. She had everything to live for."

Shook effectively demolished his own defense's theory that he could have made a mistake when he was preparing the victim's medication solutions. Always the perfect nurse, Shook recalled preparing the solutions properly and accurately just before finishing his shift at seven o'clock on the morning she died. He suggested that Mrs. Epley died because she was too ill to respond to any life-saving measures.

As Shook's court testimony went on, he began to shift the blame to his ICU co-workers, sharply criticizing the medical care Mrs. Epley was receiving shortly before she died.

He said that efforts to resuscitate her were "ineffective, and essentially a waste of time." And the heart drug that doctors tried to revive her with "was not what I have used."

Doctors and other staff members were trying to cover their own tracks by blaming him, said Shook, who said he resigned from the hospital in October 1986, and was working as an emergency medical technician with an ambulance team shortly before surrendering himself to police the following year.

Under heavy questioning by District Attorney Sparrow, Shook admitted lying to get his job at Baptist Hospital in the first place. He had pretended to be a medical corpsman in the Navy with thirteen months' active duty in Vietnam. He also said he might have told the head nurse at a hospital in Brandon, Florida, that he had been a prisoner-of-war in Vietnam and that he had seen one of his captors in the hospital where they worked together.

Asked about his lies, Shook responded: "I would think that was probably due to insecurity on my part."

He couldn't remember making a statement to SBI agent Barnes that he had "helped Mrs. Epley out" because he "just wanted her to finish dying." Said Shook: "My recollection of that conversation is that I was confused. I'm not really sure I know what I meant."

In a spirited defense, attorney Durham sang Shook's praises, telling jurors how Shook had tried every fifteen minutes that sad last night to save Mrs. Epley, tending her for high fevers, low blood pressure, and irregular heart rhythms. The patient died because an inexperienced doctor failed to follow through properly, alleged counsel.

119

"If they had responded to the high temperature, she wouldn't have died. If they had continued with Tony's treatment, she wouldn't have died. If they'd gotten enough Epinephrine into her, she wouldn't have died," argued Mr. Durham.

Instead, Tony Shook found himself facing life imprisonment just because Mr. Epley didn't like him.

But the jury didn't buy that argument. They found Shook guilty of first-degree murder but believed he acted out of mercy when he killed Mrs. Epley. They agreed that he had not only purposely withheld Mrs. Epley's life-sustaining blood-pressure medications but had also fabricated charts and medicine labels to make it look as if he had administered proper care. They didn't accept the district attorney's argument that he was simply a calculating killer.

Juror Kenneth Phillips observed: "We realize with all logic that the verdict had to be guilty, but we did feel awfully sorry for Shook."

One observer who doesn't feel the least bit sorry for Shook is Donna Mooney, a case specialist with the North Carolina Board of Nursing. A professional with ten years' nursing experience, she assisted the SBI in its investigation of Shook, and attended every day of the two-week trial.

Summing up her reading of the enigmatic killer, Nurse Mooney described him as an extremely intelligent, technically proficient nurse who seemed to lack "a nurturing, caring sense." She felt that he would be a dangerous guy to have around a hospital. "He seemed to think there comes a point where he can make a judgment as to when it's time for a patient to die. And that's not a nurse's choice," added Mooney.

"And being the technical nurse that he is, he would have all the knowledge available to him as to how best to get rid of that patient . . . and possibly not be detected."

One of the few undisputed facts to come out during the trial was Shook's intelligence and professional expertise. He always zeroed in on that most demanding and stressful areas of nursing care—intensive care. He threw himself into the field of health care so enthusiastically that he often moonlighted as a paramedic with local rescue squads when not at the hospital.

"I've always enjoyed working in the critical care area," said Shook in court. "I enjoy the challenge. You have a patient who seems stable but who could be changing very rapidly. And working for an emergency medical service is the same . . . you never know what's going to come in the door next."

If there was any respect from his co-workers at the Baptist Hospital, it was a grudging admiration. Many former colleagues judged Shook to be an arrogant individual, someone who thought he was superior to his colleagues. He thought nothing about reporting fellow nurses to his superiors when he thought they were giving inadequate nursing care. He openly criticized some doctors as being incompetent and inefficient.

As he faces his mandatory life imprisonment sentence, the last chapter in the Tony Shook story may remain unwritten.

Since it is known that a significantly higher number of deaths occurred under Shook's watch at Baptist Hospital than under his fellow intensive care workers, an SBI investigation was continuing.

And officials confirmed that agents were also looking into deaths in the intensive care unit of Pitt County Memorial Hospital in Greenville, North Carolina, where Shook worked from May 1985 to December 1985, before he joined the staff of Baptist Hospital.

All SBI agent R. Keith Bulla would say is: "The investigation of Mrs. Epley's death is over. The investigation of Mr. Shook's activities is not closed. It's just not complete yet."

Why do nurses kill? And how do nurses with personality disorders like Shook's manage to slip through the system?

Chairman of the department of psychiatric training at Georgia State University, Beatrice A. Yorker doesn't accept that mercy killing is a prime motive behind hospital murders. In an article in the "American Journal of Nursing," Mrs. Yorker theorizes that many of these disturbed nurses suffer from Munchausen's syndrome.

Mrs. Yorker said that it is common for nurses to feel that comatose or suffering patients are being kept alive unnecessarily. But those who believe in some form of euthanasia promote it openly, advocating living wills, for example, to preserve a patient's dignity. Acting on one's own goes against the whole spirit and principles of euthanasia, she said.

Dr. Arthur L. Caplan, director of the Center for Biomedical Ethics at the University of Minnesota, believes: "Whether done by a nut or a person motivated by the suffering of others, mercy killings remind us of the dangers of active euthanasia. It reminds us that it is easy to get away with it before anyone catches up with it."

As a former member of the New York State Licensing Board for physicians, Dr. Caplan says that the health care system's ability to detect impaired doctors or nurses is not impressive.

"We do better with pilots and bus drivers," he said, suggesting that at least semiannual checkups would be effective in detecting and weeding out flawed personnel.

But many organizations, among them the Board of Nursing and the Nurses Association, view cases like the Shook case as isolated incidents, particularly in a state like North Carolina where there are as many as fifty-one thousand licensed nurses.

Generally, hospitals are responsible for the supervision of their employees. Most hospitals follow the quality-assurance guidelines set out by the Joint Commission on the Accreditation of Health Care Organizations, which gives accreditation to eighty-five percent of U.S. hospitals.

There are many health-care officials who would like to see the quality-assurance programs taken one step further.

One such program is to apply epidemiology techniques, currently used in tracking diseases, to track down patterns of suspicious deaths in hospitals. Experts believe these computerized investigations would not only deter nurses from killing but improve the overall quality of health care.

Dr. Jeffrey J. Sacks, an investigator in the injury control division of the Centers for Disease Control in Atlanta, Georgia, is full of praise for statistical computer studies to help track down problem areas. The system was put into effect with unqualified success at a large Georgia hospital in 1986, resulting in the arrest and conviction of serial killer nurse, Terri Rachals (Chapter 9).

SIX

Jeffrey Lynn Feltner:
Mercy Merchant

Jeffrey Lynn Feltner's bizarre stories of death and killing were simply too wierd to be true—or so it seemed.

When the slight, five-foot three-inch nurse's aide talked about killing patients at Florida nursing homes, acquaintances attributed his grisly claims to gallows humor. It wasn't funny, but it also wasn't all that unusual for people in the health care, medical emergency, and law enforcement business. Men and women who live daily with pain, suffering, and death sometimes resort to such banter as a defense mechanism, a means of emotional relief.

At twenty-six, and so thin that he weighed just over one hundred pounds, Feltner had the innocent appearance of a choir boy. There seemed to be nothing threatening or offensive about the pale, slightly effeminate young man. But there was a thinly disguised dark side to him.

By his own repeated admission, he was a murderer, a man who had killed not once, but several times. The problem was, no one believed him when he began telling acquaintances and strangers that he had been killing elderly patients at the nursing home where he worked.

Switchboard operators at a crisis-intervention center in North Central Florida's Putnam County and nearby television stations and police agencies began fielding disquietingly curious telephone calls. Someone was phoning them and confessing to a series of mercy killings in a nursing home.

123

The anonymous caller wouldn't give his name, but he was almost as accommodating. He professed to be a certified nurse's aide, and claimed to have killed three women and two men at the New Life Acres nursing home in the tiny agricultural community of Melrose, Florida, some twenty five-miles east of the college town of Gainesville. At first, most of the calls were directed at a Gainesville television station and to the Putnam County Sheriff's Office in Palatka.

In a call to the crisis line in Gainesville, he talked of killing five nursing-home residents, including three in one three-day period. And he ominously warned: "I'm getting notions again. I want to stop, but I feel for the patients and their pain."

Crackpot confessions to imaginary crimes or to crimes committed by someone else is nothing new to experienced law-enforcement officers, the media, and mental-health workers. And many police departments keep records of people known for such confessions. The records can be a big help in avoiding the waste of valuable time and manpower tracking down false leads.

Nevertheless, the calls were sufficiently disturbing so that the Putnam County sheriff's department assigned an investigator to look into the confessions, and he was quickly led to Jeffrey Feltner. But once the nurse's aide was confronted by a law-enforcement officer, he became suddenly reluctant to talk about nursing-home homicides or to answer questions.

Except for the ominous telephone calls, there was little reason to suspect that any of the deaths that periodically occurred at the nursing home were anything but natural. It was true that when Mrs. Sara Abrams died at New Life Acres on February 10, 1988, family members requested an autopsy after noticing some bruises around her nose and mouth. But officials didn't believe that there was anything suspicious about the seventy-five-year-old woman's death, and never carried out the requested examination. Even though Mrs. Abrams had just returned from a visit with her family in Jacksonville, and was so spry that she not only walked on her own but also danced, deaths at her age are seldom considered suspicious. It was assumed she had died of a natural cause—heart failure.

Consequently, after the aborted effort to talk with Feltner, the investigation was put on hold. There was little to indicate that he should be taken any more seriously than any other emotionally disturbed citizen who pestered police and the press in twisted efforts to attract attention.

Feltner responded by stepping up his confession campaign. He telephoned both the TV station in Gainesville and the crisis intervention center there, repeating his claims that he had killed patients at the nursing home where he had worked for thirteen months. He added that he tried to kill another nursing-home resident after slipping into the patient's room through a window but at the last moment was disturbed by a knock on the door and escaped.

Investigating the alarming report, a sheriff's officer checked the room, but could find no evidence that the nurse's aide had been inside. He found a chair that had been moved from a nearby patio and placed just outside the window. But soft soil under the chair legs indicated that no weight had been placed on it after it was set up under the window. Debris on the windowsill was also undisturbed, and there were no fingerprints as there would likely be had someone climbed through the opening. The story didn't stand up, and the investigator concluded that Feltner could not have entered and left the room in the manner he described.

Nevertheless, the nurse's aide was at last arrested. But again, despite his claims of homicide and attempted homicide, he was not prosecuted on murder charges. The evidence simply did not appear to support his contention of serial homicide. And as a New Life spokesman pointed out much later, other people were present when some of the residents whom Feltner named as victims died. And when one of the patients he identified in his confessions died, the troubled nurse's aide apparently wasn't even on the property.

Feltner was eventually found guilty of making harassing telephone calls, trespassing, and filing a false report. He spent four months in jail.

His career at New Life Acres was over, and after completing his jail term, he flew to Michigan to see his father, Kasper Feltner. The young man's parents had separated three months before he was born, and Jeffrey spent most of his childhood in Miami. Although he had two older brothers and a sister, he was a private, quiet child. He didn't join in the rough-and-tumble play of his older brothers or other boys his age. Other more rambunctious boys tended to pick on him, possibly because of his small size. Whatever the reason, he preferred to remain inside the house and watch television or busy himself with domestic and private chores.

In 1979, his mother, who remarried and became Shirley Hartman, moved with her family to Melrose in Putnam County. Putnam County is redneck territory, where tiny back-country churches are outnumbered only by bars. Pickup trucks, Land Rovers, and rusted fifteen-year-old Buicks litter front yards; rough-talking, bearded men with shirtsleeves rolled up to display their tattoos are trailed by hounds or pitbulls; almost everyone listens to country music; and kids play Little League baseball and swim in canals.

Many of the men and women in the rural county look for jobs in agriculture and in the thriving commercial-boat building business. Although Putnam County is inland, the eastern edge is bordered by the St. John's River, and some of the best shrimp boats in the nation are constructed there.

For all their ruggedness, the people are hardworking and friendly, and young Jeffrey liked his new home. Despite his puny build and quiet ways, he made friends among his more rough-hewn and aggressive schoolmates. Although he didn't join in when the other boys tried out favorite fishing holes, swam in alligator-infested lakes and canals, or settled into serious girl-chasing and dating as they entered their teens, he somehow found his own entertainment. Quietly, and secretly, he began prowling homosexual hangouts.

Feltner performed adequately in his classes, bringing home mostly B's and C's on his report cards. A few years after graduating from Interlachen High School in a nearby town, he went to work as an aide at New Life Acres, where his mother was already employed as a nursing assistant.

He was industrious and so impressed his employers that he was soon promoted to supervisor over other aides. Much later, a puzzled colleague would recall that "Jeffrey really enjoyed working around all those old people, and they liked him."

But his dark side begun to surface. Old people quietly died at the nursing home. And he started making the telephone calls that eventually led to his brief jail term.

He didn't stay in Michigan long, and when he returned to Florida, he moved a few miles east to the Atlantic coast. There, he signed up with an agency in Daytona Beach that provides short-term help in the health-care field for hospitals, clinics, and nursing homes. Among his assignments were brief jobs at Bowman's Nursing Center in Ormond Beach, a seaside resort, and at the Clyatt Memorial Center in the next city to the south, Daytona Beach.

Feltner found a roommate who was willing to share the rent, utilities, and other costs of a rented two-bedroom apartment. But it didn't take the roomie long to discover that the baby-faced nurse's aide was strictly a loner who didn't talk much and preferred to keep to himself. It didn't matter, since the living arrangement was saving each of the young men more than a hundred dollars a month.

Feltner's troubles hadn't ended when he was released from jail. He had been diagnosed with AIDS, the deadly auto-immune deficiency condition that is devastating the population of homosexuals and drug addicts worldwide. The emotional toll on the sensitive nurse's aide's psyche was devastating. And the anonymous telephone calls to the media, police, and mental-health agencies began again. This time he not only confessed in soft conversational tones to serial medical homicide but added that he had killed all his victims in the same manner—by asphyxiation. And the admitted toll of dead had increased to seven.

"I'd just close the door and draw the curtains. Then I'd pull a blanket up to their necks, put on a pair of rubber gloves, climb on their chests, and seal their noses and mouths with my hands," the caller would advise. At first, he would speak matter-of-factly, almost as if he were talking about what he had eaten for supper the previous night. But then the matter-of-fact tone would change to a defensive whine, and he would plead: "I killed them because I wanted to end their suffering. I didn't enjoy doing it, you know. I didn't get my kicks off it."

Feltner made at least seven telephone calls to a television station in Daytona Beach, and additional calls to a mental-health facility and to a crime-tip agency. When one of the people he called asked why he was telling such terrible stories, he replied that he wanted someone to stop him before he killed again.

When he confessed to his roommate that he was responsible for a string of murders, the roommate notified authorities at the nurses' pool. They notified police. Homicide officers with the Daytona Beach Police Department quietly began conducting an investigation.

On August 16, 1989, homicide investigators arrested Feltner on charges of first-degree murder. He was locked up in the Volusia County Jail without bail, accused of the murder of eighty-three-year-old Doris Moriarty in the Clyatt Memorial Center. The Port Orange woman had died barely a month earlier, on July 11.

Feltner confessed to Daytona Beach homicide detective Bill Adamy that he killed the elderly woman after pulling on a pair of rubber gloves, climbing onto her chest, as she lay in bed, and covering her mouth and pinching her nose until she died.

"I'd been working there for about a month, and I seen this woman in pain," he told the police officer. "I just didn't want to do nothing for her."

He also talked about the deaths at the nursing home in Melrose and claimed that Mrs. Abrams asked him to kill her several times. On February 9, he said, he carried out her wishes. "I worked the three-to-eleven shift . . . and I killed her about 10:30 that night," Feltner told the detective. He said she was the third of five patients he murdered at New Life.

Feltner's mother was watching the noon news report on television when her son was named as a suspected serial killer. Later she described the experience as "like a bomb dropped." But she insisted that he was incapable of murder.

With Feltner's arrest in Daytona Beach, Putnam County authorities reinstated and stepped up their investigation of his activities there. Of the seven patients named at various times as murder victims by the mysterious telephone caller, now known to be Feltner, four had been cremated. One of those who was buried was Mrs. Abrams, and Putnam County authorities obtained permission from a daughter and a court order to exhume her body from a Jacksonville cemetery.

When eighteen months after her death, the autopsy was at last performed on the woman by Volusia County Associate Medical Examiner Michael Sherman, it was determined that she had died of asphyxiation. What's more, one of her ribs was broken, prompting her daughter to remark much later: "My mother was a healthy, vibrant woman. From the damage to her ribs, we believe she put up a fight for her life."

State Attorney John Tanner told the press that he would present the autopsy report and Feltner's confession to a Putnam County grand jury and seek a murder indictment. But Tanner defended the Putnam County sheriff's department for their failure to identify Feltner as a definite murder suspect after their earlier probe of his claims.

128

"This type of homicide is very difficult to detect, and even when suspected, very difficult to prove," he told reporters. Tanner also noted that none of Feltner's fellow employees at New Life had indicated they suspected patients were being killed.

But while expressing shock at the possibility that some of their patients might have been murdered by a staff member, the New Life spokesman observed that it was difficult to accept Feltner's claim of mercy killing, especially in light of Mrs. Abrams's death. Of those killed, he said, "Sara was probably in the best health of all of them. So it doesn't quite fit into the picture."

Confronted with the results of the Abrams autopsy, the press speculated that the bodies of two other former residents of the nursing home in Melrose – eighty-two-year-old Lathan Thornton of Gainesville and seventy-three-year-old William James of Jacksonville – would be exhumed. But the exhumations were not ordered, and despite his confessions to seven slayings, Feltner was formally charged with only those of Mrs. Abrams and Mrs. Moriarty.

Feltner had finally decided that it was time to talk as freely to law-enforcement authorities as he had been talking with the media and various mental health agencies. The suspect portrayed himself as a compassionate Angel of Death. He insisted that he was so upset by all the pain and suffering he saw that he tightened the sheets and blankets around the aged residents of the homes and smothered them to death with his hands to put them out of their misery.

When police agencies revealed the names on his death list, they included five reputed victims he said he had smothered at New Life Acres, one at the Clyatt Memorial Center, and one at the Bowman Nursing Center. Sixty-nine-year-old Berniece Olsen and sixty-three-year-old Rita Sugrue were the other two residents named as victims at New Life Acres. And eighty-one-year-old Ruby Swisher was named as the victim at the Bowman Nursing Center.

But Feltner was still having trouble deciding if he had indeed committed murder or not. Because of his slight build and his homosexuality, Feltner was segregated from other prisoners to protect him from sexual or other physical attacks. And as he waited behind bars for his trial, he had considerable time on his hands. He grew a scraggly beard that helped hide the sunken cheeks that caved in at the sides of his pale face. And he spent some of his time letter-writing.

In a letter to his father and stepmother in Michigan, he wrote that

129

he hadn't killed anyone, but had instead been carrying out an altruistic plan to call official attention to poor living conditions in the nursing homes.

"I wanted to spend what time I have left to do something that everyone would be proud of, but like always, I messed up," he wrote. The reference to the time he had left apparently referred to his AIDS. His case was active and he was being treated with the drug AZT.

He told similar stories about attempting to draw attention to poor conditions in the nursing homes to his attorney and to his mother.

As Feltner awaited trial in Volusia County, a Putnam County grand jury returned an indictment and first-degree murder charges were filed against him for the fatal asphyxiation of Mrs. Abrams. Despite Feltner's earlier arrest in the Moriarty death, his trial in Putnam County for the slaying of the one-time Jacksonville grocery clerk was scheduled first.

But the trial hadn't begun before the scrawny nurse's aide tried some delaying tactics. He once cut his wrists with a razor blade after being transferred to the Putnam County Jail, and another time slashed his upper arm.

He was discovered with his wrists slashed at about 8 A.M. when a corrections officer entered his cell to awaken him for a court appearance to enter a plea on the charge of murdering Mrs. Abrams. Medical personnel at the jail administered first aid until a rescue squad arrived and rushed him to the emergency room at the HCA Putnam Community Hospital. Physicians there quickly determined that the self-inflicted injuries were superficial and were not life-threatening. Jail authorities claimed that he faked unconsciousness while he was being treated there and had pushed smelling salts away when medics attempted to revive him.

While Feltner was at the hospital, his attorney entered a written plea for him of not guilty to the first-degree murder charge.

After the suspect was returned to the jail, he was transferred to a special "watch cell" where he could be closely monitored and guarded to prevent additional suicide attempts or hoaxes.

Feltner's legal counsel and some mental-health experts indicated concern after he reportedly went for days without eating, drinking, or speaking. He sometimes remained curled up in a fetal position on his cot for long periods and refused to leave.

His attorney requested psychiatric evaluations, and the professionals called in to observe him predictably ended up at odds over his competency to stand trial. One report prepared by Dr. Eric Waugh stated that the prisoner was unable to answer questions or to assist his counsel plan his defense. In an evaluation signed by the psychiatrist, Waugh described the murder suspect as "too emotionally impaired, i.e., too depressed and without psychic energy to challenge the prosecution to testify relevantly, and without the motivation to help himself in the legal process."

But in another report prepared by Dr. Umesh Mhatre a month later, it was stated that Feltner *was* competent. Dr. Mhatre reported that whatever catatonic symptoms the defendant exhibited were based on his unhappiness with being in jail.

During a brief hearing in his chambers, Circuit Court Judge E.L. Eastmoore considered the reports, as well as testimony from jail guards and the statements of opposing attorneys. Two corrections officers who worked in the vulnerable inmate housing unit at the Volusia County Jail testified that they had observed normal behavior from the prisoner. Both agreed that he seemed to experience normal depression for someone who was imprisoned.

"Just by the way he acts, you can tell he's depressed," Corporal James Belton testified. "But it's the I-don't-want-to-be-in-jail depression everyone gets."

And a Putnam County Jail guard told the judge that the razor wounds were superficial, and he believed the incidents were prompted more by efforts to gain attention than by legitimate attempts to inflict serious injury. At the conclusion of the hearing, Judge Eastmoore ruled that the defendant was not incompetent, only depressed. "I think the common thread in these evaluations is that Mr. Feltner is subject to bouts of depression," the judge said. "And that's understandable, considering the environment in which he finds himself." The judge observed that the injuries inflicted with the jail-issued razor blade were not life-threatening.

The judge also turned thumbs down on a proposed last-minute plea bargain that would have permitted Feltner to plead guilty to second-degree murder in exchange for no more than forty years in prison. Conviction in Florida for first-degree murder carries mandatory sentences of either death in the electric chair or life, with a twenty-five-year minimum of time served. Since prisoners in the state usually served only from one-fourth to one-third of their sentences, a forty-year term would mean Feltner could have been freed after serving only ten to fifteen years.

But Judge Eastmoore said he would only permit a plea of first-degree murder – meaning that even if scientists managed to conquer AIDS before Feltner's death, he would still be nearly sixty years old before he could look forward to freedom.

"It's either straight up or nothing," the judge said. He added that he did not permit plea bargains to reduced charges after the end of formal pretrial hearings, which had concluded about a week earlier.

A plea by Howard Pearl, an assistant public defender and specialist in homicide cases, for more time to prepare the defense had also been rejected by the judge, and in early January the trial opened in the county seat town of Palatka. The prosecution, represented by Assistant State Attorney David Damore, had already disclosed that they would seek the maximum penalty for the defendant, death in "Old Sparky," Florida's electric chair.

Jury selection proceeded rapidly, and a twelve-member panel was selected near the end of the first day. Feltner, with his beard shaved, his dirty-blond hair neatly combed, and modishly dressed in a pink shirt and dark necktie with white trousers, sat quietly and showed little emotion during the proceedings. Despite his prison pallor, he looked as if he could have been the boy next door.

In his opening statement, Damore told the jury how Feltner had admitted killing seven elderly people in three nursing homes in less than two years. The prosecutor said evidence would also be introduced to show how the defendant killed. "He would climb on their chests to hold his victim down. Then he'd put on plastic gloves and then hold his hand over their nose and mouth," he declared. A woman juror blanched at the prosecutor's graphic description, and unconsciously placed a hand over her own mouth.

But the woman and her fellow jurors were never asked to deliberate the case. After the prosecutor finished outlining the evidence he said he was prepared to submit, the court called a recess so the defendant could confer with his attorney and his parents in the judge's antechamber. Feltner had experienced a change of heart due to a decision by Judge Eastmoore. The judge had decided to permit the jury to listen to recordings of three confessions the suspect had made to Daytona Beach police on August 11, 15, and 16.

Feltner cradled his head in his hand as he listened to himself on

132

GENENE JONES TURK

ANTHONY JOYNER

RICHARD ANGELO

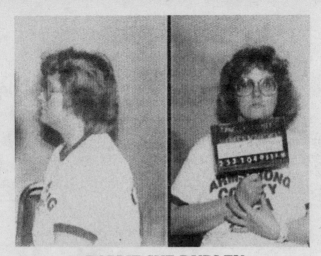

BOBBIE SUE DUDLEY

ANTHONY GEORGE SHOOK

JEFFREY LYNN FELTNER

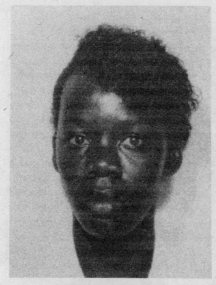

INGER LEMONT

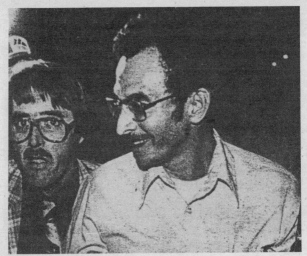

Photo Credit: Bettmann Archives

ROBERT DIAZ

Photo Credit: Lee Flanigan

TERRI MAPLES RACHALS

GWENDOLYN GRAHAM

DONALD HARVEY

RANDY POWERS

tape recount to Detective Adamy how he had murdered seven men and women, one at a time by smothering them to death. It was a chilling, and damning, recitation.

More than forty-minutes after the recess began, Feltner withdrew his claim of innocence and made a new surprise plea of guilty to the first-degree suffocation murder of Mrs. Abrams. Feltner's eyes were red, as if he had been crying, and his shoulders slumped as he stood beside his attorney and entered the plea in a soft, barely audible voice.

Judge Eastmoore immediately sentenced him to life in prison, with the stipulation that the twenty-seven-year-old man serve at least twenty-five-years before being considered for parole.

Feltner's defense attorney later told the press that he considered the decision to enter the guilty plea a wise move. "Even though he denies the charges, his statements would have damaged him. I felt it was time for damage control," Pearl said.

The attorney had sought to limit the jury's access to the tape recordings only to the parts that dealt with Mrs. Abrams' death. But the judge ruled that although the nurse's aide was on trial only for the Abrams death, his confessions to the other deaths were similar enough to reveal a pattern to his crimes, and that the tapes would be therefore admitted into evidence in their entirety.

Pearl told reporters that he was prepared to defend a single murder, but a confession to seven murders would almost certainly have doomed his client to the death penalty.

Despite the guilty plea, the convicted killer's family remained loyal and told reporters that they believed he admitted guilt solely to avoid the possibility of execution. His stepmother said that he continued to insist on his innocence when they met with him. "We're with him whatever he wants to do," she said. "We still love him."

Mrs. Hartman told a reporter: "To stop from getting the chair, I'd say I'm guilty. I know he's not guilty," she said. "I'm his mother." She added that her son was concerned about his family and didn't want them to see him die on death row.

Judge Eastmoore lifted the rule against a plea on the second day of the trial, when it was agreed that there would be no reduction of charges. The single concession of the prosecution and the court in agreeing to the plea was dropping the demand for the death penalty.

Despite withdrawing his demand for the death penalty, Damore

133

said he was convinced the nurse's aide acted out of compulsion, not compassion. "I have never felt that Mr. Feltner was motivated by concern," he said. "He has a way of trying to rationalize what he has done, perhaps so he could live with it."

Two days after his surprise guilty plea in Putnam County, Felton appeared before Circuit Judge James Foxman in Volusia County and pleaded guilty to second-degree murder in the suffocation of Mrs. Moriarty. Judge Foxman ordered a seventeen-year prison term, to be served concurrently with the earlier sentence. After a bewildering two-year ordeal of confessions and denials, the affair was ended at last.

After deputies led the frail little man away in handcuffs, Tanner said that even without trials and possible sentences in the other deaths, he believed Feltner would spend the rest of his life behind bars. Referring to the youthful killer's fatal disease, the state attorney told reporters: "I truly believe Mr. Feltner will die in prison because of his medical condition."

SEVEN

Inger Lemont:
Butcher on Call

It was a murder that should have never happened.

Every murder is a tragedy — for the victim, family, and friends — even for the perpetrator.

In the case of retired schoolteacher Ruth Ann Nedermier, of West Palm Beach, Florida, the warning signs were out. Unfortunately, the right people didn't recognize them. And someone's greed was allowed to creep up on the seventy-two-year-old spinster and kill her.

Ruth Nedermier devoted a lifetime to helping others before she found herself in a situation where she needed help. A tall, slender, dignified woman with an air of refined gentility, she was convalescing from two operations. Surgery was first performed on her for a debilitating spine condition, then surgeons implanted an artificial hip joint.

Except for the surgical problems, however, she was in remarkably good health. Her mind was as clear and sharp as it had been when she taught generations of schoolchildren. The retired teacher lived alone, but she was enthusiastic about life and lacked neither social graces nor friends.

But the back-to-back operations had left her with a pronounced limp and she couldn't move about without the help of an aluminum walker. And she needed other assistance as well. Old bones knit slowly. It simply wasn't possible for her to continue doing everything for herself during her convalescence. She needed help with her housework, shopping, and many of the other humdrum chores of day-to-day living that seem so simple for most people until the time comes when they are physically disabled by age, illness or accident.

But locating someone able and willing to come into the home either as a live-in or drop-in helper and companion can create a difficult problem. Sometimes relatives are available, occasionally friends or neighbors, but the retired teacher had neither, or at least no one whom she wished to call upon. So she consulted an agency that provided semiskilled nurse's aides for the homebound.

After brief experiences with some helpers who worked a day or so and left, Miss Nedermier again contacted an agency called Redi-Nurse and Inger Lemont was sent to her home.

Inger was a twenty-two-year-old, five-foot six-inch black woman who lived in Lake Worth, a resort town at the south edge of West Palm Beach on Florida's Treasure Coast. She was polite, experienced, and willing to work for the modest salary available in the low-paying profession. Initially, the old woman and the young woman seemed to get along well together.

Neither the convalescing old lady who brought the nurse's aide into her home nor the agency which sent her there was aware that Inger Lemont had a criminal record. The agency hadn't discovered the record because they didn't have to look. Florida has neither laws nor regulations requiring certification, licensing, or training of nurse's aides who work in hospitals or private duty. NA's who worked through agencies are required to show only that they had forty hours of training, and those who obtained their jobs privately are not required to show a regulatory agency any qualifications at all in order to offer their services.

Agencies that provide home health-care services must be licensed by the state and are checked out annually by the Florida Department of Health and Rehabilitative Services. But the department makes no investigation of the licenses of individual employees—or possible criminal records. Florida law also requires that nursing agencies send registered nurses to the home of patients to determine their needs.

But the only law regulating nurse's aides was a 1984 statute mandating training for those who work in nursing homes. Nursing or convalescent-home NA's must be certified through the Department of Education.

It was up to employers to check for possible criminal records of nurse's aides they sent into private duty or the home-care program. If employers didn't voluntarily take on the responsibility, there was no check.

Although many, probably most, nurse's aides are dedicated and sincerely concerned with providing appropriate and caring attention for their patients, like most professions, it is almost impossible to weed out the occasional bad apple. Except for doctors and a few highly skilled technicians, the health-care business offers modest pay, even when compared to the generally low-wage industries such as tourism, agriculture, and service jobs that provide employment for a large percentage of Florida's workforce. And wage-wise, nurse's aides — who can expect to earn about six dollars an hour — are near the bottom of the barrel in the health-care profession. So there is a continuing problem attracting good, dependable people.

Agency employees, and Miss Nedermier, were unaware that the quiet nurse's aide was released from the Palm Beach County Stockade just three months before she applied for a job with Redi-Nurse. Criminal court records showed that she was arrested in May 1986 on charges of stealing eight thousand dollars worth of jewelry from another elderly patient who was under her care. She pawned the jewelry for eight hundred dollars before she was arrested, and sentenced to ninety days in the stockade for grand theft and dealing in stolen property. She was also ordered to repay thirty-three hundred dollars in restitution.

When the seemingly repentant nurse's aide appeared in court, she apologized for her thievery and promised she would never steal again. She wrote a letter from the stockade to Palm Beach County Circuit Judge Thomas Johnson, pleading for a reduced sentence, insisting that she could be a productive, law-abiding citizen. She said she was very remorseful about the crime she had committed and added that she was worried that any more time spent behind bars could hinder her career. She was released after serving eighty-seven days, and shortly after that, resumed the career she had been so concerned about damaging.

Florida shares a problem with other states in the regulation of nursing assistants. The industry and lawmakers have not kept pace with the growing demand for nurse's aides. The trouble, in fact, may be even more critical in Florida than in other states because of its high population of the elderly and the spiraling residential and commercial development in recent years. Retirement and nursing homes, as well as hospitals that cater to geriatrics are bulging at the seams, and serious gridlocks are occurring in the care of the elderly and infirm. It's not so much that the services are eroding. They simply haven't caught up.

Florida's breakneck growth is straining the state's resources, and health care represents only one of a half-dozen or more critical areas that must be considered by legislators and local authorities in the scramble for priorities. Law enforcement, corrections, transportation, education, and environmental concerns are all locked in the contest for the attention of government officials and public and private dollars.

Even when the elderly, infirm, and ill do attract priority attention of lawmakers and tax dollars, home health care is one of the areas that is most easily overlooked among the crush of demands for new protective laws, regulations, and services. People cared for in their homes are isolated and out of the mainstream, conveniently hidden from sight. And they are among the most needy and vulnerable. They are pushovers for people like Inger Lemont.

The young woman could be charming and give the appearance of efficiency and industry when she wished. A graduate of high school in the upscale coastal community of Boca Raton, she was neatly dressed, clean, and courteous when she applied at the agency. She performed impressively during her interview, and did particularly well on her nursing-skills test. On her application for employment, she replied to a question asking if she had ever been convicted of a felony by checking the "no" box. Inger also submitted a 1983 Certificate of Completion for a nurse's aide course she had taken at the Federal Job Corps Center in her home state of Mississippi. When the agency asked for references, she assured her supervisors that she would provide them later. She was permitted to begin working while the references were being obtained and checked.

Inger was one of four certified nurse's aides who provided Miss Nedermier with 182 hours of care through the Redi-Nurse agency. The agency sent the eager NA to the Nedermier home for four hours on August 11, 1987, and four days later she worked there another

138

six hours.

The former teacher was so impressed with the pleasant young woman's work, in fact, that she entered into a private employment agreement with the nurse's aide that did not include the agency. When Miss Nedermier agreed to hire Inger privately, she lost important protection provided by the agency in the supervision of the NA's performance by an experienced registered nurse.

Although Miss Nedermier had been a demanding teacher, she was scrupulously fair, and she seemed to sincerely enjoy helping others to develop self-confidence and personal skills. Perhaps that helped make her too trusting and an easy mark for the unscrupulous young woman she had admitted into her life and her home. If Ruth Nedermier was a bit too trusting, perhaps it was because she had enjoyed a pleasant, useful life surrounded by people who appreciated her.

As is the case of most good teachers, the people who loved her most were her former students. Miss Nedermier had taught many years ago at Belvedere Elementary School in West Palm Beach. One of her pupils was Mary Gay-Elfreth, and the former student later recalled how Miss Nedermier had emphasized to all her students that the most important lesson in life was to cherish every day as though it were your last.

"She taught me that no matter how unimportant you may feel or how down you are, you must be virtuous in everything you do," the admiring former student wrote in a letter to the editor published in the Palm Beach *Post*. "She taught me there is no such thing as insignificance."

During her thirty-five-years as an educator, the woman touched many lives. And yet, few people knew her really well, even those who considered her a good friend. All they really knew was that she was born in a small town in the hills of West Virginia. She had few surviving close relatives, but her mother was still living and in a West Virginia nursing home. Miss Nedermier was looking forward to her own physical condition improving sufficiently so that she could return there and help care for her aging parent.

Ruth Nedermier was a giving, caring person who had spent her life teaching school. She obtained her first teaching job in 1938 in Clarksburg, West Virginia. The position paid $2,025 a year. In 1948, for reasons known only to the slender blond instructor, she

139

moved to West Palm Beach and signed a contract to teach in the Palm Beach County schools.

Over the years, her annual performance reviews repeatedly included the descriptions "excellent" and "above average." The only criticism contained in the uniformly glowing performance reports was really a kind of left-handed compliment. A supervisor had pointed out that Miss Nedermier personally resented any kind of work that took her away from her beloved classroom.

One of her last personal reviews stated simply: "She is one of the most effective teachers we have."

A major highlight of her life was a three-week trip to Europe in July 1970. She visited fifteen cities and wrote a glowing account of her experiences for the school board. In it, she described the charm of the sidewalk cafes of Paris and the people she met in the villages of Switzerland. She was thrilled that she was so close to Prince Charles in London's Westminster Abbey that she could almost reach out and touch him. She returned to her class with her eyes shining, eager to share her wonderful experiences with her students.

Although Miss Nedermier wasn't aware of it, Redi-Nurse was having problems with her personal NA. There were complaints about her unreliability, and she had failed to provide the promised references despite repeated requests. Finally, only five working days after her name was first placed on their register, the agency terminated her services. But no one at the agency informed Miss Nedermier, who was keeping the NA on as her personal helper.

It didn't take long for Inger to slip back into her old ways. While pretending to be a faithful employee, she was unashamedly forging checks and draining thousands of dollars from the teacher's bank account.

But Miss Nedermier was no fool. Her injured hip made it difficult to walk, but her mind was still functioning as well as ever. She soon realized that someone was stealing from her. Initially she didn't want to believe that it was Inger, and suspected a former certified nurse's aide she had hired. She had begun noticing troubles with her bank account and items missing from her home early in 1988, and once, after a trip to the bank where the NA had driven her, she arrived home just in time to see two strange men leaving the house. Police were notified, but no arrests were made.

On March 2, she telephoned Redi-Nurse to report the theft of money and other valuables. She wanted help tracking down the culprit and discussed the problem briefly with the president of the agency. A short time later, a nursing supervisor telephoned her to set up an appointment to further discuss the problem. Surprisingly, Miss Nedermier apologized and said the trouble had already been straightened out.

Two days later, however, an official from City Federal Savings and Loan telephoned with some alarming news. The banker was concerned about five thousand dollars that the nursing assistant had just withdrawn from the retiree's account.

Lowering her voice, Miss Nedermier asked the banker to telephone back later because Inger was in the house, only a few feet away. She had answered the telephone and handed it to her employer. Thirty minutes later, when the banker attempted to call back, there was no answer to his persistent rings.

Police, who were alerted by the suspicious banker to the old woman's absence and began a missing persons investigation, later said they believed he was the last outside individual to talk to the teacher before she died.

Although uniform officers and plainclothesmen canvased the neighborhood, there simply was no trace of Miss Nedermier. Police did pick up reports from neighbors, however, of a mysterious van with two men inside parked outside her house on the afternoon of her disappearance.

The day after the banker's frustrating conversation with the retiree, Inger cheerfully attended the wedding of a friend in Delray Beach. Ominously, the day after the wedding, according to the NA's own later statements, she gave twenty dollars to her boyfriend with instructions to buy a chain saw and three boxes of garbage bags. She said she instructed him to buy "the biggest ones [he] could find."

Even experienced homicide detectives would eventually remark that Inger, who was called "Tillie" by her friends, was smooth and cool. After her sudden freedom from the responsibilities to her missing employer, she had time to attend the wedding, shop, and munch hamburgers at McDonald's.

After the banker talked with police about his fears for Miss Nedermier, Inger was one of the first people contacted by investigators. She appeared willing, even eager to help locate the retiree, and telephoned officers from time to time to inquire about the progress of their search. When West Palm Beach Police asked her to bring her car to their headquarters so they could look at it, she agreed. But first she drove to her parents' home in Delray Beach. After talking with a friend who helped her curl her hair, the two women drove to a car wash and cleaned up her car. Inger paid particular attention to cleaning up the backseat. Her girlfriend thought it was curious that she didn't wash the outside of the car instead of merely vacuuming and scrubbing the inside. But it was Inger's car and it was her business how it was cleaned. Inger topped off the chore by spraying the interior of the car with air freshener. Then she and her helper jumped inside and drove to the Dollar Store to shop.

Late in the afternoon, she at last drove to police headquarters. By the time she arrived, detectives working on the missing persons case had left for the day. Inger returned to her home.

A short time later, she asked her brother Rudy to help her move a heavy four-foot by two-foot trunk from her apartment into her parents' house. The trunk was in the middle of her kitchen floor when her brother arrived, but when he attempted to peer inside, she slammed the lid shut, almost catching his hand. He noticed a smear of blood, but when he asked about the stain, his sister told him that it was from some wholesale meat she had stored inside.

The explanation sounded reasonable enough, and he dismissed any further questions about the stain from his mind. Inger, however, later added a touch of intrigue by telling a series of differing stories about the contents of the trunk to family members. She told her mother that she had some old clothes stored in the trunk to give to the church. She told another family member that she did have meat inside but didn't want her boyfriend to know about it. And she told yet another story of having bought the meat from thieves. She couldn't seem to settle on a story and stick to it.

Inger helped her brother move the trunk into her sister's bedroom closet. But it was there only a couple of days before the nurse's aide asked two neighbor men to help her move it outside. The meat had begun to rot, and the odor was so disagreeable that, after moving the trunk, the men returned to their homes and showered.

Once they had left, Inger removed all the packages and meticulously laid each of them on the lawn. Then she cleaned the inside of the trunk with bleach and a garden hose. Finally, she placed the packages back inside the trunk and went into the house, where she dropped to her knees and scrubbed the closet floor. Her sister helped her lug the heavy trunk back inside, and Inger sprayed everything with more air freshener.

Neither the air freshener nor the cleanup job helped at all. The odor coming from the trunk was foul, and seemed to be stronger every minute. The family had long ago lost any interest they might have had in sharing the mysterious stock of meat with Inger. The stench was becoming so overpowering, in fact, that Inger's father, Rudolph Lemont, reluctantly decided that he had to do something about it. Inger was away when he and his daughter Sharon took the opportunity to peer inside. Cautiously, they popped open the rounded lid and recoiled in horror.

Sharon shrieked and ran from the house crying. Her father simply stared in shock and disbelief. Finally, he forced himself to move, and lurched toward the telephone to call the police.

Ruth Nedermier's body was stored inside the three-foot-deep trunk in bloody chunks. The once vibrant, loving schoolteacher had been reduced to ugly lumps of ragged meat and splintered bones. The butchery had been accomplished with an unskilled primitive force. There were no traces of a trained surgeon's finesse, not even the skill of an experienced meat-market butcher. The frail body had obviously been dissected by an amateur, who ignored joints and natural junctures and simply ripped.

It wasn't difficult for homicide investigators and forensic pathologists to determine how she had been disjointed. Whoever had ripped apart the body had torn through the brittle bones and withered flesh with a chain saw. One ragged cut had chewed into the artificial hip joint. It was difficult to believe that the gory, hacked-up chunks of flesh and the once-warm, caring educator were one and the same.

Rudolph Lemont, a landscaper, later told investigators: "I knew when I looked inside, it was that West Palm Beach woman because my daughter was working there."

Aside from the fact that it was Inger's trunk, there was another reason to suspect that the body had a special connection to Inger. She had left a gory calling card—a bloody sweatshirt with the name "Inger" on the front was inside the trunk with the remains of the retiree.

Formal identification was made through a serial number on Miss Nedermier's artificial hip. Warm temperatures and the plastic bags

143

the body was wrapped in had speeded decomposition, and the remains were badly rotted. To police, one of the most disturbing aspects of the investigation at that point was the inability to determine quickly whether or not the old woman was dismembered while she was still alive. An autopsy on the grisly remains didn't immediately disclose the cause of death, and the medical examiner's office listed it as unknown, pending further investigation.

Inger Lemont remained free for four days after the remains of her former employer were recovered. Then she voluntarily turned herself in to West Palm Beach homicide detectives. During a grueling six-hour interrogation, Inger began giving police the first of what would become a series of wildly contradictory statements over the next few weeks that included five different versions of the slaying. She still didn't seem to be able to stick to a story.

In one of the versions, she admitted to investigators that she had known the trunk contained the retired teacher's body, but she blamed the outrageous crime on her boyfriend. She identified the younger man as a former Palm Beach County corrections officer whom she met while she was serving her theft sentence in the stockade.

A check of his personnel records later showed that the boyfriend worked at the stockade nearly six months before he was forced to resign in May 1987 after being accused of attempting to force sex on a female deputy.

In another statement, Inger spun a fantastic yarn about a pair of aggressive salesmen who insisted on selling her some stolen meat. She said that, although she turned them down, they left the trunk on her patio. When she opened the trunk and peered inside, she found the chopped-up body of her employer. Inger said she panicked and slammed the lid back down, but didn't inform police about the incredible and frightening coincidence.

And in yet another version of her increasingly fanciful tales, she said she found Miss Nedermier's body stuffed under her son Scooter's bed when she returned home after her neighbor's wedding. She said her boyfriend had put it there.

Inger continued to talk freely with detectives, but her stories were constantly changing. In one statement she denied she was at the teacher's house when Miss Nedermier was killed but said she had left the door open for her boyfriend and another man whom she knew by his street name "Eyes" so they could go inside and rob the old woman.

According to an eventual 108-page wrapup that provided her most consistent account, however, the retiree was murdered after discovering the latest theft attempt. Then her body was taken to Inger's Lake Worth apartment where it was temporarily stuffed under the child's bed.

In the signed confession, the nurse's aide admitted she was in her employer's house when Miss Nedermier was robbed and killed. She said she tried to distract the retiree, but the old woman saw the two men going through her things and began hobbling toward her bedroom. Ingrid said her boyfriend hit Miss Nedermier in the head with a brick. Then after the woman fell to the floor, he hit her again. The NA said that Miss Nedermier pleaded with him just before she was struck the second time: "What did I do to make you do this?" Then the old woman had looked at her and asked the same question. No one replied.

Inger said that after the woman was killed, the men continued ransacking the house, looking for money and jewelry. Then her boyfriend covered the old woman's mouth with a scarf and dragged her out of the house. Forensic pathologists and homicide investigators later determined that the cause of death was suffocation, occurring when Miss Nedermier was gagged and a plastic bag was pulled over her head.

Inger said that after the assault and robbery, she left to pick up her three-year-old son, Scooter, and took him to stay with her parents for the weekend.

Inger attended her friend's wedding that Saturday, as if nothing had happened. The next day, she gave her boyfriend money to buy a chain saw, gloves, and large plastic grocery bags, she continued. She claimed she stood guard outside the room while the body was cut up so that it would fit into the new steamer trunk she had purchased a week earlier for two hundred dollars. The pieces of flesh were triple-wrapped in plastic bags before being placed inside with mothballs and air fresheners.

The room was a terrible mess when Inger finally went inside, and she scrubbed it down with strong cleansers and followed up by spraying air freshener.

She said she threw Miss Nedermier's purse into a dumpster in Delray Beach, and dropped the chainsaw into another dumpster a few miles away. Inger told detectives that she was upset at her boyfriend because he had promised to take the trunk away and burn it, but instead he disappeared and left it on her patio with the incriminating corpse stored in chunks inside.

When police asked the suspect about the seventeen thousand dollars she had looted from her employer's bank account, she defended the thievery. She said she deserved the money, and that she gave most of it to her boyfriend to buy drugs.

Portions of the stories sounded legitimate and fit in with other information investigators had gathered. A teenager rummaging through a trash bin behind a department store only six blocks from the Lemont family home had found a garbage bag that contained the purse and other items – Miss Nedermier's credit cards, personal papers, her house keys, shattered eyeglasses – and a bloodstained brick.

A used typewriter ribbon had also been discarded with the other items. It carried the impression of Inger's name and address, and a note to her boyfriend telling him, "I love you." Miss Nedermier's name had also been typed with the ribbon.

The discovery in the dumpster fit in with Inger's conflicting statements. But other elements of the confessions were simply too hard to swallow, and some made no sense at all. The frustrating jumble of admissions, retractions, and curious memory lapses promised to make interesting grist for lawyers to joust over at a trial.

With the assistance of banking executives, detectives also compiled copies of all the checks Lemont had written to herself on her employer's account.

Preliminary charges of first-degree murder were filed against the nurse's aide, and a judge ordered her held without bail. A few days later, a Palm Beach County grand jury returned a multicount indictment that included charges of first-degree murder, assault and battery, robbery with a deadly weapon, kidnapping, grand theft, and multiple forgery offenses.

As Lemont waited out the lengthy pretrial process and the trial itself in jail, her attorney accused police of prematurely dropping the investigation after her arrest. He claimed that it would have been physically impossible for the 135-pound woman to have murdered the victim, cut up the body, and moved it around in the trunk without help from someone else.

He also injected the question of race into the already sensational case. "What you have here is a black female with a prior record of grand theft and a white lady well known in the community," he told reporters. "There's a lot of sympathy on her behalf, and the sympathy is convoluting the facts."

The lawyer told journalists that Inger's remarks to police during the interrogation amounted to a statement, not a confession. He claimed she was frightened and wasn't lucid when she provided the statement, and said she would plead innocent to the charges and request a jury trial.

Detectives didn't totally disagree that it would be difficult for a 135-pound woman to carry out the killing and dismemberment, then move the body around by herself. But suspecting that someone else was involved in the grisly crime and proving it were two different things. One frustrated homicide detective pointed out that she had told so many stories that it was hard to conceive of any jury believing her testimony in court. "All we have to link her male friend with the murder is Inger Lemont's word," he said. "There isn't a shred of evidence to back her up."

No charges were filed against the boyfriend, because police had no solid evidence of his involvement in the crime. When authorities issued a subpoena asking him for a sworn statement, he cited his Fifth Amendment rights against self-incrimination and refused to discuss the case. Police were left with only Inger's string of unsupported crazy-quilt accusations.

Inger's troubles continued while she waited out the tangled legal process in the stockade. Jailers reported that she made one half-hearted effort at suicide. And she told another inmate that she killed her employer after listening in to the telephone conversation with the banker about the looted funds.

She had experienced other problems since her arrest, as well. Immediately after her first interrogation session with detectives, she complained of feeling ill and was rushed by ambulance to a nearby hospital. But after emergency treatment for an undisclosed condition, she was quickly released to custody of law enforcement authorities.

As part of the pretrial maneuvering and jockeying for position, Inger's attorneys filed a motion asking for the case to be moved to a court outside of Palm Beach County because of the heavy publicity

147

in the local print and electronic media and the fact that so many people in the county had known the victim. Judge Thomas Sholts declined an immediate ruling but said he would consider the motion when jury selection began.

Before he had an opportunity to make a ruling, however, Inger's attorneys and prosecutor's representatives worked out a plea bargain. Investigators had collected some damning evidence against the suspect, and her attorneys conceded to reporters that they were concerned she might be convicted of first-degree murder. If that happened, considering the particular helplessness of the victim and the gruesome aspects of the case, conviction might be followed up with a death sentence. Inger Lemont had no desire to be executed, so she agreed to plead guilty to a reduced count of second-degree murder, a charge that in Florida carries a maximum sentence of twenty-two-years in prison, although in actuality she could expect parole much sooner.

Despite the agreement to plead guilty, however, she continued to blame her ex-boyfriend for instigating the crime. In a deposition, she claimed he repeatedly told her they should "rob the old bitch."

But it was Inger who was charged with the murder. Assistant State Attorney Allen Geesey summed up the prosecution's position in regard to her unsupported accusations against her former sweetheart when he remarked: "Inger Lemont claimed her boyfriend did it all, but she was the one in possession of the body parts."

When she appeared in a packed courtroom before Circuit Court Judge Thomas Sholts for sentencing, he questioned her in an effort to shed more light on her motivation for the horrendous crime.

"Why did you do it?" he asked. "Why did you kill her and dismember her body?"

The defendant, dressed in a baggy olive-drab prison uniform, hung her head, peered at her feet, and mumbled, "I spent a lot of time thinking about it and I don't know."

The judge warned that he did not have to accept the scaled-down plea, and reiterated that he wanted to know exactly what she did and why she did it.

Inger turned and peered in desperation at her attorneys, pleading, "What did you tell me to say?"

Under the judge's persistent prodding, she eventually provided some answers to his questions. But most of her replies were in monosyllables. She continued to blame her ex-boyfriend and she continued to show her reluctance for further discussion. "I made a statement to police already," she told the judge. "I knew what was going to happen . . . I just left the door open to help him do it," she said of the purported robbery scheme.

"So you did it for money, material gain?" the judge asked.

"Yes."

"Was it worth it?," he wanted to know.

Inger hesitated again, studying her feet. Then, in a barely audible whisper, she told him, "No."

Judge Sholts accepted the pleas of guilty to charges of second-degree murder, burglary with assault, armed robbery, uttering forgeries, and violation of probation. Then he sentenced her to seventy-five years in prison, three times the guideline sentence for second-degree murder. The prosecutor had refused to accept the plea bargain without her agreement to accept the longer sentence. Sentences on the lesser charges were scheduled to run concurrently with the murder term. Inger Lemont never apologized for the cruel betrayal and murder of her gentle employer.

Ruth Nedermier did not leave a will. But she left a legacy to the old and to the infirm, as well as to the thousands of students whose lives she helped shape during their time together in the classroom.

Her grisly murder forced the Florida Department of Health and Rehabilitation Services, HRS, to begin considering measures to toughen regulations governing the rapidly burgeoning home-care health industry. State Senator William "Doc" Myers of Hobe Sound took the lead in the move for reform, calling for laws to require firms in the business to verify prior employment history of job applicants before hiring, and to allow access by the companies to the state's Abuse Registry.

HRS began maintaining the statewide registry to record cases of abuse against children, the disabled, and the elderly. Home health-care agencies were already required to report accusations of abuse to the registry, but they were not allowed to use it to screen job applicants. Politicians were now insisting that information in the registry be made more easily available to home health-care agencies.

"It's just a shame that it takes a catastrophe to solve a problem," Myers declared.

Individual nurses, nurses' associations, and agencies which employ them were also anxious to improve their services, and especially to better protect their clients and patients. Paula Massey, director of the Florida Nurses Association, pointed out that patients were getting out of hospitals sooner and returning to their homes in need of a higher level of health care than in the past. And she called for involvement of more skilled nurses in home care.

Lee Pearson, assistant manager of criminal justice for the American Association for Retired People, pointed out that his agency was also concerned with the need for better protection of people requiring home care. He said that AARP was investigating strategies to come up with improved standards and background checks for people in the home health-care industry.

"Criminals don't present themselves as criminals," he told reporters.

Officials with the Redi-Nurse Agency were understandably distressed over the tragedy, and responded to the wave of negative publicity with various statements, including remarks during a press conference in their offices.

A spokesman pointed out that there was nothing in Florida law mandating reference checks of nurse's aides working in health home care. References are frequently worthless anyway, he said. The spokesman estimated that only about fifty percent of reference requests were being returned from former employers with meaningful information, primarily because of fear of litigation. Employers are afraid of lawsuits if they give poor recommendations to former workers.

The Redi-Nurse official also told reporters that no check was made for a criminal history on the NA because local police agencies didn't make such records available. Although a Palm Beach County sheriff's office spokesman confirmed that criminal records are not given to employers, he said that they *will* advise employers if applicants have criminal records in the county.

But state legislators and health-care professionals are well aware that a mere tightening of the regulations in no way means that the problems are solved. There are just too many opportunities for abuse. And the old and infirm in Florida and in other states continue to be robbed – emotionally, physically, and sexually abused, and sometimes murdered by the people they are most dependent upon.

A few months before the Nedermier case reached the courts,

ninety-three-year-old Lena Grimes of West Palm Beach telephoned the Visiting Nurse Association of Palm Beach County for assistance in hiring a part-time helper to do her shopping and run errands. She subsequently hired three women at various times. Some four months later one of the women was arrested and charged with grand theft for allegedly stealing more than twelve thousand dollars by writing checks to herself from the old woman's account. Mrs. Grimes also filed a civil suit in an effort to get back both the money and china and silver she reported missing from her home.

In another Palm Beach county case about the same time, a night nurse was on duty when a catalogue company telephoned to say that a three-thousand dollar order was ready for the blind, ninety-year-old resident. The old woman had placed no such order. Following a four-month investigation, Delray Beach police arrested the woman's day nurse and charged her with grand theft after discovering nearly twenty-five thousand dollars missing from the patient's savings account.

Alarmed activists working to improve protection and care of the elderly and infirm point out that there are dozens of similar cases filed in Florida's courts every year, and it's highly likely that there are many more cases of thievery and physical or sexual abuse that will never be reported. Each incident that occurs is a tragedy. And unless meaningful reforms are made rapidly, the system is ready-made to undergo another staggering calamity like the brutal murder of Ruth Nedermier.

EIGHT

Robert Diaz
Prophet of Death

Soft-spoken Robert Diaz, a forty-six-year-old father of three, never ceased to amaze his co-workers at the southern California hospitals were he worked as a coronary care nurse.

A frustrated and impatient man who loved to play doctor, and who claimed psychic powers, Diaz was able to predict with uncanny accuracy exactly what time certain heart patients were going to die.

One co-worker, Nurse Sandra Wingo remembers one occasion when Diaz asked her of two elderly patients: "Who do you think will go first?" Wingo said she was confused by the question because both the patients he was talking about were in stable condition.

There was no mystic power behind the Diaz prophesies of death. The bespectacled, quiet-spoken Angel of Mercy, whom associates and friends described as having a morbid fascination with "blood and gore" was the protector of the wards in whom elderly patients entrusted their lives.

And he was systematically murdering them one by one.

When twelve elderly patients died mysteriously in two Los Angeles-area hospitals in the spring of 1981, an alert nursing supervisor badgered her superiors into launching a full-scale investigation.

The probe revealed one common link: Diaz had worked at both hospitals, and the deaths occurred during his shifts.

All the victims were elderly, and all experienced the same ghastly symptoms just before dying, first turning red, then blue, finally succumbing to violent seizures. Each of the victims died at 1 A.M., 4 A.M., or 7 A.M. In every case, these were the times Diaz went off duty.

Riverside County Assistant District Attorney Thomas Hollenhorst, appalled by the obvious premeditation in the killings, vowed early in the investigation that he would be seeking the death penalty, drawing attention to the fact that "there almost appeared there was a time for dying."

As evidence against the self-proclaimed "psychic doctor" mounted, Diaz was eventually arrested later in the year and charged on twelve counts of murder. When arrested, the temporary or substitute nurse was also under investigation for another fifteen suspicious deaths at other California hospitals where he worked part-time.

Diaz, one of sixteen children, was born and raised in Gary, Indiana. He started his working life at an auto parts factory in the Midwest, but made a career change because of his preoccupation with becoming a doctor and took up nursing as a career while in his thirties.

And what a career it turned out to be. At one stage during the height of the investigations into his activities, one detective suggested that Diaz could be responsible for "the largest hospital-related mass murder case in U.S. history."

Diaz's reputation as one of the most prolific institutional killers of all time seemed secured when a six-month investigation sought answers to the suspicious circumstances surrounding the deaths of sixty elderly patients in three southern California counties: Los Angeles, where thirty died, and Riverside and San Bernadino where thirty more had died. All the victims were elderly and ill, and all experienced the same symptoms before dying, first turning red, then blue, then suffering violent seizures. The primary function of the drug Lidocaine, whose presence was the common denominator in most of the cases investigated, was to stabilize cardiac patients by correcting arrhythmia or irregular heart beat, but which in large quantities could induce a heart attack. Diaz had been a part-time worker at all three locations.

Investigators decided to zero in on only the twelve killings supported by the strongest evidence—eleven victims at the Community Hospital of the Valleys in Perris and one death at the San Gorgonio Pass Hospital in Banning. Another suspicious death of sixty-two-year-old Estel Jones in Chino Community Hospital in northern California on March 25, 1981, was also probed, said the Riverside district attorney's office.

The death in Chino of Mrs. Jones had first been attributed to "natural causes," but was later recorded as a homicide. Because of the high mortality rates among elderly patients at the Chino hospital during the period Diaz worked there on "the graveyard shift," attention turned to the quiet, bespectacled nurse with the neatly trimmed mustache and shock of dark wavy hair who had moved his area of expertise to hospitals to the southern area of the state. Coincidentally, the death rate at hospitals farther south was accelerating, and Diaz came under investigation for these matters. He was never investigated further or charged for the killing of Mrs. Jones or any other Chino Community Hospital patient.

His name, however, still hangs like a menacing pall over every hospital he was associated with during his relatively short but checkered ten-year career as a so-called Angel of Mercy. In an effort to divorce itself from the Diaz stigma, the Community Hospital of the Valleys has reorganized and reopened under new management as Perris General Hospital.

Since there was no apparent motive for the slayings, which occurred in the southern California region in the four-week period between March 30 and April 25, 1981, elderly victims were described as being in "decrepit" condition; there's no telling how long Diaz's killing spree might have lasted.

Thanks to a vigilant nursing supervisor, Patricia Christensen, horrified at the repeated similarities in the rapidly increasing number of deaths at the Perris hospital where both she and Diaz worked, an investigation was initiated.

Without pointing the finger at Diaz – or at any other employee, for that matter – nursing supervisor Christensen recommended to her administrators at the thirty-six-bed Community Hospital of the Valleys that a coroner's inquiry was necessary in light of the alarming series of questionable deaths. Initially, her pleas were ignored.

But the concerned nurse didn't back down and, when an inquiry was eventually launched, twenty-four bodies were exhumed.

Sophisticated autopsies revealed heavy doses of the heart-regulating drug Lidocaine, although none of the deceased patients had injections of Lidocaine entered in their medical records, indicating to investigators that the drug had not been prescribed.

The fact that the dosages were so lethally high also helped to eliminate the possibility of accidental overdoses. Twelve of the cadavers had as much as a thousand milligrams in their bodies. A single, normal dose to control irregular heartbeat is fifty to a hundred milligrams.

Suspicion began to center around Diaz soon after the investigation began on April 23, 1981, when investigators routinely questioned him about the deaths. Diaz's indignant denials were followed by a one-million-dollar lawsuit against the authorities for allegedly destroying his career. That lawsuit was quickly dismissed, but authorities felt that Diaz was a man who protested too much, and he remained a principal suspect.

A month later, Diaz had another run-in with the law when he was arrested for the illegal possession of a quantity of drugs, including morphine, in his home. Like Diaz's first lawsuit, these accusations didn't get far, either. The charges against him were dropped because of legal technicalities related to the police search warrant.

Not one to sit back and keep a low profile, Diaz decided to do battle with the authorities again. In August 1981, three months before his arrest for murder, he and his wife Martha filed a second lawsuit against the authorities. This time they claimed four and a half million dollars in damages for defamation of character and libel.

Diaz was to persist in a charade, with indignant civil counterallegations throughout the investigation. In fact, shortly before his conviction, he upped the price of his shattered career to a mammoth three-hundred-million-dollar suit – the staggering sum total of his final lawsuit against the county.

Meantime, as inquiries proceeded, investigators uncovered more incriminating evidence – three telltale syringes, each containing traces of Lidocaine and each bearing labels in the handwriting and carrying the signature of coronary care nurse Robert Diaz. They were found in the coronary care units of each of the private hospitals where the mystery deaths occurred, and where Diaz had worked as a temporary employee on overnight shifts.

Two of the syringes were discovered at the Community Hospital of the Valleys where nursing supervisor Michelsen had first sounded the alarm.

The prosecution spoke with many of Diaz's co-workers, who were able to place Diaz at, or very near to, all the death scenes. They were later to testify how Diaz always seemed to be carrying syringes of Lidocaine in his pockets and how he became increasingly agitated as certain patients neared death.

Diaz is best remembered by co-workers for his delight in casting himself in the role of doctor and, after the awful truth began emerging, his sinister penchant for playing God by accurately predicting the time that certain patients would die.

Diaz, remember former colleagues, was enthralled with Egyptian history and reincarnation and claimed to have psychic healing powers. Friends and relatives have tried to piece together clues in Diaz's otherwise undistinguished life which could explain his weird interest and bizarre behavior.

"Robert was basically an uneducated kid from the Midwest who knew he was never likely to fulfill his lifelong ambition to be a real doctor. That's why he was always talking about ancient Egyptian healing secrets, reincarnation, his psychic powers, and all that crap," recalled a family friend. "He was trying to cover up what he didn't know by talking about all other kinds of crazy stuff. He wanted to be a doctor. He wanted to be a bigshot. He wanted to draw attention to himself – I guess that's why he killed all them people."

A few days before Thanksgiving Day 1981, Diaz was arrested and charged with twelve murders, eleven of the charges arising from deaths of patients ranging in age from fifty-two to eighty-nine at the Community Hospital of the Valleys between March 30 and April 22, 1981.

The other murder charge stemmed from the April 25 death of a seventy-nine-year-old male patient in San Gorgonio Pass Memorial Hospital in Banning, California, where Diaz had worked a single night shift before being let go.

Inspite of strong evidence from other hospitals, Los Angeles County Coroner Thomas Noguchi announced his unwillingness to help prosecute Diaz for the private-hospital deaths in his area because he felt the medical evidence was lacking.

Diaz opted to be tried in neighboring Riverside County. And that's where he eventually did go to trial – in November 1983, more than two years after his arrest. Until then, the Diaz case had been punctuated with interminable and exhausting preliminary hearings, lawsuits, wild allegations, and counterallegations. Diaz milked the system for all it was worth.

Diaz elected to be tried before Superior Court Judge John H. Barnard, foregoing his right to a jury trial. And after an equally exhausting trial, Judge Barnard had little hesitation in finding Diaz guilty on all twelve counts of murder. Judge Barnard also declared there were "special circumstances," since these were multiple, premeditated murders. Under California law, this qualified Diaz for the death penalty.

He currently awaits death in the gas chamber. During his lengthy trial, prosecutors were never able to establish a cut-and-dried motive for his abominable behavior.

Diaz's journey to death row was a long and circuitous one from his arrest in 1981, his conviction on March 29, 1984, and his death sentence handed down on April 11 the same year. He was held in prison without bail from the date of his arrest until the day he was sentenced to die, all the time stubbornly protesting his innocence. By that time even his wife Martha was disgusted with the behavior of her litigious spouse, and had given up visiting him in prison by August of 1982. Diaz kept up an elaborate smokescreen while instructing public defenders how to conduct his defense, dragging out the process by obtaining countless trial postponements, and by his spurious lawsuits against investigators and the county, who, he claimed, were only out to besmirch his good name.

For the first time in his life, Robert Diaz was getting the attention he had always craved. Born into a large and poor Indiana family, Diaz was made aware at an early age that the odds were stacked against him ever becoming a qualified physician.

He battled several bouts of illnesses during childhood, and, as a result, never really completed more than ten full years of formal education.

To improve his health and his mind — and more likely to get away from Gary and his large family — Diaz signed on for a stint in the U.S. Marine Corps when he was eighteen. Shortly after signing up, he went AWOL and was discharged from the service soon after his return to duty. It was back to Indiana and a dead-end job at the auto parts factory where other members of his family worked. Diaz's first attempt at marriage also turned out to be less than successful. Married in Jacksonville, Florida, in 1971, he was divorced by 1972.

It was after his divorce that Diaz reevaluated his life and decided to

157

go into studies which could propel him back into his first love and interest – the world of medicine. He enrolled at a local school for vocational nurses, although later he was to tell co-workers in California that he had studied nursing at Purdue University in Indiana.

Diaz took his studies very seriously. He was proud of his new-found medical knowledge. At family gatherings, he insisted that relatives and their children introduce him to their friends as "Dr. Diaz."

For Diaz, the change in careers so late in life must have required a considerable degree of self-determination. But was it worth it? That's the question he must have been asking himself when he was placed under official scrutiny during those long, relentless months of homicide investigations beginning in 1981.

Although he wasn't arrested at his Apple Valley, California home until November 1981, murder investigators were on to him as early as April 23 of that year, said Assistant District Attorney Hollenhurst. As they slowly began building their case during a three-county probe, autopsies were done on selected bodies exhumed from a number of southern California cemeteries. The investigation also included batteries of toxocological tests and reviews of patient medical charts by cardiologists and pathologists.

There appeared to be a "common plan and design" in all the deaths – and Diaz was "the common denominator," said Assistant D.A. Hollenhurst.

Deputy District Attorney Patrick Magers got into the fray when the Diaz case eventually came to trial in November 1983. Despite Magers's evidence of the lethal doses of Lidocaine found in the bodies of Diaz's patients, public defenders Michael B. Lewisr and John J. Lee insisted to the bitter end that there was only circumstantial evidence against their client. They claimed there was no proof that the massive doses of Lidocaine had been administered at the one time.

"The levels of Lidocaine found are not necessarily exclusive to massive doses, but may have been caused by therapeutic doses – doses customarily ordered under clinical conditions," argued Defender Lee. "What we propose is that the prosecution has ignored a number of very crucial factors, and further that the prosecution's case is circumstantial. Circumstances can be equally suggestive of innocence."

Lee's remarks were intended to challenge evidence given by Mi

158

chael A. Peat, forensic toxicologist at the Center for Human Toxicology in Salt Lake City, Utah, who first reported the lethal one thousand milligram drug doses in patients' tissues. Under cross-examination, Peat did concede that other factors could have led to the seizures and subsequent deaths of patients. The defense made much of the fact that most of the victims were already in advanced stages of chronic heart and lung diseases, such as emphysema or hardening of the arteries.

Diaz testified on his own behalf that doctors gave him a free hand with patients, and that he administered only therapeutic quantities of Lidocaine and other drugs.

But Superior Court Judge Barnard, in light of the heavy body of evidence linking Diaz with Lidocaine, and the fact that prepackaged doses of Lidocaine found at the Perris hospital had been tampered with to increase their strength, supported the strong prosecution arguments.

His twelve-count guilty verdict was made under a "special circumstances" finding—that of multiple, premeditated murder which, under California law, qualified Diaz for the gas chamber or life imprisonment without the possibility of parole.

Diaz sat impassively, his fingers drumming a tattoo on the table in front of him, as the verdicts were announced. Immediately, he turned to his co-counsels Lee and Lewis and calmly began discussing the next phase of the proceedings—the hearing to establish whether or not he should be executed.

"The evidence pulled it off. I feel wonderful," said D.A. Magers after Diaz was found guilty on March 29, 1984. Magers said Diaz was "nothing but a killer" who betrayed the trust of patients, fellow nurses, and doctors, adding that the single most significant piece of evidence which swung the case in the prosecution's favor was the discovery of the three telltale syringes laced with Lidocaine which the prosecution successfully proved had been prepared and "loaded" by Diaz. These constituted "the smoking gun."

Deputy D.A. Magers conceded that he had never at any time offered any explanation of motive behind the bizarre murders, and wasn't about to go about hunting for reasons of motive at that stage in the proceedings. "It's not the typical kind of motive such as you would expect to see—like murder for financial gain," observed Magers. "It's rather obtuse."

Public Defender Lewis said he and his client were "disappointed" with the verdict. However, he added: "I'm satisfied we got a fair hearing from the judge."

The verdict represented the conclusion of the longest court trial in Riverside County history, with over seventy witnesses offering testimony over a five-month period.

A surprise courtroom visitor as the judge announced his verdict was Diaz's thirty-three-year-old estranged wife, Martha, making her first-ever trial appearance. She sat quietly in the courtroom with new thirty-three-year-old boyfriend, Randy Smiley. Asked why she was there, Martha Diaz responded: "I'd rather hear it from the judge than read about it in the newspapers." And how did she feel about the verdict? "I really don't know. I still haven't made up my mind."

What had made up Martha Diaz's mind about leaving her now-convicted killer husband was the fact Diaz had even instituted legal proceedings against *her* in an effort to take her three children away from her. One of the children was Diaz's; the other two were hers from a previous marriage. Now that her children were safe and the case finally dispensed with, Martha Diaz was free to start immediate divorce proceedings.

For her estranged husband, however, freedom was a thing of the past. At his sentencing hearing, less than a month later, Judge Barnard handed down twelve death sentences. The judge noted that he could have limited the number of death sentences to two, but said he believed the maximum number of penalties was warranted because of the nature of the crimes.

The judge also ignored a request by the defense to modify the verdicts against Diaz to life imprisonment, based on the accused's willingness to forego a jury trial. The prosecution also felt that the rather illogical plea of mitigation—claiming that Diaz deserved "compassion and sympathy" because he saved taxpayers the cost of a jury trial—was not worthy of consideration.

Citing the unusual circumstances surrounding the case, Judge Barnard ordered that Diaz be sent immediately to await execution on San Quentin's death row. Deputy District Attorney Magers recalled how Diaz accepted the judge's curt pronouncement: "He just sat there with a smirk on his face. He didn't say anything. He just got up and left the courtroom."

Perhaps Diaz was saving his bluster and humbug for the prison cell interview he gave a few hours later to local radio station KCAL. Still protesting his innocence, he shocked listeners when he pronounced the Community of the Valleys Hospital in Perris, where most of the bizarre deaths had occurred, "a slaughterhouse."

Said Diaz: "Heck, the defense didn't even allow me to say some things to my family because they were afraid what it would do to my case. Now it's all over, I think people should really know what went on at that hospital."

Diaz claimed he had documented 155 deaths from April 1980 to April 1981, documents that "would dispute everything the district attorney said in this case." He said sixty-two deaths had occurred the first three months of 1981, before he arrived at the hospital.

"All this is just a cover-up," he claimed. "They never said anything about the ones who died on the days I wasn't there, or on preceding shifts. A lot of those people died under unusual circumstances. There was a lot of negligence on the part of the physicians. The mistake I made was telling the district attorney about them."

Diaz said he felt he should have been exonerated, and claimed he did not kill anyone, particularly for his "own amusement or enjoyment," as alleged by prosecutors. "I'm asking that this investigation not be closed out. Too many deaths went on; too many things were unexplained. There were a lot of things I gleaned from patient charts when I went through them that will show what was going on in there.

"That place was a slaughterhouse."

Since Diaz is unable to come to grips with his guilt even as he sits on death row, it is unlikely the whole truth or scope of his reign of terror in the nursing profession will ever come to light. It is likely he will take the true story of the horror and magnitude of his crimes to his grave.

As one psychologist observed: "This man's life is one long chronicle of denial, procrastination, and a total inability to accept authority or responsibility. We are not likely to see this change."

NINE

Terri Maples Rachals:
Licensed to Kill?

Terri Eden Maples Rachals: Was she the ultimate Nurse Jekyll and Mrs. Hyde of the American nursing profession?

Acquitted of six counts of murder and nineteen counts of serious assaults on patients, authorities are still puzzling whether she was a hopelessly, mixed-up mental case or a cool, calculating would-be executioner.

"A dangerous tigress stalking the wards" was how the prosecution described her.

In spite of her taped confession—which she later recanted—to five counts of injecting patients with a potentially lethal heart-stopping drug, an Albany, Georgia, jury opted to find her guilty on only one of the less serious charges—aggravated assault on an eighty-nine-year-old male patient who survived.

The sole suspect behind a wave of senseless killings and callous assaults that rocked Albany's Phoebe Putney Memorial Hospital to its foundations, twenty-five-year-old Mrs. Rachals was convicted of the single assault charge but judged to be mentally ill.

She was jailed for seventeen years, although under state guidelines she could be eligible for parole in two years.

The serene-faced young mother, whose own childhood and background is a heartbreaking tale of tragedy and tears, showed little emotion when her lawyer, George P. Donaldson III, presented the court with a simple statement, void of any remorse or feelings of guilt. It read:

"As a Christian, I know that to hurt or to take another life is wrong. There is a real war inside of me because I do not know whether I committed the acts or not. I honestly don't think I did. But if I did, I could never have done it with hurt as the intention. All I can ask is that I be allowed to have the mental counseling necessary to once again be a productive member of society."

Everyone connected with the hospital and elaborate prosecution of little Terri Rachals found this an unusually bland reaction with no mention of the word "sorry", not what they expected from the woman who, when first suspected of being responsible for murder at the hospital, hung her head and asked state investigators: "How do you tell your husband you're a murderer?"

Who then is the real Terri Maples Rachals?

Rachals, a church choir member and doting mother of a two-year-old son, was described by her counsel, Donaldson, as a person of "incredible compassion who had devoted her life to other people."

This was far from the Rachals who critical care nursing director for the Phoebe Putney Hospital, Ann Rambusch, said was "more dangerous than a tigress," and who had "written a sorry chapter in nursing history."

There was also no doubt in the mind of Dougherty County District Attorney Hobart Hind who, pushing for a maximum sentence, told a court: "The state proved that there was only one person who, in every instance, had access to the injured and destroyed patients. That person was Terri Rachals."

Suspicious deaths and near-death emergencies had been troubling officials responsible for the critical care unit at the Phoebe Putney Hospital from the summer of 1985 into the early part of 1986.

The problems stopped as suddenly as they began with the March 13, 1986, arrest of registered nurse Terri Rachals, charged with the murder of seventy-three-year-old retired construction worker, Andrew Daniels, who was recovering from a hernia operation at the prestigious Albany hospital. Daniels died on November 14, 1985, poisoned by the potassium chloride injected into his intravenous line. Rachals, tipped off by officials that charges were pending, had entered a hospital for psychiatric treatment the night before her arrest for Daniels' murder. On being charged, one of her first requests was for a Bible. Her nursing license was immediately suspended.

Disclosure of the Daniels murder was the first break in a complex, intensive investigation at the hospital which included the use of a new, highly-efficient computerized tracking program. Statistical analyses by this new technique led investigators to suspect Terri Rachals. But the Daniels murder was only the beginning. The investigative floodgate was open, and more suspicious deaths surfaced.

When three-year-old Norris Morgan died in the same hospital on November 26, 1985, two days after he was struck by an automobile, his mother, Mrs. Lillian Morgan, was too upset to go into details with doctors about the exact cause of her son's death. She knew he was in bad shape, but was hoping and praying he would pull through after doctors told her his prognosis was fifty-fifty.

Then, suddenly, little Norris was dead. "I just couldn't understand it. I was so upset about it that I never did go back to the hospital for the doctor to explain it to me. I just didn't want to find out anymore," remembered Mrs. Morgan. She was to relive that horror four months later, on March 25, 1986, when the hospital told her her son might have been a murder victim.

That was the same day a grand jury indictment accused Nurse Rachals, a six-year veteran at Phoebe Putney, of murdering six patients – including the elderly Daniels and the Morgan boy – by injecting them with potassium chloride. She was additionally charged with 20 counts of aggravated assault on other patients who survived poisonous injection attacks. All the murders and assaults happened between August 19, 1985, and February 22, 1986.

A harrowing six-month reign of terror had come to an end. Authorities at a hospital under siege could breathe easily again.

Investigators still hadn't come up with a motive for the killings and assaults which involved a total of eleven patients, some white, some black, some young, some old, one of them a sick convict – many of whom had been victims of aggravated assault several times over. In addition to murder victims Daniels, of Moultrie, Georgia, and the Morgan toddler from Albany, the other deceased were: Milton Lucas, a sixty-eight-year-old man from Sylvester, Georgia, who died on October 19, 1985, while recovering from an operation to remove a tumor from his right leg; Minnie Houck, a fifty-nine-year-old Moultrie lung cancer patient who died November 7, 1985; Joe Irvin, a thirty-five-year-old Albany head injury patient, who died November 10, 1985; and Roger Parker, a thirty-six-year-old Ashburn, Georgia, gunshot victim, who died November 15, 1985.

According to the indictment, four of the six who died received at least one other dose of deadly potassium chloride before their fatal dose. In addition to killing Mrs. Houck, Nurse Rachals was also charged with three counts of aggravated assault for allegedly injecting her with two doses of potassium chloride on November 6, and twice more on November 7, 1985, the day the woman died.

Five other patients who Rachals was said to have injected with potassium chloride incredibly survived the silent attacks.

Lucky survivor Jack Delmus Stephens, a seventy-two-year-old retired warehouse manager from Cordele, Georgia, pulled through after his heart stopped beating twice on November 18, 1985, and he was recovering from heart bypass surgery.

Another patient, Frankie Lee Creech, a twenty-six-year-old inmate from nearby Lee County Correctional Institution, reportedly received six injections of potassium chloride between November 10 and November 24, 1985, and survived — only to die later at another hospital from an unrelated head injury.

Like most of the other victims, Creech, who was in a coma after being struck on the head during a prison fight, had no history of heart problems. His trouble was a dangerous brain clot. But his heart inexplicably stopped six times while in the Albany hospital.

His mother, Mrs. Charlotte Creech, said she knew something was terribly wrong. "It got to the point when I dreaded when Sunday and Thursday came around. The attacks always happened on a Sunday or a Thursday."

The other victims named were George Whiting, fifty-six, Frances Freeman, fifty-five, and Sam Bentley, eighty-nine, all of Albany. This trio survived the cardiac arrest induced by the aggravated assault.

As she was hit with this barrage of charges, Nurse Rachals was already undergoing treatment, at her own request, for mental problems in the psychiatric unit of the very familiar Phoebe Putney Hospital. She was later transferred to other state mental health facilities, first to the Southwestern State Hospital in Thomasville, Georgia, then to Central State Hospital in Milledgeville, Georgia, for psychiatric treatment and evaluation.

Around this time, doctors and other investigators started probing the background of this bright and intelligent career nurse with a seemingly vast portfolio of guilty secrets. And they lifted the curtain on a past checkered with personal pain and tragedy.

165

Rachals' early childhood really began in a little town named Hopeful, Georgia, a sleepy rural community nestled between peanut farms and pine trees in the southwest part of the state. She was only two years old when her natural mother had a nervous breakdown and her father gave her up for adoption to the Maples family in Hopeful. Then when she was eleven, her adoptive mother suffered a massive stroke and died. Her adoptive father became an alcoholic soon after.

For much of her troubled adolescence, the confused young girl spent a lot of time desperately seeking an identity and substitute parents to give her the love and attention she craved, but never had in her life. She developed close relationships with her friends' mothers; she sought to find out all she could about her natural parents; she was constantly volunteering to spend time with the sick and elderly.

She tried to bury all the bitter memories of her unloved childhood by immersing herself in her new friendships and studies. She became a studious, caring bookworm. It seemed only natural when, early in her life, she chose nursing for a career.

That's why residents of Hopeful were saddened, shocked, and even a little disbelieving over what became of Terri Maples Rachals, the grown-up wife, mother, and nurse.

"If I had to describe her in one word, it would be compassionate," says Betty Baggs, who taught Terri Maples in Sunday school at Hopeful Baptist Church. "Even as a child, she wanted to be a nurse. Of all the children I ever taught, she was the last one I would have predicted this to happen to."

Not long after Mrs. Rachals' arrest, Dougherty County District Attorney Hobart Hind told reporters: "I understand what we have here is a girl who had a horrible, horrible background."

But friends from the nurse's past don't like to dwell on the horror and the tragedy. They prefer to remember the studious and devout young girl who lived comfortably among them, eagerly performing good deeds at the local church.

She had moved to Hopeful from Albany when she was six years old. Her adoptive parents—retired Navy enlisted man Jim Maples and his wife, Louise—settled the family on a fifty-acre farm.

Just five years later, Louise Maples suffered a massive stroke while at work at her civil service job on the Marine Corps Logistics Base in

Albany. She died shortly after.

Terri continued to live in Hopeful with her father, but Mr. Maples remembers how difficult it was for them after the death of his wife.

"Sure she took it bad. We both did," says Mr. Maples, now sixty-one and disabled from a stroke in 1982. He says he developed a drinking problem soon after, something that plagued him until he sought help from Alcoholics Anonymous at his teenage daughter's insistence. "I took the cure," he says. "She's the one who suggested it."

Those outside the family also noticed the change in Terri Maples.

"She lost her mother at a time when all girls need their mothers very badly," recalls Mrs. Baggs. "It was very, very hard on her." She says the girl eagerly visited elderly shut-ins in the community.

Kelli White, a friend and fellow student at Mitchell County High, remembers that, as a teenager, Terri was particularly close to the mothers of her friends.

"You could definitely tell that she felt a void there," says Mrs. White.

She also longed to find out the identity of her natural parents. "One time she tried to find out who her real parents were," says Mrs. White, who did not know if the search was successful. Jim Maples says he and his wife never even knew the identity of the couple who gave Terri up for adoption.

"We were only told that the mother had a nervous breakdown and the father put Terri up for adoption," he says.

Despite the problems she faced in her personal life, Terri excelled in school, winning membership to the Mitchell County High School Council and Beta Club for top scholars.

Her classmates and teachers at Mitchell County High School recall that as a student there in the late 1970's, Terri was shy and sometimes self-conscious, but well behaved and studious, compiling a spotless academic record.

"You remember students for the good they do, and Terri was a very good student," says Kathryn Lofton, a biology teacher at Mitchell County High who taught her in the tenth grade.

Before her senior year began, Terri Maples decided she wanted to attend school in Albany and left home in 1978 to live with a first cousin and his family.

In Albany, Terri continued with her solid academic record, helping to launch a school newspaper at Westover High School from where she graduated in 1979.

167

She went on to fulfill her childhood dream of becoming a nurse, attending Albany Junior College for two years and receiving an associate degree in nursing in 1981 before working at Phoebe Putney, a 432-bed public hospital.

She also became active in a church, transferring her membership to Byne Memorial Baptist in Albany, where she joined the church choir. There she met Roger Rachals, a young printer and cerebral palsy victim. They were married in 1980, and four years later had a son, Chad.

She was a pillar of her community. Even during her trial, fellow members of the Byne Memorial Church choir would gather outside the courtroom, talking among themselves, shaking their heads in disbelief. "She sang in our choir. I went to this girl's bridal shower. How could this thing happen? She seemed so normal," said close friend Mrs. Mearl Hall.

Until Terri Rachals' arrest, the family lived together in a new house in a suburban Albany neighborhood where homes are valued in the ninety-thousand-dollar range.

Friends in Albany recall her much the same way as those in Hopeful.

Valerie Anderson, a close friend who sang with her in the church choir, also describes Terri Rachals as "compassionate," adding: "She was the kind of person who never forgot your birthday. I feel in my heart that if she did the things they say she did, then the only reason was that she could not bear to see the patients in pain."

After her arrest, Rachals went through a court-ordered psychiatric examination at the Milledgeville state hospital. Afterward, Dr. Thomas Hall, director of the hospital's forensic services division, submitted a report to the court that the young nurse was suffering from a form of depression known as "dysthymic reaction." However, the doctor felt she was capable of understanding the charges against her and assisting in her defense, and was therefore competent to stand trial.

Dr. Hall said Terri Rachals might have been motivated to kill patients to end their suffering. "She feels that the patients she allegedly terminated were asking to be terminated, and she felt she had to do something to relieve their discomfort and misery," he said.

Defense Attorney Donaldson, who hinted that mental competence could be a key factor in the subsequent trial, pleaded not guilty on all charges on Rachals' behalf, and requested a second mental evaluation of his client, to be conducted this time by psychiatrist Dr. Everett

Kuglar at Georgia Regional Hospital in Augusta.

Pretrial motions and postponements delayed the start of the hearings against Rachals until mid-September, 1986, to the chagrin of District Attorney Hind, who maintained throughout: "Our position is that she knew right from wrong when she committed the crimes."

But Defense Attorney Donaldson hinted to the jury that Mrs. Rachals was suffering from a severe personality disorder, much like the split personality characters in the books *Sybil* and *The Three Faces of Eve.* This stemmed from prolonged abuse she suffered as a child, he claimed.

Added Mr. Donaldson: "We believe the evidence will show that Mrs. Rachals suffers from a mental disorder that causes periods during which she can't remember what took place, and during which she does some unusual things."

The prosecution got a tremendous break at the beginning of the trial when Superior Court Judge Asa D. Kelley, Jr., went against defense objections and said that jurors would be allowed to listen to an incriminating tape recording in which Nurse Rachals confessed to Georgia Bureau of Investigation agents that she had injected five patients with deadly potassium chloride, killing three of them.

In her confession—ruled by Judge Kelley to have been given voluntarily, and therefore valid evidence—Mrs. Rachals admitted administering injections to victims Lucas, Creech, Houck, Bentley, and Daniels, when they all were patients in the Phoebe Putney Hospital's surgical intensive care unit. She said she had become emotionally attached to these patients and their families. Creech and Bentley recovered from their ordeal; the other three died.

"I just couldn't stand to see them suffering . . . they would just ask me to let them die," a tearful Nurse Rachals told investigators. "I just wanted to stop doing it, but I did not know how. I know I was under a lot of stress at the time with marital problems. I probably wanted to get caught. I didn't know what to do. Once it got started, I couldn't stop."

Nurse Rachals's confession was limited to only five victims. She denied injecting any of the other six patients mentioned in the charges, or any other patients in the hospital for that matter.

But Mr. Donaldson, for the defense, submitted that Terri wasn't guilty of any killing or assault. Her mental disorder, he said, was such that it made her confess to crimes that "in all probability she did not commit."

169

In a forceful and uncompromising attack on all of Nurse Rachals' possible lines of defense, District Attorney Hind refuted any suggestion that mercy killing might have been a motive. "Mrs. Rachals was so obsessed with power and control that she ruthlessly killed six of her patients with injections of potassium chloride, and tried to kill five others," he said.

In its clear form, potassium chloride is used by several states to administer fatal injections as capital punishment. The drug is used an estimated 250,000 times a year to slow down the heart when preparing patients for open heart surgery.

"The evidence will show that she knew right from wrong every second," DA Hind told the jury of seven men and five women. "We believe the picture you will see is that of an individual who has felt second-class all her life, who has been mistreated all her life, who could not handle power and control." Because of her horrible childhood background, Mr. Hind said the prosecution had no intention of seeking the death penalty.

Hind painted a picture of a bitter and twisted woman overcome by malicious evil, who exulted in a feeling of personal power as she watched doctors and nurses scurry down the corridors of the Albany hospital to try to save unfortunate patients whose hearts had stopped beating after being injected by potassium chloride.

One of these luckless victims was little Norris Morgan, aged two. His parents clung to the hope that he would pull through after being run down by an automobile. But, claimed the district attorney, Mrs. Rachals had different plans for him.

"The parents happened to believe in God's miracle . . . but the evidence shows that they were throw out of the room by this individual before the baby passed away," said Mr. Hind, indicating a sobbing Rachals, herself the mother of a two-year-old boy.

District Attorney Hind paused to let the enormity of the offense register with the jurors. He went on to say that Rachals had succeeded in "manipulating everyone at the hospital, and has now become a nationally important person. She has accomplished what she set out to do. And she stalked her victims like a tigress," declared the district attorney, pounding the front of the jury bench for emphasis.

Then there was the case of Minnie Houck, the Moultrie lung cancer patient. She survived three potassium chloride injections, but died after the fourth dose. "If Minnie Houck wanted to pass away, would she not be looking for a merciful death?" asked the district attorney. "But what did she get? She got three individual attacks where, in order to be resuscitated, she was beaten on the chest."

And Terri Rachals was familiar with the pain a patient had to endure when being revived after cardiac arrest, Hind added. "She was an authority on the agony she was creating in these patients. I submit that the evidence is going to paint a picture of a person who is criminally responsible for what she has done."

The wave of unexplained deaths which swept Phoebe Putney Hospital's fourth-floor surgical intensive care unit—with November 1985 the peak period—was so distressing to the hospital staff that they nervously referred to the incidents as "Disaster on the three-to-eleven shift."

Cardiac arrests were cropping up in the most unlikely cases. Doctors and nurses were alarmed and frustrated. One physician became so angry that he transferred a patient out of the unit and even suggested that a new five-hundred-thousand-dollar cardiac-monitoring machine could be the culprit, by "leaking" electrical charges and causing patients' hearts to stop beating.

But, the courtroom was told, a methodical, sophisticated investigation—using a new computerized tracking system—had narrowed down the suspects, and all the indicators pointed to the quiet, but nevertheless much-respected Nurse Rachals.

Phoebe Putney's cardiac arrest rate normally numbered around three or four in any given month. But during that black November, nine patients suffered cardiac arrest, some of them several times, despite the recent purchase of the state-of-the-art cardiac-monitoring units.

Recalling these disasters on the three-to-eleven shift, critical care nursing director Ann Rambusch observed: "Everybody said, 'Here we've got these wonderful new machines, but our patients seem to be getting sicker.' "

Medical experts worked around the clock to track down the cause of the cardiac arrest epidemic. Eminent cardiac anesthesiologist Dr. Donald Findlayson from Atlanta's Emory University helped supervise security precautions—monitors were checked and found to be working properly, drug solutions were tested to ensure that they contained the proper ingredients, patients whose hearts stopped beating were immediately blood-tested for potassium chloride, and intravenous lines were checked on a regular basis for traces of potassium chloride.

As a result of these precautions, said nursing director Rambusch, the panic eased. Although unexplained traces of potassium chloride had been found by Dr. Findlayson in some blood samples, there were no more sudden cardiac arrests. The mystery remained, but everyone was relieved that the silent terror had lifted.

Then, just ten days after the security measures were lifted on February 1, 1986, eighty-nine-year-old Sam Bentley's heart stopped beating under mysterious circumstances.

By this time, revealed the nursing director, suspicions were being drawn to Nurse Rachals, who frequently worked the three-to-eleven P.M. disaster shift and was present when the eleven patients mentioned in the charges suffered cardiac arrests.

Nursing director Rambusch did concede, however, that many other factors, such as drugs or even salt substitutes, could cause a person's potassium levels to rise. But in these particular cases, electrocardiograms established that at least ten of the eleven victims had received concentrated doses of potassium.

The accused had become emotionally distraught over the case of lung cancer patient Minnie Houck, who was in so much pain that she even pleaded with nursing director Rambusch to "Please let me go." Nurse Rachals was particularly upset over Mrs. Houck's suffering after the patient's family refused to agree to allow the hospital to abandon life-support procedures should another cardiac arrest occur.

But chilling testimony about the events surrounding Mrs. Houck's death tended to refute the idea of mercy.

Mrs. Houck's daughter, Carrie Kight, wept loudly in the quiet courtroom as she remembered those awful days when her mother suffered heart attacks, one after another, on November 6 and 7, 1985. "I told them, 'You better not let my mama die.' I looked in and saw them pounding down my mama's chest, her laying there cut open, and I saw them run electricity through her twice.

"Her body just flew all over," said Kight tearfully, close to breaking down emotionally. "I told them, 'Don't hurt her no more.' That's when I said, 'Let her go.' I didn't know what else to do."

Nursing director Rambusch was aware that Nurse Rachals had had some degree of emotional problems in her personal life. The year before the suspicious deaths, Terri Rachals complained to her that her husband was beating her. The supervisor referred Nurse Rachals to a marriage counselor and a shelter in Albany for battered women.

A year later, Rachals sent Ann Rambusch a gift with a note attached to the effect that she had overcome her marital problems.

Outside the court, nursing director Rambusch remembered how her intensive care nursing staff had all gone through hell during this period. She had pushed for a complete investigation, never suspecting foul play was involved. "I wanted to absolve my nurses," she said sadly. "And it turned out to be one." She had no reason to suspect Rachals, the meek, overweight country girl with the expressionless face, who had performed well as a nurse for six years, including three years' ICU experience. "She was not one of my best nurses, nor was she one of the worst, either," said the nursing director, adding softly: "We'll know what happened. But the terrible thing is that we'll never know why. If she hadn't confessed, we would never have known. It's almost impossible to prove."

Even with the taped confessions, Nurse Rambusch's observation was to prove prophetic.

The most damning evidence against Terri Rachals concerned the cardiac arrest of eighty-nine-year-old Sam Bentley, the one patient she was eventually convicted of assaulting. Prosecution officials agreed that the Bentley incident was "the smoking gun" in their case against Rachals.

Despite his advanced years, Bentley had valiantly come through more than five hours of risky abdominal surgery on February 10, 1986. But the following day, as he was receiving a routine bag of plasma into his bloodstream, his heartbeat suddenly became erratic and he went into cardiac arrest. Amazingly, he was revived and survived.

Medical director of the surgical intensive care unit, Dr. David Calhoun, was baffled. Another attending physician gasped: "It looks as if something just all of a sudden poisoned his heart."

Terri Rachals was the nurse who delivered the plasma to victim Bentley's room. And tests showed that the plasma's potassium level was thirty times higher than normal.

Confronted with this direct evidence, Rachals told investigators in a tape-recorded confession: "I watched the heart monitor because I knew something was going to happen." She admitted injecting the plasma with potassium chloride, and admitted she knew what it would do. "It stops the heart," she said.

Rachals's confession was played to a hushed courtroom. Like her taped confessions to other incidents, it was delivered in a matter-of-fact tone of voice. In the course of the trial, the jury heard Rachals's own voice submit a number of reasons why she allegedly committed the crimes – most of which had to do with their pain and their families' pain.

In her own defense, Nurse Rachals denied injecting patients at Phoebe Putney Memorial Hospital with potassium chloride and totally recanted the confession she gave investigators. "They showed me some charts," Mrs. Rachals said of the interview with Georgia Bureau of Investigation agents. "I was real confused. They told me they thought I had done it. I started thinking about it very seriously. I thought maybe I did do them."

Mrs. Rachals said she began to "visualize" the alleged injections after the investigators related details of the crimes.

The interview with the state investigators came during a period when she was going through marital and emotional problems, Rachals told the court. There were previous instances in her life when she couldn't remember where she had been or what she had done. "I have had so many things happening to me that I could not explain," Rachals said when asked why she had thought she might be guilty. By way of explanation, she told how there were several occasions when she would arrive home from work several hours late and wasn't able to recall where she had been.

Rachals said she once found a new purple jogging suit in her chest of drawers, but could not remember buying it. She said she would open her pocketbook and find several hundred dollars in cash and not know where it had come from.

"For the life of me, I could not remember where I'd been. I was confused. There were so many things going on that I couldn't explain or understand," said Rachals.

She said she had agreed to talk to the investigators without an attorney present because she was also concerned about the suspicious deaths at the hospital. "We all knew there was an investigation going on," said Rachals. "I didn't feel I had done anything wrong. All I wanted to do was clear my name."

Earlier in her testimony, Mrs. Rachals described a troubled childhood, including the death of her adoptive mother when she was eleven and alleged sexual abuse by her adoptive father.

Until just three weeks ago, she said, she had suppressed a horrible memory of being raped at gunpoint by her drunken, adoptive father, Jim Maples. She was seventeen at the time.

Alleged Rachals: "I was asleep on my bed and he came into my room and started hitting me. He had a pistol with him. He said he was tired of me trying to avoid him, and that he would teach me a lesson for telling people he was a drunk."

But the alleged sexual abuse – totally denied by Jim Maples – had really begun shortly after her adoptive mother's death, the defendant testified. "I felt so dirty," Mrs. Rachals said. "I was just real confused. I just didn't want him to touch me. I just wanted to get out."

Mrs. Rachals said she began experiencing marital problems about a year after her marriage, and she attributed those problems to her alleged sexual abuse as a child. She said she frequently was unresponsive to her husband. "I just kept seeing my father's drunk face," she testified.

As defense testimony began, a former high school classmate recalled that when Mrs. Rachals was seventeen year old, she went to school in tears, so nervous she kept dropping her textbooks.

"She said, 'Last night, my dad tried to rape me,' " Kelly White, the former schoolmate, testified as Mrs. Rachals's murder and aggravated assault trial entered its second week.

But to Mr. Hind, Maples denied ever molesting his daughter.

"Are you the type of man who would molest your daughter?" District Attorney Hind asked Maples, who suffered a stroke in 1981.

"No, sir," replied Mr. Maples.

Mrs. Rachals's husband testified about the couple's marital problems and his wife's unusual behavior the previous fall, when she allegedly was injecting patients at the hospital with potassium chloride.

His wife was often sexually unresponsive during their six-year marriage, said Rachals. Only once did she mention childhood sexual abuse to her husband, Mr. Rachals said.

During arguments with his wife, Rachals would sometimes get violent, he said on the witness stand.

Defense psychiatrist Dr. Everett Kuglar, an Augusta physician and superintendent of the Georgia Regional Hospital there, testified that Rachals suffered from "dissociative disorder," which causes her in times of stress to lapse into periods of amnesia during which she experiences personality changes.

"These are states of mind when the individual essentially becomes a different person," said Dr. Kuglar. He added that Terri Rachals's mental condition might have caused her to confess to crimes she did not commit.

"These are very suggestive people," Dr. Kuglar said of people with dissociative disorders. "You can suggest to these people that they did something. Since they cannot remember what they did, they visualize. They cannot separate the fantasy world from the real one."

A Central State Hospital psychiatrist claimed, however, that Terri Rachals was capable of knowing the difference between right and wrong when she allegedly injected patients with the heart-stopping chemical.

"I feel, from my examination, that during that period of time, she did know right from wrong," Dr. James B. Craig, a psychiatrist at Central State Hospital in Milledgeville, testified after Rachals's defense rested its case.

Dr. Craig was called by the prosecution to rebut testimony by defense psychiatrist Dr. Kuglar that Terri Rachals was incapable of distinguishing between right and wrong. Dr. Craig testified that Rachals suffered from severe depression, low self-esteem, and other personality disorders. But he said he found no evidence of a "dissociative" disorder which would cause her to have periods of amnesia or personality changes.

During his first interview with Terri Rachals in March, no evidence of "memory defects or amnesia" was found, Craig testified. But in August, there were "certain things she couldn't remember as good as she could when we first saw her."

Terri Rachals's attorneys did not pin their defense wholly on her mental instability. Instead, attorney Donaldson told the jury that natural causes, not injections of potassium chloride, were to blame for the unusually high number of cardiac arrests. "Nobody committed the crimes," declared Mr. Donaldson.

Assistant District Attorney John Hogg pointed to Mrs. Rachals's confession of March 13, 1986 as definite proof of her guilt. "You don't confess to murder unless you did it," Hogg said.

Another expert defense witness, Dr. E. Mansell Pattison of the Medical College of Georgia, agreed that Mrs. Rachals, whom he

176

found to be highly susceptible to suggestion, could have been persuaded to confess to the alleged crimes because of a strong desire to please.

Georgia Bureau of Investigation agents obtained a confession from Rachals, by first "educating" her about the alleged crimes, claimed her attorney. "Terri's mind got confused, and then they showed her evidence," Mr. Donaldson said. "Slowly, she began to say, 'That's got to be right.' "

In closing, Mr. Hind charged that Mrs. Rachals, her attorneys, and two psychiatrists had presented their defense of mental illness so Mrs. Rachals would not be held responsible for injecting patients with potassium chloride.

"She had the ability to be the nurse of the year," Hind said, "but she is the murderess of the century. You have a right to be ashamed of Terri Rachals. She betrayed her God and violated her pledge to Him and his people."

Mr. Hind also accused Mrs. Rachals of making her adoptive father "Victim Number Twelve" by falsely accusing him of sexually molesting her as a child. "This is a dirty, rotten thing that has been done to Mr. Maples," the district attorney said. "If you're willing to do that to Mr. Maples, then there's not much that you're not willing to do to somebody else."

D.A. Hind said it was sad that "she has destroyed the life of her father, her husband, and affected the life of her son. There are some folks who are just meaner than a snake."

Urging the maximum sentence, her former boss, nursing director Ann Rambusch told the judge: "Never before have I seen the rights of patients violated in such an obscene and brutal way by a member of my profession as they were by Terry Rachals. She knew the difference between right and wrong. She was in control then and remains in control today.

"The first responsibility of a hospital and the people who work there is that they do the patient no harm. As she gave no mercy, so she should be given no mercy herself. She has caused unknown terror in the hearts and minds of her victims. She has written a sorry chapter in nursing history."

But these vehement pleas and arguments against Rachals by and large fell on deaf ears as far as the jury was concerned. Their verdict — guilty on only one charge of assault — showed clearly where their sympathies lay, and what story they accepted.

Later, jurors explained that they felt the prosecution failed to present sufficient evidence to warrant a conviction on all but one count. They also said they accepted the defense psychiatrists' testimony that Mrs. Rachals suffered from a mental disorder, partially resulting from childhood sexual abuse that may have caused her to confess to crimes she didn't commit.

Under State Board of Pardons and Paroles guidelines, Rachals is eligible for parole as a first offender after serving twenty-four months of her seventeen-year sentence, although, said spokesman Silas Moore, the board sometimes overlooked these guidelines, requiring a lengthier stay in prison.

On completion of her sentence, Rachals will be required to undergo three years' probation. For a five-year period, she will also be required to undergo a "psychological stress evaluator," a test somewhat similar to a polygraph examination, every two months to determine whether she is engaging in any criminal activity.

Saying he planned to appeal, Rachals's attorney said of the sentence: "We are disappointed. We were not expecting anything that severe."

After further psychiatric evaluation, it was decided that Rachals was fit enough to serve out her sentence in the Georgia Women's Correctional Institute at Hardwick rather than in a state mental hospital. She could continue to have treatment for her mental problems on an outpatient basis although, if her condition worsened, she could be transferred to a state facility.

Since the incidents, Phoebe Putney Memorial Hospital has made surveillance of mortality and cardiac arrests a routine part of its quality review. Once the initial information is logged into the computer, it takes only a few hours of work each month to keep it up to date.

Such a surveillance can help spot problems with high-tech machines, or drug mixtures, or innocent human error. And it can also highlight what a hospital is doing right.

Nurse Rambusch said the key to the surveillance is the encouragement of questioning and healthy suspicion. "Hospitals can protect patients against these rare circumstances only when we begin to look at them and say, 'It does happen, it can happen.' It does not mean that we are a bad hospital, that we give bad care," she added.

TEN

Nicholas Robert Giesa:
Lethal Aide

Peter Stodolka was one of the friendliest, most outgoing men you could ever expect to meet. Friends of the retired construction worker and shoemaker said he seldom had a harsh word for anyone. He had just passed his seventy-eighth birthday, and despite the loss of a leg, he maintained a cheerful, positive attitude.

And when he obtained an artificial leg, he was so happy he vowed to dance a jig – and followed through in front of a crowd of smiling and hand-clapping neighbors in his home near Olympia, Washington.

A friend later recalled that "Pete always acted and talked like he had two good legs. His handicap was strictly physical, definitely not mental. He was one of the neatest guys I ever met." The glowing endorsement was typical of the way people who knew Stodolka felt about him.

The artificial leg meant a lot to Stodolka, and he took pride in the renewed independence that it provided him with. He had been living alone and had gotten used to taking care of himself since 1983 when his wife, Ethel, had died of a stroke.

When a lifelong problem with diabetes got the best of him a few months later and doctors were forced to amputate his leg, he was depressed for a time. But the depression didn't last, and it wasn't long before the plucky old fighter dug in his heels and resumed his life with the same rosy attitude he had maintained in the past.

He even managed to hold on to his good humor when a stump infection made it too painful for him to wear the new artificial limb for a while. It wasn't easy, even for Stodolka. He hated to be dependent on anyone. He was an independent man who had worked hard all his life, and he was proud of his accomplishments. He was especially proud of his modest home along Old Highway 99, which at one time was the main corridor between Olympia and Tacoma, Washington. When Interstate 5 was constructed, Stodolka found himself a bit more off the beaten path, but it didn't bother him a bit. He enjoyed the increased privacy provided for the neighborhood and the opportunity to pass his time among friends. And he had many friends.

About the only thing about Peter Stodolka that bothered his neighbors was his habit of carrying large amounts of money around with him. The habit worried them, and some of them urged him to bank more of his money and to carry only the amount of cash he might need for his day-to-day living. But Stodolka was a trusting man, and he also considered himself to be a good judge of character. When his friends persisted in their warnings, his pat response was to simply smile and ask: "Who would want to hurt an old man like me? I'm no threat to anybody."

"Pete had a childlike faith in people," a neighbor later recalled. "He trusted everyone the way he wanted them to trust him. And that's what got him killed!"

During the year between the summers of 1985 and 1986, Stodolka's problems with his amputated leg forced him to give up some of his prized independence. He was a big, solid man with short hair, who had an infectious roaring laugh and enjoyed a good joke. He was also an excellent amateur musician, and when he was feeling good, he sang and played the saxophone or guitar for his friends.

But his health problems had made it difficult for him to move around, and he spent much of his time resting or sleeping. He faced the sad fact that he had to have help.

Neighbors looked in on him and helped with the cooking, housecleaning, shopping, and other chores, but eventually he had to obtain professional assistance. He brought several nurse's aides into his home to help him care for himself and the house. It was then that his skill in character judgment became most obvious.

The old man was quick to praise aides he believed were honest and industrious, but if he had second thoughts about one of the men or women he contacted through health care agencies, he quickly

acked off. The aide he was uncomfortable with wouldn't be asked
o return, and before long someone new would be helping him.

When Stodolka contacted Sound Home Health for a nurse's aide,
spokesman advised him that they didn't provide the in-home health
are he needed but put him in touch with another company they sub-
ontracted with. That company, Advanced Health Care, sent Nicho-
as Robert Giesa to his home.

Giesa was a man who had never managed to get his life firmly on
rack. Blond and beefy, he had worked at a number of jobs, none of
which he kept for very long. After graduating from high school in
orrance, California, near Los Angeles, he worked for a short time
or a fast-food restaurant. But he wasn't happy with that work and
oon enlisted in the Navy. He served his hitch with neither serious
roblems nor special distinction, and after accepting an honorable
ischarge, went to work for a McDonald's restaurant in South Caro-
na.

While busy earning a modest living on the Southeast coast, he
lso continued his education, taking computer science and other
lasses. Soon he crossed the country again, and accepted a job with
computer software company in California. But he stayed with the
oftwear company only briefly before pulling up stakes once more
nd moving to the Pacific Northwest.

The person responsible for his move to Washington State was an
ttractive woman he met at a church function. Giesa was interested
n the Church of Jesus Christ of Latter-day Saints and was studying
o become a Mormon when he met the woman. She admired his
oncern with spiritual matters and took an interest in helping him
ind himself. She suggested they move to the Olympia area and
hare the expenses of an apartment. It was made plain that the ar-
angement would be purely platonic. Giesa agreed.

They found an apartment in the small Thurston County town of
umwater at the southern edge of Olympia, the state's capital city.
lowever, the relationship of the two roommates quickly began to
our. Giesa was a man who would rather lie around the house than
vork or look for a job. He grumbled about his father, whom he re-
ented. And he spun outrageously fanciful tales that rapidly began to
vear out his roommate's patience. He once showed off a stethoscope
nd blood pressure cuff, bragging that admiring doctors had given
he equipment to him as a reward for saving a woman's life in a shop-

ping mall by administering cardiopulminary resuscitation to her She didn't believe him. She had purchased equipment that was exactly the same at the local drug store. They quarreled loudly and incessantly. After a few weeks, the woman abruptly packed up her things and moved out.

Giesa was devastated by the rejection. Overnight he became a recluse. He was morose, and went to great lengths to avoid his neighbors. Dishes were stored unwashed in cabinets and piled up in the kitchen sink, he dropped his clothes in listless piles on the floor, and began to skip showers and left his hair uncombed. He pulled the drapes closed over his windows, and often refused to answer knocks at the door. And he developed an obsessive interest in crocheting and knitting. A resident of the apartment complex later recalled seeing him sitting at a table, so engrossed in knitting that he was seemingly unware of anyone or anything else around him.

With no one to share the rent, Giesa was forced to find a job. But he was a thirty-year-old loser with an unimpressive employment record. The longest he had ever held a job was his time in the Navy, and he had apparently found more acceptance there than he ever did in civilian life.

Despite his lack of experience in the health care field, he applied for a job as a nurse's aide. The prospective employer turned him down. The woman who interviewed him later described him as "obnoxious . . . very pushy and aggressive. He claimed all these skills that he obviously did not have," she observed. "I found him a no-hire situation in every respect."

Giesa had more luck when he approached Advanced Health Care in Olympia. When he applied, he brought along a recommendation from an employment referral service working in conjunction with the Church of Jesus Christ of Latter-day Saints. Early in April, he was hired and sent out on his first job. His pay was six hundred dollars a month.

The office coordinator for the health care agency said later that she believed the Mormon employment referral service had checked Giesa's qualifications. But the placement counselor with the service said he had merely referred Giesa to the agency. He said he expected Advanced Health Care to screen the job applicant.

Giesa had written on his job application that while he was in the military service in 1977 he studied to be an emergency medica

182

technician. But Navy records showed that he had worked as a store-keeper, the same job rating that is referred to in the Army as quarter-master. He had apparently never work in the medical field.

But when he was sent to Stodolka's home, the old man and the young man didn't get along well.

Giesa worked only one twenty-four-hour shift at Stodolka's home, and the elderly man knew right away that he didn't want to keep him around. He just wasn't comfortable with the nurse's aide. For one thing, Giesa wandered around the house all day and most of the night. Giesa was replaced on the job by another nurse's aide after his first night at Stodolka's.

It was shortly after Giesa's around-the-clock stint at the house on Old Highway 99 that Stodolka approached a neighbor and gave her a thousand dollars, asking her to keep it for him because he didn't want to carry it around. Stodolka conceded that he just didn't like the new nurse's aide who had been sent to help care for him. The neighbor agreed to hold the money and put it away for him in a strongbox.

Stodolka wasn't the only one who was uncomfortable around the nurse's aide. Another resident of the neighborhood described Giesa's personality as "bizarre."

"The guy was an enigma in the area," he said. "Everybody knew everybody's business, but we didn't know a thing about him. It was like he didn't need anybody."

One of Stodolka's neighbors remembered Giesa because he didn't own a vehicle and often rode the bus or walked miles to and from work. "He was weird, always talking to himself and looking around. He gave people the creeps," the neighbor shuddered.

When Stodolka's stump infection subsided enough so that he could reattach his artificial leg, he kept his vow and danced for his friends. He grabbed a delighted neighbor, and his glasses bounced up and down on his nose as he led her in a lively jig around the kitchen. For the first time in weeks he was less dependent on his neighbors and the home-care nurse's aides. He behaved like a child with a new toy.

He didn't know then, but horror and tragedy were only a few hours away.

Carol Starovasnik, a friend and volunteer for the Salvation Army Meals on Wheels, later recalled that Stodolka was "happier that day than I ever saw him before. He was so pleased that he could walk."

183

As she reminisced about him, her voice softened. "He was such a trusting man," she said. "He trusted people the way he wanted them to trust him, and that is what killed him."

Another neighbor recalled that Stodolka once paid a man in advance to deliver a load of firewood and lost his money when the wood-cutter never showed up.

If there was one person Stodolka didn't trust it was Giesa. Even though he had been replaced – and, in fact, dropped by the agency – Giesa continued to stop by from time to time.

Giesa used the money Stodolka paid him to catch up on his rent, but he was still behind. In fact, his landlord was becoming irritated at his failure to pay on time and began collecting every other week instead of monthly.

Several times in July, Giesa stopped by Stodolka's home. Nobody knows what occurred during those visits, but he never stayed long and most people assumed they were merely social calls.

On July 29, Giesa showed up at Stodolka's house again. This time when he left, the cheerful one-legged man was lying in a pool of his own blood, his chest and back ripped open by three deep stab wounds.

A neighbor who stopped by to look after the old widower found him dead in his bed. But he was covered with blankets, and when Thurston County Coroner W.W. "Tag" Frazier was called to investigate, it was assumed he would eventually announce a determination of death from natural causes. However, when he pulled the covers off the corpse, he found Stodolka's upper torso and the bed clothing he was lying in soaked in blood. Frazier was peering at the victim of an especially grisly homicide.

The Thurston County Sheriff's Department launched an immediate and intense investigation. Technicians dusted the house for fingerprints, and came up with more than they knew what to do with. Friends, neighbors, deliverymen, workmen – and nurse's aides had been trooping in and out of the house for months.

Except for the body and the bedclothing surrounding it, there was surprisingly little blood in the house: no bloody fingerprints on the walls, no smeared murder weapon, and no indication that the killer had washed up in the kitchen or bathroom. Curiously, a blood-stained pillow that had been carried from the bedroom was found stuffed in a paper sack in another room of the house.

While technicians were going over the house, other investigators were canvasing the neighborhood, talking with area residents, looking for people who may have seen or heard something suspicious. The effort quickly turned up information about Stodolka's disturbing habit of carrying large sums of money. One neighbor confided that she believed he might have had as much as $1,800 in his billfold. Homicide detectives and evidence technicians searched the house thoroughly, but they could find no sign of the worn billfold. It wasn't in the old man's pants pockets when his clothing was searched, and it was nowhere to be found in the modest home he had lived in for so many years. Robbery seemed to be a good bet as a possible motive in the killing.

Suspicion quickly focused on the nurse's aide with the bizarre behavior after detectives learned that he had been hanging around the house following his one-day stint caring for the old man. Investigators determined that Giesa had made a substantial down payment on a van he was buying, and they wondered if there might be a connection between the financially troubled young man's sudden riches and the missing wallet. They obtained search warrants for Giesa's Tumway apartment and the new van. And they struck paydirt!

Detectives had hardly begun their search before they found an athletic totebag that contained, among other items, a sheathed ten-inch knife with a serrated blade. The forensic pathologist who performed the autopsy on Stodolka concluded that, based on its shape, the length of the blade, and the jagged cutting edge, the hunting knife could have inflicted the stab wounds found in his body.

Police also found Stodolka's missing wallet containing cash, his driver's license, and other personal cards with his name on them. The thirty-year-old nurse's aide was taken into custody and transported to the Thurston County Sheriff's office for questioning. It was about 7 P.M., the same day Stodolka was killed.

Once Giesa was in custody as the prime suspect, he appeared surprisingly eager to talk about it. He made two statements to homicide detectives. In one, he said that he stabbed the old man in the back, then, still in a rage, pulled the knife out and plunged it into the widower's heart.

In the second statement, Giesa said that he wanted to go for a ride and decided to stop by Stodolka's house for a visit. He said the old man was resting in bed when he arrived. From that point on, however, the statement drifted. It became erratic, jumbled, and unintelligible.

But basically, Giesa contended that they chatted briefly before he gave the elderly man a backrub and Stodolka fell asleep. He said Stodolka slumbered only a few minutes before he awakened in an angry mood.

"What the hell are you doing in my house?" Giesa claimed the old man shouted at him. A moment later, according to the murder suspect's account, Stodolka grabbed a knife from a nearby bookshelf and tried to stab him.

It may have seemed perfectly reasonable that Stodolka would order the obnoxious aide from his home. But after talking with neighbors, investigators knew it was unlikely that he would keep a sheath knife lying around on a bookshelf. And everyone acquainted with the old man agreed that he was a gentle man. It would have been completely out of character for him to attack someone with such a deadly weapon unless he was protecting his home or fighting for his life. Giesa's story was difficult to believe.

But he stubbornly stuck to his guns, insisting that as they fought over the knife, they tumbled onto the bed and the blade somehow ended up thrust deeply into the old man's back. Giesa said that when he realized Stodolka had been stabbed, he pulled the knife out. Then he stabbed him in the chest to end his misery. Giesa said one of his hands was slashed during the desperate fight for life.

The nervous young man's story became even more confusing and bizarre as he ended his account of the stabbing. He told the stone-faced detectives that he had believed Stodolka was his dead father and the knife was a flashlight. But after Stodolka was stabbed in the back, his mind suddenly flashed back to the reality of the present and he realized that the old man was hurt and in pain. It was then, he said, that he knew he had to finish killing him as an act of mercy.

Giesa's statement was about as strange as they come, and it seemed that if his attorneys later wished to build an insanity defense for him, he had just provided some handy groundwork. But he had also admitted committing the fatal stabbing of the physically handicapped old man. Giesa was jailed on charges of first-degree murder. A few weeks later, the charge was upgraded to aggravated first-degree murder, a more serious count that carried either a possible death sentence or life in prison without possibility of parole.

Bond was set at two hundred thousand dollars. Giesa's court-appointed lawyer pleaded for a bail reduction, pointing out that his client was indigent and couldn't even afford to post twenty thousand dollars. Giesa had been fired from the home-care nursing agency in June, weeks before the murder. The lawyer's motion was rejected.

While the accused killer was sitting in his jail cell awaiting trial, friends recalled the victim as a "delightful man," who had lived for his wife, his church, his music, and his gardening. Peter Stodolka's home-grown vegetables had become an institution in the neighborhood, and what he didn't eat himself or give away to neighbors, he sold at a small produce stand.

A woman who knew him for years said the only thing that seemed to bother him were the grisly stories he read in newspapers about murders. He couldn't imagine anyone killing another person for money – or any reason. It was inconceivable to him and completely alien to the life he had lived.

When his wife died, the old man seemed to lose some of his grit. He became softer, more gentle, and more accepting of his own mortality. Neighbors agreed that he grieved terribly over her death.

Born in Perham, Minnesota, on August 1, 1907, Stodolka migrated early in his life to the Pacific Northwest. In Olympia, he belonged to St. Michael's Roman Catholic Church. And according to the Reverend Michael Feeney, the Church became Stodolka's life and the only family he had after his wife's death.

Giesa's bizarre behavior continued after he was jailed. Shortly after he was locked up, he wrote a grotesquely curious letter to his deceased father that helped expose his apparent rage, frustration, and mental turmoil. It read:

"If Dad were alive today – 8-16-86.

"Dad, you are a son of a bitch. You keep telling Mom and I you love us, but by your actions tell us you don't care. You cut me down saying I couldn't learn anything, but when (sic) asked questions of you, who is it who never had time for me? Who always shoved me away?

"Who was it that wouldn't listen to his own family or doctor? Even though the doctor told you it was OK to go back to work but take it slow. Did you listen? Hell no!

"We all love you. Even Mom whom you abused for so many

187

years with your damned drinking. You don't even know how many times I have heard Mom crying in bed because she was afraid of you having an accident hurting you or someone else. Between your damn drinking and excessive working you are killing yourself. Why don't you listen to anyone who cares about you? You never listen to anyone but yourself. We all love you and care about you."

Giesa didn't sign the letter. At his trial much later it was admitted as evidence to demonstrate his reputed emotional state at the time of the slaying.

The trial began in October 1986, before Superior Court Judge Carol Puller in Olympia, and Giesa pleaded innocent by reason of diminished mental capacity. The prosecution was prohibited from revealing to the jury that the victim was an amputee. Defense attorneys contended the information would prejudice the jury against their client, and the judge agreed.

The state's team, headed by Thurston County Prosecutor Phil Harju, argued that Giesa murdered Stodolka during a robbery. The prosecution contended that Giesa needed money and went to his former patient's home to commit the robbery. The defense claimed that their client was trapped in such a disturbed mental state that he was unable to consciously form the intent to commit murder.

Mental health professionals testifying for the defense claimed that because of the mental trauma stemming from the death of his father, his father's destructive history of alcoholism, and the traumatic effect of the previous deaths of two patients under Giesa's care, he was not mentally capable of forming an intent to murder on the day he fatally stabbed Stodolka.

They said Giesa became upset when Stodolka began talking about pleasant memories with his wife and got up to leave and perform exercises to work off his anger. But he tripped and bumped his head. They contended that he closed his eyes and when he opened them again he had a vision of his father in Stodolka's bed. It was then that Giesa grabbed what he believed was a flashlight, but was really the hunting knife.

The prosecution scoffed at Giesa's fanciful tale of being caught up in a deadly hallucination during the stabbing, and presented their own mental health experts to counter the claim. Tacoma psychologist Richard Peterson testified that he believed Giesa was fully capable of forming intent to kill the old widower. Peterson branded Giesa's story as unbelievable. He described the tale as "sounding like a bad movie script."

The prosecution witness pictured Giesa as a malingerer who lied in his psychological tests, and during the testing showed no remorse for Stodolka's death. Peterson said that if the defendant had actually suffered a psychotic episode that was responsible for his inadvertant killing of Stodolka, he would have cried and mourned for the widower. Instead, Giesa repeatedly stated that he cried over his father.

Psychiatrist James Bremner testified that Giesa admitted to him that he intended to kill the old man. He said that during an interview, Giesa told him that he and Stodolka began arguing, and he didn't know what was happening when he stabbed the old man twice. But Giesa realized what was going on *before* he plunged the hunting knife into Stodolka's chest the third time, to put him out of his misery.

The psychiatrist said Giesa told him he pressed a pillow over Stodolka's face after the stabbing to make sure he was dead.

Nor was the psychiatrist ready to accept Giesa's story of killing during a hallucination.

"I felt some kind of rehearsed fabrication," Bremner said of the tale. And he agreed with the testimony of the earlier expert who said he believed Giesa was falsely claiming to be mentally ill as a ploy to stay out of prison.

Dr. Bremner told the court that although Giesa exhibited mild depression and had mixed personality disorders, he wasn't suffering from any mental disorders serious enough to prevent him from forming intent to kill the victim.

"He had the mental capacity to do it," the psychiatrist testified.

Other witnesses cast suspicion on Giesa's story that Stodolka had willingly admitted him to his home as a guest on the day of the murder. They said the old man had admitted to them that he was afraid of the odd nurse's aide and didn't want him around.

And the woman Giesa had followed to Washington State and briefly lived with testified about the ex-sailor's tall tales. She drew an unflattering word picture of a man who was a slob and a liar who couldn't be taken seriously. Giesa sat with his head in his hands, crying through much of the testimony.

After conclusion of testimony, and summing up by the prosecution and defense, the jury took less than nine hours of deliberation to return with a verdict. They found the former nurse's aid guilty of aggravated first-degree murder.

Unlike his behavior during the trial, Giesa displayed no emotion when the verdict was read, and he was equally stone-faced when he was handcuffed by two burly guards and led back to his cell.

The prosecutor had not sought the death penalty, so there was no mystery over what Giesa's sentence would be. But when he appeared for sentencing, Judge Fuller asked if he had anything he wished to say.

Giesa walked to the front of the room, and speaking quietly but with apparent emotion, he told the court: "I am here with a broken heart and spirit. In my heart and according to Scriptures, the only sentence that I can receive is death.

"Shedding innocent blood is against the Lord," he said. "There is only one judgment to be placed. I pray to you and to my Heavenly Father for mercy. In some way I may be able to repay mankind and my Lord for that mercy. I am truly sorry and regret the act I have done. In the name of Jesus Christ, Amen."

The judge explained that according to the law there was only one sentence she could order. Then she sentenced him to life in prison with no possibility of parole.

Jury foreman Herb Larson later told reporters that the jurors felt the prosecution did a good job proving that Giesa knew what he was doing when he killed Stodolka. He said they also believed that the defendant was being untruthful in his statements to police and mental health experts. "There were so many stories and they got progressively elaborate," Larson added. "Apparently he never told the truth."

The jury foreman added however that he believed there were two victims of the crime. "One was Mr. Stodolka," he said. "The other, unfortunately, is Giesa. I think he's very unfortunate. He needs psychiatric treatment. We all feel sorry for him and wish there was a way we could make him whole. But that was not our charge."

ELEVEN

Catherine Wood
and Gwendolyn Graham:
Night Stalkers in White

MURDER, spelled out in capital letters, was a tension-relieving game for lesbian lovers Catherine May Wood and Gwendolyn Gail Graham.

They methodically planned to dispose of vulnerable elderly victims under their care in a cruel and bizarre alphabetical sequence so that the first letter of their names spelled out the name of their sicko game—MURDER.

And cold-blooded executioner, twenty-five-year-old Graham, and her lover callously boasted that one of the principal reasons for their sadistic slayings of her pathetically, defenseless prey was to ease stress if she was having a "bad day."

Their alphabet murder game backfired because many of their targeted frail victims struggled too much. Despite the efforts of their strong young executioner Graham, many patients, finding hidden strengths in their desperate struggle to cling to the last vestiges of their lives, fought back too vigorously for Graham's liking. They just refused to die.

So the murderers were forced to change their game plan. Instead of continuing with the alphabet fun and games, they set their sights on weaker prey, and settled for collecting souvenirs from their pitiful victims, most of whom suffered from Alzheimer's disease. The souvenirs, which they showed to other nurse's aides and lesbian friends during leisure moments when they boasted about the murders, included pathetic trinkets and personal items, anklets, handkerchiefs—even a novelty gift balloon and a set of dentures.

It was early in 1987 that nursing home aides and lesbian lovers Wood and Graham first came under suspicion of murdering eight elderly patients at the Alpine Manor Nursing Home in Walker, Michigan, a suburb of Grand Rapids. Wood's ex-husband Ken had at last taken the bizarre confessions seriously and gone to the police.

According to the grisly story pieced together from other aides, nurses, and lesbian friends of the pair, Graham suffocated the elderly patients in their beds holding washcloths firmly over their nose and mouth, while Wood acted as lookout, sometimes listening to the stifled death throes and gurgles on an intercom at the nurse's station.

In one case—that of sixty-year-old Mrs. Marguerite Chambers—Wood had watched from the door as Graham murdered and was able to observe the death convulsions and jerking legs of the helpless elderly lady.

The two self-appointed executioners had made a lovers' pact so that they could be bound together for eternity, their perverse love fueled by shared secrets of cold-blooded killings.

The final act was staged in Grand Rapids on November 2, 1989, when Gwendolyn Graham was sentenced to six life imprisonment terms with absolutely no chance of parole. She was convicted of suffocating five of the patients under her care.

Ironically, as details of the Alpine Manor killings began to emerge, the love affair had soured. The lesbian lovers' pact had become a pointless evil memory.

At an earlier hearing, Wood admitted she often acted as a lookout or diverted the attention of the supervisors while her buxom young friend with the plain, open features and dirty-blond hair smothered their frail victims.

For her part in the crimes and for turning against her former lover, Wood pleaded guilty to second-degree murder, and at a separate hearing before Kent County Circuit Judge Robert Benson in Grand Rapids, Michigan, she was sentenced to twenty to forty years.

She wasn't in court a week later when Judge Roman Snow threw the book at her ex-lover. Doomed to spend the rest of her life behind bars, Graham displayed no remorse or emotion and declined Judge Snow's offer to speak before sentencing. Her one request was that she not be sent to the same prison as her former lover-turned-betrayer.

Wood had been more talkative the week before when she confessed to her role in the bizarre pact to kill. In a prepared statement read by her attorney Christine Yared, Wood expressed remorse:

"Saying, 'I'm sorry' is just not enough. Mere words cannot express the remorse and guilt. I'll have to live with this for the rest of my life. I was caught up in a mess but do not excuse any action or try to blame anyone for my part in this."

That's when Judge Benson gave her the twenty-to-forty year sentence with the mitigating observation:

"Without you, I'm sure this matter would never have been cleared up. I'm convinced that you truly show remorse. I'm also convinced you are a follower and not a leader."

During the earlier trial of ex-lover Graham, Wood, as the principal witness for the prosecution, made an effort to set the record straight. Her evidence was a horror story which convicted Graham of five counts of murder in the first degree, and a sixth count of conspiracy to commit murder in the first degree.

In hushed tones, Wood chilled everyone in the courtroom as she told how she sometimes served as a lookout or diverted supervisors' attention as Gwendolyn Graham suffocated six patients in their rooms while they worked as nurse's aides together at Alpine Manor Nursing Home in Walker, Michigan.

Wood shocked the jury further when she told how the killings were part of a weird pact to bind their love together forever. She revealed the calculated iciness of her co-conspirator when she recalled how Graham told her that murder helped her "relieve tension."

This horrifying tale of lesbian love, jealousy, and cold-blooded murders began to unfold early in December 1988, when both women were arrested—Graham in her hometown of Tyler, Texas, a hundred miles south of Dallas, and Wood in Walker, Michigan—and charged in the killing of a ninety-eight-year-old nursing home patient Edith Cook. Graham initially announced that she was going to fight extradition to Michigan to face the charge and was held in custody with bond set at one million dollars; she later withdrew her extradition fight. Wood was held without bail in Michigan, her home state, charged in the death of Mrs. Cook and another nursing home victim, sixty-year-old Marguerite Chambers. Both bodies had been exhumed and autopsied.

Both women were frail and terminally ill, Mrs. Cook with coronary artery disease and Mrs. Chambers with the Alzheimer's disease she had suffered with for fourteen years. Medical Examiner Stephen Cohle was to testify later that he formally changed the cause of death on their death certificates from natural causes to asphyxia due to suffocation. However, he said he had no scientific evidence to support that conclusion, and based his findings on information from the police. That lack of "scientific evidence" was later to prove a weak link in the prosecution's case against Graham—but fortunately Graham's bragging and boasting to friends about her evil acts were enough to sway the jury.

Walker, Michigan, Assistant Police Chief Bill Brown said that the two women were initially suspects in eight deaths, Graham was finally convicted of five murders at the peaceful Alpine Manor Nursing Home, a facility for "total care" patients in the conservative town of Walker, which borders the northwest side of Grand Rapids and has a population of twenty thousand.

Murder investigations were concentrated on the January to April 1987 period during which a total of forty patients had died.

Shortly before her arrest, Graham was working as a nurse's aide at the Mother Frances Hospital in Tyler, but was fired less than two months before her apprehension when Texas hospital officials were tipped off she was being investigated for the Michigan killings.

Graham had returned to Tyler in 1987 after her year long affair with Wood had fallen apart amid scenes of jealousy, threats, and violence. Graham fled with a new live-in companion, Heather Barager, a young woman embarking on her first homosexual love affair.

Although born in Santa Maria, California, Graham felt more at home in Tyler, Texas, than any other place. She had lived in the Gresham area of town, had gone to school there, was brought up there, and held several jobs in the town before her trip to Michigan

194

and her meeting with Wood and murder.

At Tyler's Grace Community School which she attended from 1975 to 1980, Graham was remembered as a "quiet and respectful" young girl, according to school principal Jerry Burgess. "She always had a sad look on her face. She was never happy," recalled Burgess. From a broken home, she seemed to have a problem with self-esteem. She never graduated, although her transcript from Tyler Community College, which she attended in the spring of 1984, shows she did earn a Graduate Equivalent Diploma. Before leaving Texas, she held a number of dead-end jobs in town—as a Mini Mart convenience store clerk and as a newspaper carrier.

Although she was later to claim she was a product of an unhappy family, with a father who sexually abused her and a mother with whom she had absolutely nothing in common, townsfolk could only remember good things about her as a child and in her early working years. They were staggered when they heard the vicious charges against her.

Later, Graham was to appeal to the sympathy of the court when she described that sad and lonely childhood. As a teenager, she had burned her own arms dozens of times with cigarettes—her only way of venting her frustration, and a misguided attempt to get back at her father for his alleged abuse.

Tyler resident Ruth Weaver, a newspaper distributor for the Dallas Morning *News,* who employed Graham from 1983 to 1985, said: "Gwen always seemed a nice, friendly person to me." Gasped a family friend: "Not Gwen . . . I liked Gwen. Gwen wouldn't kill anybody."

Wood was a longtime employee at Alpine Manor. She had begun there in July 1985, and was promoted to nurse's aide supervisor at Alpine Manor. But she was forced to quit as the homicide investigations got under way in October of 1988. She was working in a fast food restaurant at the time of her arrest on December 4.

As in other cases involving death-stalkers, both women got high marks for their job performances at the 285-bed nursing home. "Both had very good reviews. In surveys, both were found to be very well liked by patients," said Ginny Seyferth, an Alpine Manor spokeswoman.

And how did the home cope with the mind-shattering news that

195

it had two killers in its midst. "I think the staff is overwhelmed," said Seyferth. The nursing home was forced to provide counseling for patients and employees. Later evidence was to prove that the majority of the home's two-hundred-strong nursing staff already had strong suspicions about Wood and Graham. Co-worker and nurse's aide Patricia Patterson, for example: "Wood had a quick temper, and Graham was unpredictable. Wood would throw diapers at me and cuss at me." On the other hand, the inseparable girls used to enjoy laughing and joking around, particularly about their callous deeds when they showed off their "souvenirs."

Tragically, everyone chose not to believe the joking girls. The only person to take the killing stories seriously was Wood's ex-husband. Remorseful, his ex-wife confessed her complicity in the nursing home killings. Mr. Wood went to the police, the investigation was begun, and in less than two months the two killers were in custody. No one can honestly blame the officials and staff for being taken in by the two murderous aides. "There was nothing anyone could have done to prevent it," observed Walker Police Chief Walter Sprenger. "There was no reason to believe such terrible things were going on. As a result, it's the sort of thing that could have happened anywhere."

Like everyone else involved in this horrific case, Police Chief Sprenger was at a loss to pinpoint motives for the killings with any degree of accuracy. He ruled out the possibilities of mercy killings, or killings for financial gain, but felt that the women's lesbian relationship was "part of a complex web that brings the whole thing together."

Devastating testimony by Wood's ex-husband Ken and Graham's final lesbian conquest, live-in lover Heather Barager, helped the prosecution bring the killing team to justice at a fast clip.

Wood told how his ex-wife—they were separated in 1986, divorced the following year after a total of eight years' marriage—tearfully confessed the crimes to him shortly after Graham had run off to Texas with her new friend Barager. "She said, 'You wouldn't believe the things we've done.' She said that she and Graham had killed six people at Alpine Manor," said Mr. Wood, who reacted to her incredible confession in stunned, numbed silence.

The patients' deaths had been dismissed as natural causes until

196

Wood told police of his ex-wife's confession in October 1988, about fourteen months after the conversation. Wood explained that he had taken his time about going to the police because he had promised his wife he wouldn't tell anyone. "And I thought about the families of the victims; so many people were going to get hurt," added Wood.

But he decided eventually to tell the authorities. "Cathy wasn't getting any better. She couldn't let go of what happened . . . I went to the police because she needed help."

It was in August 1987, that his ex-wife first told him about the killings, said Mr. Wood. She described to him how her roommate Graham killed six patients as Wood stood guard. He said Wood told him she and Graham had committed the crimes "just for fun," and that they selected only seriously incapacitated patients because there was less chance of a struggle.

His ex-wife also told him about the M-U-R-D-E-R spelling game that Graham and she had devised—although this plan was abandoned when some would-be victims put up too much of a struggle. It was then the terrible duo decided to forget the alphabet game and stick to weaker, more vulnerable prey.

Graham's girlfriend Heather Barager, who was at one time Wood's bitter rival for Graham's affections, said she at first believed no killings had taken place. She thought Wood and Graham were kidding about murdering patients. Then she thought that a vindictive Wood was making up vicious stories to get back at her and Graham.

Barager said Graham was still living with Wood when they first became lovers. But when Barager and Graham planned to set up a home together, Wood threatened to turn in Graham to the police. Graham decided to stay with Wood. "She got in my car and said she loved me and always would . . . but she had to go back to Cathy."

Barager said she was shocked when she first heard police were conducting a serious murder investigation and her lover Graham was the prime suspect. "She said she wasn't going to take the whole blame for the killings," said Barager. "She then asked me to check some books dealing with the criminal justice system and prison out of the Tyler public library for her."

Barager said she had never taken Graham's confessions about the killings seriously during all the time they were together. It was her first homosexual affair. It gradually dawned on her that Gwen was indeed telling the truth all along when detectives arrived on their doorstep in Tyler with a warrant for Gwendolyn's arrest. "I kept saying I didn't believe it. But Gwen said it was true. She had killed those people." At no time did she implicate Wood. Barager admitted she had first concealed Graham's confessions from the police "because I didn't want to lose Gwen, and because I was scared."

Barager said she had now cut all ties with Graham. She had quit writing to her and had returned home to live with her parents.

As yet another young former lover turned against her, Graham, looking very much the abandoned woman, sat beside her attorney weeping, blotting tears from her eyes with a crumpled handkerchief.

Two other friends of Graham's, Deborah Kidder, an ensign with the U.S. Navy, and Lisa Lynch, another former nurse's aide at Alpine Manor, said that Graham had freely confessed her part in the murders with both of them on a number of occasions. "But it was just too incredible. I just didn't believe it," said Kidder.

Lisa Lynch said that Graham and Barager had wanted to run off to Florida together, but Graham was scared to take off because she knew Cathy Wood had something on her which she could use against her. That's when she not only repeated her guilt in the suffocations, but rhymed off names of victims—Mrs. Cook, Mrs. Chambers, Myrtle Luce, 95, Mae Mason, 79, Belle Burkhard, 74, and a hapless sixth patient she could only remember struggling with.

Miss Lynch also recalled Wood talking about how Graham's "souvenirs," which she stole from her victims, were displayed on a shelf in a bedroom of the home the two women shared.

Yet another two former nurse's aides at Alpine, Dawn Male and Russell Shawn Thatcher, were two more witnesses to the lesbian lovers' bizarre collection of souvenirs from dead patients. Among the mementoes were a sock and a decorative heart ornament.

Graham was later to claim that the odds and ends she showed visitors and friends, which she kept on a shelf in her bedroom, were just silly little personal items—certainly not the property of murder victims.

"Gwen Graham said she also used a pillow to suffocate patients. I didn't believe either of them, I thought they were joking around with me—a sick joke," said Miss Male who also admitted to having sexual relationships with both Wood and Graham.

All the co-workers testified how Wood told them she acted as lookout while Graham did the suffocating. Both Miss Male and another friend of Cathy Wood agreed that Graham was the more violent of the pair. She had physically abused Wood.

Wood told a new friend, witness Nancy Harris, whom she met in June 1987, that she was afraid for her life. "Wood told me that she was very worried about this woman Graham. She said she had seen this woman suffocate Marguerite Chambers. She felt this woman was capable of killing anyone," testified Miss Harris. Wood said Graham had even tried to suffocate her, added Harris.

In an early confession to police, Wood told how she and Graham were "involved as lovers in a homosexual relationship." Graham told her that the killings had provided her with a kind of "emotional release"—with the exception of what Mrs. Wood called the "mercy killing" of ninety-eight-year-old Mrs. Cook who was suffering from gangrene at the time of her slaying.

There was no mercy, however, in the January 18, 1987, murder of the Alzheimer's disease patient, Mrs. Chambers. Graham coldly and methodically executed helpless Mrs. Chambers, her strong arms pressing down on her, suffocating her by pressing a washcloth under the patient's chin and another over her nose and mouth.

Mrs. Wood said Graham would flippantly talk about the murders and the victims either immediately before or after they occurred, and claimed she had not come forward earlier with the whole sordid story because Graham had repeatedly threatened her with physical harm.

"She was always happy when one of the patients died," Wood was later to testify against Graham, adding that Graham had plotted the deaths of at least another five patients, but was thwarted when some of the elderly men or women fought back. Wood disputed the assertion by Graham's defense counsel, Mr. James Piazza, that Wood was just out to revenge herself on Graham for taking off with another woman and that the Alpine Manor deaths had always been from natural causes.

Wood claimed she was distraught after Mrs. Chambers' suffocation in January 1987, and Graham promised to stop. Soon after, when another patient died after a deadly struggle, Graham seemed to take the incident as a sign "that it was supposed to go on."

The reason Wood gave for going along with the killings in the first place was because "I thought Gwen was the first person to ever love me and I didn't want her to leave me, no matter what."

Wood was frank in the picture she painted of the obsessive sexual attraction she felt for Gwen. Weeping during her testimony against Graham, Wood said her lover used to frighten her, taunting her with the rolled-up washcloths she used to smother her victims. At one stage, said Wood, Graham tied her to a bed and began smothering her. She only stopped when Wood began crying.

Wood admitted that she helped Graham select victims by checking out total-care, uncommunicative patients—the weakest of the weak—to see how vulnerable they were. She would check them out by pinching their noses and obstructing their breathing to see how much they resisted. But she said the only patient she ever picked out for Graham to kill was the frail Mrs. Cook, because she was so ill, and this one would be more of a mercy killing. "I thought that if someone had to die, at least it could be someone who wasn't healthy," said Wood.

To prove her undying devotion to her, Graham told Wood that she would have to kill a patient herself. But Wood lost her nerve when the poor patient she had targeted for death peered pathetically up at her. She couldn't go through with it.

The slayings came to an end, said Wood, when she was promoted and moved to another shift.

As the grisly testimony began spilling out in Michigan courtrooms, relatives of the victims, hearing the true, full horror stories for the first time, were aghast at the evil enormities inflicted on their loved ones. "The dying part is not the bad part. I expected her to die," said Nancy Hahn, daughter of one of the victims. "The bad part is that somebody killed her."

Mrs. Hahn, the only child of Mrs. Burkhard, added: "I was kind of hoping that we would never really know whether they killed her or not . . ."

Mrs. Maxine Luce said the death of her ailing mother-in-law Myrtle Luce was "a blessing. But when you think of someone deliberately taking her life, well, that's another thought entirely. When you think of somebody lying there helpless, being smothered, that's taking another person's life, and nobody has a right to take another person's life . . . whether she was close to death or not."

One of the biggest bombshells during Graham's trial was dropped by key witness Wood when she claimed one of the primary reasons she wanted Graham arrested and put behind bars was a strong fear that she would kill again—and that helpless babies would be the victims this time around!

Wood said she finally implicated Graham after her return to Texas in the summer of 1987 because of disturbing telephone conversations between the two about Graham's new job as a nurse's aide at the Mother Frances Hospital in her hometown of Tyler.

Now living apart, with their killing days at Alpine Manor behind them, Graham apparently had not gotten the bloodlust out of her system. She told her former accomplice that sometimes she got an uncontrollable urge to pick up one of the helpless babies under her care at the new hospital and bash its brains out against a glass wall.

"When she was killing people at Alpine and I didn't do anything, that was bad enough," said Wood in answer to questions about why she had spoken so freely to police about her former lover in the fall of 1987. "But when she would call me and say how she wanted to smash a baby . . . I had to stop her somehow," said Wood, sobbing heavily as she continued her testimony. "I didn't care. I knew she was working in a hospital there. She said she wanted to take one of the babies and smash it up against a window. I had to do something. I didn't care about myself anymore."

Fortunately, according to officials at Tyler's Mother Frances Hospital, Wood's fears for the safety of babies at the facility were unfounded. Dawn Jenich, director of community affairs at Mother Frances, said Graham only worked on the neurology-orthopedic floor and would not have had any access to babies in the nursery.

"The nursery doors were locked twenty-four hours a day. There was no way staff members—other than authorized nursing personnel—could get in there," said Mrs. Jenich, adding: "During her employment here, there was nothing that ever happened that was unusual."

However, Graham had been swiftly fired once the Mother Frances officials were notified of her background.

In her own defense, Graham maintained that the whole question of killing patients was a sick joke which had gotten out of hand. The pair had originally made up the stories of smotherings to shock another lesbian co-worker at the home, a woman with whom both had been sexually involved. "Cathy would start it . . . and I'd just go along with the stories," explained Graham.

Wood and Graham, in their convoluted way of thinking, liked painting a picture of themselves as hardened killers. That way they could command fear and control people. And it also safeguarded their love affair. Who else would want to become involved with a couple of self-confessed killers? Their shared secret meant they were perfect for each other.

Recounting stories about murders was just the two of them playing head games, said Graham, because Cathy Wood just loved concocting stories. It was only after she began seeing another woman, said Graham, that Wood threatened to "make someone believe the story that we had been killing patients."

The reason Wood kept insisting the murders were real was because Wood was consumed with jealousy and wanted to get revenge on Graham, who left her for the other woman and returned to Tyler, Texas, in August 1987. When police investigators first approached her, said Graham, she realized Wood "was going to get even, just like she said she would."

An ironic twist in the events leading up to the conviction of both women is that Cathy Wood, in her remorse and her misguided crusade to save the babies at the Mother Frances Hospital from Graham's barbarism, never dreamed for one minute that she would leave herself wide open for a long spell in prison herself.

A pathetic case in the witness box, Wood told Kent County, Michigan, Assistant Prosecutor David Schieber that when she first spoke to police she was totally unaware there was a possibility that charges could be filed against herself. "The first time we went into Walker police headquarters I wasn't even thinking about charges. I

202

did not think that I would be charged." She thought that if there were any charges filed against her, they would be dismissed in return for her cooperation in prosecuting her ex-lover.

Although a self-confessed accomplice, Wood maintained to the end that she didn't physically participate in any of the suffocations. She did promise Graham at one stage that the two would alternate killing patients so that the secret they shared would help cement their relationship until the end of time. "We were supposed to be together forever," added Wood softly.

Wood's life was totally transformed when she first met Graham, the court was told. They were an odd couple; a couple of misfits. Graham derived some kind of weird pleasure in washing the bodies of her victims after they had been murdered. And Graham and Wood could get so excited talking about the suffocations that they sometimes got an uncontrollable urge to have sex together, said prosecutor Schieber.

Graham was certainly unlike any person Cathy Wood had known before. Before Graham entered her life, when they first met at Alpine Manor, Cathy Wood was leading the life of a recluse. Her weight had ballooned to 450 pounds, her marriage was in trouble; she had no friends or outside interests.

Life for Cathy Wood was in a rut. Married as a teenager, she was in many respects naive about the ways of the world. Feeling fat and unloved, she was highly susceptible to a new lifestyle. She was to find this with her new friend, the tough little country girl from Texas who had survived the school of hard knocks and who was also looking for an exciting new life in Michigan and a risqué new love style.

All of a sudden both of them found themselves thrown together in a brand-new social whirl, introduced to a new and daring kind of love. Gwen and Cathy found comfort and love with each other, probably for the first time in their unhappy lives. Also for the first time, their daring confessions, hinting at a darker, even dangerous side to their personalities, brought them the warped respect and twisted admiration of their sexual peers. The two plain Cinderellas basked in this glow of newfound attention.

Cathy Wood lost a great deal of weight and her social life picked up. All thanks to her new friend Gwen. It was only a matter of time before she ordered husband Ken out of the house and Gwen was installed as her new roommate and lover.

Life was sweet at last for Cathy. "I was drinking a lot. I went wild. I went to bars. I thought it was all great fun," said Cathy. But soon the laughter was replaced with cold-blooded horror. When Graham first brought up the idea of killing people in October 1986, said Wood, she thought she was kidding. "The conversations were quite wild. I thought we were just playing," she said.

When the killings began, she was very careful about having no direct role apart from playing sentry and preventing other workers from seeing what was going on. As the plot grew more and more macabre, she thought about going to the authorities, but gave up on that idea after Graham became abusive and threatened her. "In a way I tried to pretend it wasn't happening," said Wood. "There was just so much going on . . ."

It was around this stage in their relationship that the games turned into real-life nightmares. During sex, Graham liked to tie Wood up and try to suffocate her, said prosecutor Schieber. At one time, Graham threatened Wood with a gun.

The pair got so carried away with murder plots that they even discussed killing other nurse's aides at Alpine Manor—eliminating jealousy from their lives by disposing of possible threats to each other's affections.

Defense Attorney Piazza and his client Graham presented a totally different picture, the flip side of this strange coin. Wood was "a spiteful, aggressive, vindictive manipulator" who made up the story. He said Graham went along with it, "thinking it was a mind game . . . a big joke." Beefy, heavyset Wood was the dominant partner in the relationship, with the most forceful personality, claimed the defense.

"I wanted to leave Cathy . . . mostly I was tired of playing games, hurting people emotionally and mentally," argued Graham. "She told Heather that she would kill us both if we left the state, and make someone believe our story about killing patients."

When Wood saw there was little hope of her persuading Graham not to run off with Heather Barager, Wood coaxed Graham to spend one last night with her for old time's sake. Graham testified how Wood coaxed her to a darkened basement and tied her up—

not an uncommon sexual practice between the two. Only this time, claimed Graham, Wood menaced her with a gun, threatened to kill her, then shoot herself. Eventually, she freed Graham, who took off for Texas with Barager.

Mr. Piazza said it was then that Wood concocted the story of the killings, presenting it as real to get her revenge on Graham for running out on her. He said Wood, Graham, and their lesbian friends and co-workers "used to always play mind games . . . to control, to dominate."

Said Mr. Piazza: "Once Wood started bragging about murders, Gwen Graham went along—thinking it was another game, another joke. She loved Catherine Wood, so she wanted to please her, so she went along with this joke," he said, contending it was the much larger Wood—who outweighed Graham by more than two-hundred pounds—who menaced Graham with a gun during sex and threatened to accuse her with the murders when she went off with another woman.

After police began investigating Wood's confession to her ex-husband, Wood needed "a sacrificial lamb." She offered up Gwen Graham, said the attorney.

Both the prosecution and defense made emphatic points to the jury about not dwelling at length on the sexual aspects of the case. Prosecutor Schieber told the 11-women, three-man jury: "This is not some kind of referendum on homosexuality or lesbianism. This is not a typical example of a typical gay relationship. The dynamics of this relationship were destructive, almost cancerous."

Defense Attorney Piazza urged the jury "not to judge these individuals' morals or lifestyles. You'll hear about love, jealousy, hatred, and revenge . . . all familiar to people in heterosexual relationships. Gwen Graham is gay and proud of it. There is nothing to hide there."

In his impassioned, often emotional defense of Graham, lawyer Piazza raised his voice when he told the jury: "All this case is, ladies and gentlemen, is talk—and talk is cheap. To quote Sir Arthur Conan Doyle, 'Without imagination there would be no horror.'

"Gwen Graham is living in horror because of the bizarre imagination of Cathy Wood. Just because Wood has pleaded guilty does not mean that Gwen Graham is guilty of anything . . . other than

205

going along with some bad jokes."

Earlier, Mr. Piazza had requested that all charges against Graham be dismissed or reduced, a motion Judge Roman Snow denied. Later, Judge Snow was to cite a Michigan Court of Appeals ruling that the deaths need not be proved beyond a reasonable doubt and that a defendant may be convicted "solely by the uncorroborated testimony of an accomplice."

After deliberating the tangled maze of allegations and counterallegations for a total of seven hours over a two-day period, the jury found Gwendolyn Graham guilty on all six counts.

Graham, who had waived her extradition rights to be brought from Smith County Jail in Tyler, Texas, to the Kent County courtroom in Michigan, sat, head bowed, showing no emotion whatsoever as the verdicts were announced.

Immediately, defender Piazza announced he was shocked at the verdict and planned an appeal to get the verdict set aside. Protesting what he claimed was the lack of physical evidence against his client Mr. Piazza said: "There are several legal issues on which to base an appeal. I'm disappointed. I don't think it was a proper verdict. But it's the jury's prerogative. We're just done with round one."

His staunch belief in Graham's innocence was echoed by Fran Shadden, a former lover of Graham, who was in court. Once the verdict was announced, Miss Shadden raced to a telephone to relay the outcome of the trial to Graham's family in Texas. "I don't understand how she could have been convicted with no evidence—just hearsay," said Miss Shadden.

Miss Shadden had not lost faith in Gwen Graham. She did not believe her guilty of murder. "I don't believe her capable of that. She may be capable of a lot of things, but not murder," said Miss Shadden.

Friends and relatives of the victims who had crowded into a packed courtroom every day of the trial had different thoughts.

"My mother can finally rest in peace," said Jan Hunderman, daughter of victim Marguerite Chambers. "The scars will always be there, but it helps knowing the truth."

And Linda Engman, daughter of victim Mae Mason, said she was "thrilled" with the verdict. "I didn't have any doubts at all. I

206

wish we had the death penalty," she said.

Peace returned—at least temporarily—to the scene of the crimes, the nursing home Alpine Manor. It issued a terse statement: "Even though we still find it difficult to believe that any of this actually happened, we will continue to place our trust in our system of justice."

Prosecutor Schieber remained unshaken in his belief that true justice had run its course. He objected to defense claims that Graham was convicted primarily on the shaky evidence of a co-conspirator. Mr. Shieber said his only surprise was that the jury had taken so long to reach a verdict. "Cathy Wood's testimony was only a cog . . . other witnesses's testimony was just as devastating", he said.

Jurors declined to comment after the verdict, although one juror who declined to give her name said that the jury was "very much shaken up" by the case. "It was a very difficult case to decide," she said.

Only a few days after Graham was sentenced to life in prison, Alpine Manor, the suburban Walker nursing home, was in the news again. A St. Joseph County, Michigan, woman whose mother was smothered to death filed suit against the home.

The suit was filed by Nancy Hahn of Buchanan, Michigan, the only daughter of Belle Burkhard, and Mrs. Burkhard's eight living siblings. Claiming more than a hundred thousand dollars in damages, the suit accused operators of the home of hiring dangerous or unbalanced personnel, failing to properly supervise them, and failing to keep the facility safe.

Alpine Manor spokeswoman Ginny Seyferth declined comment on the legal action. "At this point, the nursing home is just focusing on quality care for its patients," she said.

The legal papers against the home made graphic use of part of Wood's testimony against Graham when she recalled the death of Nelle Burkhard at the home on February 26, 1987. The suit contended Burkhard died "experiencing the conscious terror of a vicious attack before succumbing to death."

Wood testified that Graham told her that Burkhard struggled so hard she had to put her knee against the woman's arm to complete the suffocation. At the time, Wood was getting an audio blow-by-blow play of the execution through an intercom at the nursing station as the killing was taking place.

As the saga of the star-crossed lesbian lovers drew to a conclusion, experts continued to be bewildered about the motive for the crimes. How had sex fantasies suddenly turned into such shocking reality?

Prosecutor Shieber probably hit closer to the truth than anyone when he speculated in his closing argument at the Graham trial: "I don't think Graham even knows why. It was murder for murder's sake . . . for pleasure's sake . . . It was something intensely personal."

TWELVE

Randy Powers:
Code Blue "Hero"

Trouble seemed to follow nursing assistant Randy Powers wherever he worked.

He was fired from several hospitals—on one occasion for making sexual advances toward four male patients, on another, after writing an anonymous obscene letter to his superiors.

Incredibly, no matter how many times he was fired, no matter how scandalous his behavior, Powers was able to walk into job after job after job. No questions asked.

Except for one stage in his odd career—when Powers was the center of a mammoth investigation into a number of suspicious deaths of elderly hospital patients at places where he worked, he was never linked to possible murders. Because of lack of strong medical evidence, the homicide investigation was shelved.

The young Californian was arrested, convicted, and jailed for five years for assault with a deadly weapon—a hypodermic loaded with the dangerous heart drug Lidocaine; unlawful practice of medicine; and endangering the life of a child.

That jail sentence for the assault on eleven-month-old Sarah Mathews should have spelled the conclusion of Powers's erratic career as a health-care worker.

Incredibly, that wasn't to be the case. He completed only two years of his sentence, satisfactorily met the requirements of a brief period of probation, then went on to legally change his name and was successful in getting a new medical technician's certificate.

Less than five years after his first arrest for the baby attack and an even shorter period of time after being named as a principal suspect in the inconclusive probe into a series of hospital homicides, Powers, now thirty-one, was back patrolling the wards of another hospital in the southern California area. It was only after an alert nurse recognized Powers from photographs taken earlier in his infamous career that embarrassed hospital officials terminated his services and equally embarrassed county officials revoked his license—for the second time.

The fact remains: Randy Powers—reincarnated under his new name, Randy Kato—had successfully thumbed his nose at the health-care system. His story is arguably the most dramatic in illustrating how known misfits, with even marginal determination and imagination, can walk off the streets and, with the most appalling records, be allowed to don white coats and stalk wards at will.

Slender respiratory therapist Powers was twenty-six when he first hit the headlines, gaining near legend status as a health-care maverick. Powers fit the maverick or drifter label because he never really showed enthusiasm about holding down a permanent job. He preferred to belong to a nursing registry service which landed him part-time work in several hospitals. That way, no one really understood the shy loner who yearned to be a real doctor. No matter the job, sooner or later Powers could be relied upon to foul up and either quit or be fired. That was the pattern of his weird hit-and-run career. Soon people were questioning: Was there something sinister behind Powers' erratic work pattern?

How he managed to keep his horrendous work record hidden from employer to employer for so long remains a mystery—a mystery that is a common theme through this random look at the dangerous misfits who are drawn to careers in health care. For a variety of reasons, Powers was kicked out of a number of hospitals in southern California and told never to return.

But like the proverbial bad penny, he seemed to keep popping up in key hospital jobs.

While working for the Los Angeles County Department of Health Services, Powers was dismissed after four male patients at the Olive View Medical Center in Van Nuys reported he had made improper sexual advances toward them.

But despite that blot on his record, Powers didn't have much trouble landing himself a new job shortly afterward—as a nursing aide at Sherman Oaks Community Hospital just a few miles away.

It was while he was at the Sherman Oaks facility that elderly patients started dying at an incredible rate. And the deaths always occurred on the shifts Powers worked.

On the surface, Powers was quiet and studious. Sometimes he allowed himself to be drawn into conversation, particularly when asked about his burning ambition to be a doctor one day. Otherwise, he came across to colleagues as withdrawn and a loner.

True to form, Randy the loner found himself fired from the Sherman Oaks center after only a few weeks.

His dismissal had nothing to do with the epidemic of suspicious deaths that was driving hospital authorities crazy. Randy's offense was writing an obscene letter to hospital administrators!

Coincidental with his leaving, the hospital death rate slowed down perceptibly. Because of this rapid turnaround in the mortality statistics, hospital authorities smelled a rat. Perhaps Powers was linked in some way to the unexplained deaths.

After his departure, details of the deaths were forwarded by the hospital to the district attorney's office. But the investigation was agonizingly slow in getting off the ground. Meantime, Powers's career in the field of health care was continuing—typically, not without controversy. His next incarnation was as an ambulance driver for a San Fernando Valley company. And in this job he was hailed as a hero . . . temporarily. His cool-thinking diagnosis and treatment was credited with saving the life of eleven-month-old toddler Sarah Mathews. The unfortunate child had become ill while attending an unlicensed day-care center—coincidentally run by Powers's mother Hazel from her home in Encino, yet another town in the sprawling San Fernando Valley where Powers seemed to flit from medical facility to facility, according to his whim.

Baby Sarah was suffering from a dangerously high fever and convulsions resulting from what was believed to be an insect bite. She became critically ill in Powers's home, while under the care of his mom.

But Powers was on hand to save her life. After giving little Sarah first-aid treatment on the spot at the request of his anxious, unsuspecting mother, Powers persuaded a neighbor to drive both him and the girl to the emergency room of nearby Northridge Hospital.

When physicians at Northridge eventually conducted an in-depth examination of the little girl, they couldn't find the insect bite referred to by emergency medic Powers. Instead, tests revealed a needle mark on her thigh and toxic levels of the heart drug Lidocaine in her system.

That led to Powers's arrest. He was jailed a few days after his so-called medical heroics, facing charges of assault with a deadly weapon and practicing medicine without a license for injecting the child with a massive dose of the powerful heart drug. He found himself deeper in trouble when he admitted stealing the drug, Lidocaine, from yet another hospital with which he had been associated, the Queen Of Angels Medical Center in Hollywood.

But there were more serious allegations in store for Powers.

On October 3, 1984, while in jail charged with assaulting the Mathews baby, medical and law-enforcement agencies dropped two more bombshells on the sinister nursing assistant turned ambulance driver.

Bombshell number one was District Attorney Robert H. Philibosian's revelation that he had requested exhumations on several elderly patients who had died of sudden heart attacks at the Sherman Oaks Community Hospital while under the care of Powers. In addition, D.A. Philibosian announced that the inves-

212

tigation surrounding Powers had expanded to a search for more suspicious deaths at three other Los Angeles-area hospitals where Powers had worked as a respiratory or inhalation therapist.

Bombshell number two was the revelation that, prior to his career at Sherman Oaks, the Los Angeles County Health Department had fired Powers for reported "sexual advances and acts" toward and on male patients at the Olive View center in Van Nuys.

He had worked at the county-operated medical center in Van Nuys for five months, from December 27, 1982, through May 20, 1983, according to Robert C. Gates, the county's health director.

Powers's unsavory past was fast catching up with him. Initially, investigations into his background were concentrated on his short stint at the Sherman Oaks facility. D.A. Philibosian was initially cautious not to jeopardize any future case when he told a press conference: "It may be that those deaths had nothing whatsoever to do with Randy Powers or anything that was administered to them prior to the time they expired."

Powers's attorney, Sammy Weiss, was quick to jump on the district attorney's cautious statement. "These impending exhumations are nothing but a fishing expedition," said Mr. Weiss, adding that his client was "in total shock" about the investigation.

Hospital authorities revealed that there was evidence to indicate that the Sherman Oaks patients may have been injected with Lidocaine—the same drug Powers injected into the eleven-month-old toddler before "saving" her life. Again, Defense Attorney Weiss countered: "Even if Lidocaine is found in the bodies, there's no proof my client actually gave them the Lidocaine."

Weiss's confidence was borne out when after months of investigation it was announced that the medical tests for the drug Lidocaine in the tissues of deceased Sherman Oaks Hospital patients had proved inconclusive and there were to be no charges forthcoming. The investigation of the suspicious deaths, however, was not closed out. It was being "shelved," announced officials.

That's why hospital and police authorities had treaded very carefully early in their investigation and were ultra-cautious in statements about Powers. They were extremely apprehensive that a panic would set in among patients and personnel in every Los Angeles-area hospital.

And with good reason.

Earlier that year in the same general area, coronary care nurse Robert Diaz was convicted of murdering twelve elderly heart patients in two Riverside County hospitals. Forty-six-year-old Diaz was sentenced to die in the gas chamber.

These fears prompted D.A. Philibosian to issue a further statement, hopefully to allay public trepidation and avoid a hospital panic situation: "We do not have any indication that this is a Nurse Diaz situation, but we are not ruling that out. I don't want to alarm large numbers of people and hospitals. But based on the information we have, the most prudent course of action is to check out every single death that occurred at a time following the attendance of this particular individual."

As the question of whether another possible mass hospital murderer was going to be uncovered was being debated in headlines and on television, licensed ambulance driver-respiratory/inhalation therapist-nursing assistant Powers was in Los Angeles County Jail waiting to be released on twenty thousand dollars bail. Police said he had confessed to the deadly assault on little Sarah. Powers was familiar with Lidocaine, a drug used to regulate heartbeat and which can be fatal in large doses, a police spokesman added. Powers's mother, who ran the babysitting service attended by little Sarah, had been cleared by police of any suspicion in the assault on the toddler. Baby Sarah, however, was still in the hospital, but no longer in any danger.

It wasn't until medical reports revealed that Powers had assaulted the baby in Encino with a Lidocaine injection that the possibility that the same drug could have been used on the Sherman Oaks victims became a major issue. The tentative inquiries involving Powers and his job at the Sherman Oaks center was suddenly escalated into a priority investigation.

214

Mr. Marc Goldberg, chief executive officer at the Sherman Oaks Hospital, confirmed that Powers's name was linked to the hospital deaths and information to that effect had been forwarded to the district attorney's office, said Mr. Goldberg.

Cautiously, Mr. Goldberg said that bringing the matter to the attention of the district attorney's office was "not an indication of wrongdoing. However, it was statistically remarkable, and we felt we had a moral and legal obligation to draw it to the attention of the authorities.

"They were all elderly people, mostly moribund, and the cardiac arrests they suffered were certainly no surprise to the hospital or their doctors," said Mr. Goldberg, adding that the patients were all over seventy. All of the patients were afflicted with respiratory illnesses and died "over a several-week period between April and May. Powers didn't discuss the deaths with anybody at the time. He treated a lot of people in our hospital during that same time period—fifty to a hundred—and didn't have problems," observed Mr. Goldberg. Powers, in fact, was the one who reported the cardiac arrests, and he had also participated in the emergency cardio-pulmonary resuscitation efforts.

Mr. Goldberg said Powers was never at any time authorized to inject any type of medication into a patient. He did work in a facility, however, where Lidocaine was easily obtainable. "The control of Lidocaine is not really that tight, because it's an anesthetic that's used in the emergency room all the time," said Mr. Goldberg. "It's on every floor. It's on every cart. It's available for anesthetizing skin before suturing."

Powers, who had worked at Sherman Oaks on a referral or per diem basis, was fired from the facility in mid-May that year for "administrative reasons, unrelated to the deaths." Despite his firing by L.A. County's health department for his sexual misbehavior at the nearby Olive View center in Van Nuys, in May, 1983—exactly a year before his Sherman Oaks dismissal—Mr. Goldberg said Powers's work performance at Sherman Oaks had been satisfactory. He came across as a shy person to his coworkers, and he had never discussed or commented on the sub-

215

ject of euthanasia, mercy killings, or other types of wrongdoing.

Subsequently, Mr. Goldberg explained that the "administrative reason" which led to the firing of Mr. Powers was an obscene letter he had written his superiors. The letter was received by the young respiratory technician's supervisor. "We had a certified graphologist determine that samples of Powers's handwriting and the writing in the letter were the same." Explained Mr. Goldberg: "It was an allegation on our part. We did provide him with an opportunity to have his handwriting reexamined, but he never came to the meeting." The letter, dated May 11, 1984, was a poorly written diatribe, laced with foul language and signed from "the people in respiratory."

But despite the obscene letter and the sexual misbehavior assaults on Powers' work record, Defense Attorney Weiss painted an entirely different picture of Powers: "He's a very shy boy who seems to me to be harmless, and he has a pleasant personality."

Apart from the letter that led to his dismissal, there was never any indication during Powers's stint at the Sherman Oaks hospital that he had a potential for violence. There was nothing about him that could have put him in the "walking time bomb" category, argued hospital authorities. His job there was similar to that of nursing attendant—an entry-level position with an hourly wage ranging from $5.85 to $7.84. His salary level was equal to pay for laboratory assistants, switchboard operators, staff secretaries, and payroll clerks.

The technical nature of his duties included oxygen-supply checks and the performance of intermittent positive pressure-breathing treatments that help patients breathe more freely by use of a respirator. "If there were any problems in the course of his professional duties, they would be in the area of communicating with patients," said hospital spokesman Goldberg. "He was counseled on one or two occasions concerning his verbal communication with patients."

Sherman Oaks authorities were totally unaware Powers had gotten into hot water with the L.A. County health department for depraved behaviour toward patients in his previous job.

In fact, disclosures about Powers's unsatisfactory earlier work record at Olive View in Van Nuys were not available for public consumption until the Los Angeles *Daily News* got hold of a confidential memo prepared by L.A. County Health director Gates to county health officials on September 26, 1984—two weeks after his arrest for the deadly assault on baby Sarah.

The memo triggered off investigations into any kind of untoward behavior at every facility where Powers had been employed. Administrator of the Olive View facility in Van Nuys, Douglas D. Bagley, immediately announced he had launched "an internal audit to screen anything that might be relevant, which encompasses everything that happened at the hospital during the five months Powers worked here—from thefts to deaths that may have occurred at the hospital."

While Powers's principal job at Sherman Oaks was as a respiratory therapist, he had lesser duties during his five months at the county's Olive View center in Van Nuys. "He was nothing more than a Nursing Attendant One—a pan carrier—while he was at Van Nuys," said a hospital source. The same source reserved comment, however, on how a lowly "bedpan carrier" could have walked away from the hospital facing no criminal charges after molesting four of the patients under the care of the facility.

Another bizarre incident cost Powers another job, this time at Van Nuys Community Hospital. This was early in his career, back in 1981, and his duties there were very mundane. He had to serve meals, help bathe patients, and change bed pans. Hospital spokesman Ron Rider said of Powers: "He had high concern for the patients he worked with and was meticulous in fulfilling his job duties."

But after a strange incident in March 1981, Powers and the hospital went their different ways. "We found that he was stockpiling patient personal-hygiene items such as combs, brushes, and toothpaste in the patients' rooms," said Rider. "There was never any indication he was stealing any of it. Whenever he'd order from central supply, he would order two or three of the items and just keep them in patients' rooms." When told of a

217

hospital administration inquiry into the situation, Powers apparently became very upset. He did not show up for work for a couple of days; the hospital called his home. A woman answered the phone to say he had taken a job elsewhere.

The Sherman Oaks investigation began with the exhumation of three elderly women patients, Viola Ames, 78, Victoria Rose, 72, and Fannie Talbot, 95. Tissue samples from the three women were sent for testing at the Center for Human Toxicology at the University of Utah, the same hospital that provided the evidence against hospital serial killer Robert Diaz. These were the tests that proved inconclusive.

Powers denied ever confessing to the crime, and pleaded not guilty when he eventually came to trial on the Baby Sarah case. More serious charges of attempted murder of the baby and assault with intent to cause her great bodily injury had been dropped. Van Nuys Superior Court Commissioner Alan B. Haber found him guilty, after a ten-day trial without a jury, of assault with a deadly weapon, unlawfully administering medication, and endangering the girl's life.

Deputy District Attorney Michelle Rosenblatt successfully argued that Powers had injected Baby Sarah with a potentially lethal dose of Lidocaine in an attempt "to get a little bit of the glory; he was looking for recognition as the saviour of a baby."

Defense Attorney Weiss attempted to convince the judge that the mistake had been made by an emergency-room doctor at Northridge Hospital, not Powers. Physicians at the hospital, he contended, had mistakenly administered the baby Lidocaine—and then conspired to frame Powers. "I'm not sure whether this case should be called the Powers case, or the Northridge Hospital coverup," argued Weiss.

Weiss also submitted the argument that Powers had, in fact, saved the infant's life, pointing to doctors' testimony that the child would have died without a plastic airway Powers inserted in her throat before rushing her to the hospital when she lost consciousness.

Doctors also testified that the baby was in critical condition, her blood containing more than twenty times the normal dosage of Lidocaine which would be administered to an adult to correct irregular heart rhythms.

Tears in his eyes, Powers held his face in his hands and sobbed as Commissioner Haber sentenced him to the maximum sentence of five years' imprisonment on July 10, 1985.

Baby Sarah's father, twenty-five-year-old Brian, an employee with a San Fernando Valley moving company, and his twenty-eight-year-old wife Maria, were satisfied with the verdict. "Maybe he wanted to be a hero, but if he wanted to experiment, he should have bought a chemistry set," said the girl's father. Now twenty-months old, their daughter had spent five weeks in the hospital, running up forty thousand dollars in medical bills, which had been met thanks to state medical benefits, insurance, and a trust fund made up of donations.

Mr. Mathews said he and his wife had tried not to get too bitter about Powers after the attack on their baby. "We are not real mad at him, saying 'Kill him! Kill him!' What would that accomplish? I forgive the guy. We do pray for Randy," said Mr. Mathews.

"If we were to get too involved in this case, then we would be taking our minds away from our main concern—the child. We don't want our children growing up to be mad at the world," he said. Added his wife: "I do feel bad for Randy's mother. And as far as he's concerned, there is certainly something that needs to be taken care of in his life. I hope he's never allowed to do this to anyone else. I'm just glad my daughter is alive."

Northridge Hospital's prognosis for baby Sarah's complete recovery after her twenty-nine-day stay as a VIP patient was more than encouraging. "She is a very active little one. She likes to run around in her walker, and our nurses had a tough time keeping up with her," said Northridge spokeswoman Ann Bethel. "She has really bounced back. I don't think people expected that much of a recovery so quickly."

The Lidocaine drug, with which Powers injected the baby, turned out to have been stolen from Queen of Angels Hospital in Hollywood, another L.A.-area medical facility where job-hopping Powers had worked, according to police. But there was further bad news from Queen of Angels hospital officials—six patients who had been under Powers's care at the hospital had died in suspicious circumstances. Two deaths that occurred on August 9, 1984, occurred within ten minutes of each other. Details of all the deaths had been passed on to D.A. Philibosian's fast-growing dossier on the shy but personable Powers.

During his term in custody waiting trial on the Baby Sarah charges, Powers—described by his brother as "an aspiring physician"—remained an enigma to investigators. He had originally told police he was guilty of the assault on the baby. And on the question of hospital deaths and the related flurry of exhumations, he chose to let attorney Weiss do the talking. On the advice of Weiss, he refused to be interviewed about the controversy that surrounded him.

People were curious about this strange, introverted man. Officials at hospitals where he had worked and had been fired or quit described him as a "quiet employee" whose "only problem was communication with patients." He was also described as "meticulous," with "high concern for the patients he worked with."

Nor did Defense Attorney Weiss waver in his praise of the accused, even at the height of the alleged homicide investigations. Weiss commented on the little Sarah case: "This is a case where he was acting in an emergency situation. Perhaps he went beyond the call of duty and his expertise. But I don't think he intentionally hurt anyone, nor does his past indicate there is anything of this nature."

There was, however, no question at all that Hawaiian-born Powers harbored an obsession to be a doctor. As his brother said: "All he ever does is study . . . he wants to become a doctor." A neighbor in Hesperia Street, Encino, John Clerique, confirmed Powers's obsession. In fact, said Clerique, everyone on the block thought Powers was a paramedic.

A few years before his name hit the headlines, Power amazed family and neighbors as he raced out of his home with a first-aid kit to administer caring medical attention to a dog that had been injured in a dog fight in the street. "He seemed to know what he was doing. He looked real professional," remembered one observer.

Powers wrote his own bizarre footnote to the story of his decline and fall from the health-care field not too long after his release from prison on the assault conviction. Although he had been decertified as a health-care worker, Powers surfaced again in October 1989, as Randy Kato. He had legally changed his name and falsified an application to obtain a new emergency technicians' certificate. He was working as a volunteer in a Valencia hospital, until a nurse recognized him and informed authorities.

After further investigation by police and the Los Angeles County Department of Health Services, Kato's second license was revoked. Health department investigator Larry Smith reassured the public that Powers would never have slipped through the security net if he hadn't changed his name to Kato. "He falsified his application," said Smith. "We have a flag on Randy Powers . . . that name wouldn't have gotten through. It would have come up in our files."

Ironically, it is unlikely Powers, aka Kato, will ever have to answer any penalty for sneakily trying to resurrect his career. On his reapplication he had denied ever having had a license revoked before or having ever been convicted of any kind of defense. These new facts were released to the Los Angeles district attorney's office, where Powers was not exactly an unknown. But no charges were to be filed against him, announced Deputy District Attorney Robert W. Dawson. Not even a misdemeanor charge, said Mr. Dawson. Apparently the application that Powers falsified neglected to state that falsifying information was a punishable offense.

Again, Powers's behavior ran true to form. Interviewed by authorities, he maintained his private posture and gave them minimal information. As Randy Kato, he acknowledged he had previously used the name Randy Powers. He agreed to accept, without appeal, the second revocation of his emergency medical technician's certification.

According to health department records, Powers applied under his new name for his second certificate on May 24, 1989 – just three days after the expiration of his parole from prison. The health department issued him a new license less than a month later.

His plans were rumbled in August 1989, after a nurse at Henry Mayo Newhall Memorial Hospital in Valencia contacted L.A. police detective Phil Quartararo. Quartararo said the nurse contacted him because he was the investigator in the Baby Sarah case five years earlier. She told him that Powers, now calling himself Kato, had been accepted as a volunteer worker at the hospital.

Quartararo's inquiries showed Powers had been released from prison December 27, 1987, and completed parole five months later. While he was on parole, he applied at the county clerk's office to have his name changed from Zelaan Escott Powers to Randy Kato.

"I have gone by the name Randy for most of my life," his application for a name change reads. "I prefer the name Randy Kato. The change is not for the purpose of misleading creditors, or any other persons." Detective Quartararo said that Powers, or Kato, who was then living with his mother, completed a 152-hour emergency medical technician's instructional program at College of the Canyons in Valencia, prior to successfully applying for a license which, in effect, allowed him to offer treatments involving basic life support in hospitals and other locations.

"I was shocked that he could have obtained another certificate after what he had done to that little girl," observed Detective Quartararo.

A copy of his application shows that he checked a box marked "No" following a question asking if the applicant had been convicted of a crime in the previous ten years. Another question, asking if he had ever been the subject of a decertification disciplinary action was also checked "No."

Known as Kato, Powers began working as a volunteer at the Valencia hospital that summer, while applying for a full-time emergency medical technician position there. He was let go and his application rejected when he was revealed as Powers, said the detective.

A spokeswoman for the Valencia hospital, Caroline H. Korth, cited hospital privacy rules and refused to comment on Powers, aka Kato. A spokeswoman for the local College of the Canyons also refused to discuss Powers because school policy forbade releasing any information about a student.

Powers's reappearance on the hospital scene prompted more questions about the possible hospital homicides that focused suspicion on the young therapist back in 1985. Confirming that investigation, Deputy District Attorney Brian R. Kelberg, head of the office's medical-legal department, added: "The demise of these patients is not what one would have expected given the nature of their illnesses."

But none of the bodies exhumed and examined in 1985 showed evidence of drug injections. However, stressed Mr. Kelberg, the investigation has never been officially closed. Samples of tissue from the exhumed corpses had been preserved so they could be retested one day in the future when better medical research technology becomes available.

"We exhausted all recognized and acceptable toxicological studies, but there are certain drugs which can be lethal . . . which are not presently detectable," Mr. Kelberg said. "We have not closed our investigation because technology may produce additional tests that may be relevant."

THIRTEEN

Donald Harvey:
Poison PN

A grotesque sixteen-year killing spree through hospitals and nursing homes in Eastern Kentucky and Southern Ohio that may have claimed the lives of more than fifty victims ended the same way it had begun—by curious chance.

Forty-four-year-old John Powell was a husky, physically active man who worked as a plumber and welder at the General Electric plant, and was a diligent "Mr. Fixit" at the home he shared with his wife, teenage son, and two teenage stepdaughters. When he wasn't at the plant or energetically puttering around his home busying himself tiling the kitchen, enclosing the porch, or putting in new flower boxes, he liked to roar away on his motorcycle for a relaxing ride.

He owned a motorcycle helmet but didn't like to wear it on hot days. His helmet was off one day in July 1986, a sultry midsummer scorcher in Cincinnati, when his bike and a car collided. Powell was thrown to the pavement and struck his head. The injured factory worker was rushed unconscious to Drake Memorial Hospital where doctors and nurses worked desperately to save his life. The skillful emergency treatment kept him alive for months, but his brain had been terribly damaged and he sunk into a deep coma from which he never recovered. On March 7, 1987, he was found dead in his bed by

224

a nurse's aide.

Early the next morning, Powell's body was stretched out on its back on the cold stainless-steel slab of an examining table for what was expected to be a routine autopsy. In Ohio, as well as in many other states, the law requires autopsies on the bodies of anyone who is believed to have died an unnatural death, either by accident, suicide, or homicide. Determining the exact cause of death of traffic victims can be important steps in establishing legal liability.

Dr. Lee Lehman, Hamilton County (Cincinnati) deputy coroner and senior pathologist, was selected to perform the autopsy, and from all appearances it promised to be as routine as most of the more than six-hundred others he had carried out. With practiced expertise, the skilled pathologist leaned over the cadaver and neatly sliced open the chest cavity. As he began to inspect the lungs, Dr. Lehman recognized the telltale signs of severe pneumonia, a not uncommon condition among patients who are seriously ill and spend long periods of inactivity in bed. The presence of pneumonia appeared to bear out a finding of death from natural causes. Dr. Lehman recalled, sometime later, that he was about to enter that information in his journal. But autopsies require that all major organs be checked, and the pathologist continued the autopsy, opening the stomach. Almost immediately he recognized the unmistakable, acrid odor of cyanide.

Cyanide was the poison that the Reverend Jim Jones dropped in Kool-Aid to snuff out the lives of more than eleven hundred of his followers during the Peoples' Church tragedy in Guyana in November 1978. A form of the poison, known as Zyklon B, was used in Nazi gas chambers during WW II to eliminate Jews, Gypsies, Communists, homosexuals, and others considered to be enemies of the state.

When cyanide is breathed or swallowed, it prevents oxygen from being distributed by the body. The body's cells are unable to utilize the oxygen they have absorbed and they cease to function. This shuts down the portion of the brain that controls breathing, and victims smother as surely as if they had a pillow pressed over their face or were caught in the constricting coils of a giant anaconda.

And it is a favorite poison of suicides and murderers. Suicides choose it because it is swift and deadly efficient. A crystalline powder that is present in some seeds such as wild cherry pits, the barest taste can kill a healthy, grown man in mere minutes. It is a handy murder tool for the same reasons, and has the added appeal of being almost undetectable in the bodies of victims after embalming, since embalming fluid destroys the substance.

Due to genetic factors, only some twenty to forty percent of the population can smell the poison. By chance, Dr. Lehman was one of those who had the right olfactory sensitivity to the odor. In addition to his fortuitous olfactory abilities, the pathologist was not only a medical doctor but possessed a Ph.D. in chemistry from Indiana University as well, and had previously worked in laboratory settings with cyanide. He knew from experience what it smelled like.

Described by experts as resembling the smell of bitter almonds, the odor was unmistakable. And once recognized, there were other signs. The blood was a particularly deep scarlet, and there was evidence of corrosion of the stomach lining.

But pathologists, like police and prosecutors, are not quick to make accusations without backup evidence. They are methodical about collecting information and although there were strong indications that deliberately, or inadvertently, Powell had been poisoned, there was no immediate outcry. Samples of the former patient's blood and stomach contents were analyzed in the coroner's laboratory to check for toxins. The analysis confirmed that a lethal dose of cyanide was present in both the stomach and blood.

Still, the medical sleuths were unsatisfied and sent the samples to an independent laboratory for analysis. The laboratory's report was negative. There was no finding of cyanide in the samples. Perplexed, the coroner's chemists ran the tests again, and for a second time there was a positive indication of the presence of cyanide. The independent laboratory was contacted again and asked to repeat their tests on the samples. This time the laboratory confirmed the findings of the coroner's experts.

Spokesmen for the independent laboratory blamed equipment failure for the negative finding on their initial tests.

With the suspicions of cyanide poisoning confirmed by the latest tests, coroner's authorities ordered autopsies on the bodies of everyone who had died at Drake in the several days that had elapsed since Powell's death. Although no evidence of additional foul play was turned up, the results of Powell's autopsy were reported to city police and to administrators at Drake, and a full-fledged investigation was launched.

As part of the inquiry, police officers began the awesome task of interviewing the 750 men and women employed on a full- and part-time basis at Drake, as well as doctors, members of Powell's family, and anyone else who might have had access to the factory worker while he was hospitalized. Many of these questioned were given lie detector tests. Among those asked to submit a polygraph testing were hospital employees who had worked on Powell's ward. One of these was a polite, soft-spoken, slender nursing assistant named Donald Harvey.

The aide missed his appointment for the test, and was rescheduled. Everyone else scheduled for tests had taken them and passed. But when the day for Harvey's rescheduled test arrived, he flatly refused to submit to interrogation while hooked up to the device. Instead, he surprised investigators by nervously admitting in a verbal statement recorded on videotape that he had injected cyanide into a gastric tube hooked up to Powell. Harvey was arrested on a charge of aggravated murder.

The murder suspect was the same nurse's aide who had discovered Powell dead in his bed. Suddenly he was the focus of an investigation that would broaden and accelerate until he was exposed as one of America's most ruthless and prolific modern-day serial killers—a heartless monster who preyed on the helpless because he liked the feeling of power.

The morose mountain boy had told friends and co-workers that he sought a career in health care because he wanted to help others. But years later, after the deaths of scores of patients he had attended, as well as several acquaintances outside his workplace, detractors would dispute that. He was attracted to jobs in hospitals, nursing homes, and morgues because of a twisted compulsion to kill, or to witness death, they would insist.

Harvey had had an unhappy childhood. He was a Mama's boy, Grandmama's boy, and teachers' pet. But his scrappy peers near the isolated backwoods hamlet of Island Creek where he was raised considered him to be a sissy because he preferred to play with girls instead of boys. He didn't take his own part in the rough-and-tumble play of small boys, and would cry or run away instead of fighting when he was challenged. And he was the defenseless target of sexual abuse by an uncle and by a neighbor that began before he was old enough to attend junior high school. The abuse continued for years.

But he was considered to be a nice boy and a good neighbor. As a schoolboy he was polite to his teachers, did his homework faithfully, and was an honor student before dropping out of classes in the ninth grade. Throughout his childhood and early teenage years, he faithfully attended the Walnut Grove Baptist Church with his family. And as a young adult, whenever he was home he paid courtesy calls on neighbors who had been kind to him, stopped in to visit with his former teachers, and amiably chattered for hours with his family while watching television game shows. If he knew poverty growing up in the mist-shrouded hills and mountains, he was no different from most of his neighbors, who shared the Harvey family's hardscrabble existence.

Harvey was born at Mercy Hospital in Hamilton, Ohio, on April 15, 1952, to seventeen-year-old Goldie Jane Harvey and thirty-two-year-old Ray Harvey. Ray had a job as a machinist's helper with the Mosler Safe Company when his first son was born. But soon after Donald's arrival, the family moved back to Island Creek, about midway between Sturgeon and the Owsley County seat of Booneville. Donald's sister, Patricia, was born there in 1958. Two years later, his brother, Anthony, was born.

There isn't much except poverty, misery, and a handful of poor families in Island Creek. A single paved two-lane road runs along the creek that the settlement takes its name from, and every so often a clapboard and tarpaper house is nestled among the tree-lined and rocky hollows and hills.

228

Ray Harvey was blind in one eye, a condition that might have contributed to his difficulty in holding jobs. Like most of his neighbors, he knew a bit about farming, but the meager patches of bottom land suitable for crops were in such short supply that the profession couldn't be counted on for a living. He worked awhile on a power-line construction job, but had difficulty keeping up with the other men and was laid off. Mostly the family barely subsisted. Sometimes there was no food at all in the house.

It was during those hungry years that Donald later claimed he was sexually abused, first by an uncle, then by his neighbor. When the boy walked up the road to the neighbor's house, the man would give him food and allow him to sleep there. The price of such kindness was sex.

As he approached his teenage years, young Donald's relationship with both his parents disintegrated. There were bitter disagreements with his mother, whom he later accused of treating him more like a brother than a son. And there was serious friction between him and his father, who blamed himself for the boy's blossoming homosexuality. Donald stayed away from his home as much as he could, camping at the pedophile neighbor's home or helping out the elderly parents of another neighbor, with cooking and other household chores in exchange for food and a place to sleep.

Harvey was seventeen in 1969 when he traveled about thirty-five miles southwest to London, Kentucky, at the edge of the Daniel Boone National Forest to visit his grandfather who was a patient at the Marymount Hospital. During the visit, he was befriended by a young orderly. Less than a year later, after Harvey had turned eighteen, the orderly helped him get a job at the hospital. He had barely settled in to life on his own when he became involved in a homosexual affair with a youth who worked in a local funeral home. And almost as soon as he had begun his new job, patients at Marymount Hospital began dying in unusual numbers. Especially on Harvey's ward. The emotional strain began to show.

Early in 1971, Harvey broke into a neighbor's apartment in London and stole a coat and a small amount of money. Then he went to another apartment and set a fire. Much later, he would say the fire represented his first clumsy effort at suicide. He was arrested the same night, and eventually fined fifty dollars on a reduced charge of petty theft, and released to custody of his parents. Part of the court's sentencing agreement called for the disturbed young hospital attendant to submit to outpatient treatment at a mental health center in Frankfort, Kentucky.

Harvey's father didn't know what to do about his troubled, effeminate son. Desperate to find help, he urged him to join the military. A hitch in the armed services might make a man out of the boy, the elder Harvey reasoned. So Donald joined the Air Force. His first duty assignment after recruit training was at Travis Air Force Base, a few miles outside San Francisco. The young military recruit quickly found his way to Castro Street in the center of San Francisco's bustling homosexual community. He took two drug overdoses before he was released from the Air Force on March 9, 1972. The honorable discharge cited a "character/behavior disorder."

Harvey returned to Island Creek in disgrace. Family members said they were ashamed of him. He took another overdose of pills, but survived and was transported by ambulance to the Veterans Administration Hospital in Lexington, Kentucky, where he stayed in the psychiatric ward for four months. He was treated as a psychiatric outpatient for another eighteen months after that.

During his stay in Lexington, Harvey took a job at the Cardinal Hill Hospital. Then he moved on to a job as a ward clerk at St. Lukes Hospital in Fort Thomas, Kentucky; to Christ Hospital across the Ohio river in Cincinnati; then in 1975, to the Cincinnati Veterans Administration Medical Center. For eight years, he worked as an autopsy assistant in the VA hospital's morgue. Even when he was off duty, he liked to hang around and watch as autopsies were performed.

His proximity to death apparently satisfied his homicidal urges during the near decade he worked at the morgue, and Harvey would later insist that he killed no one during that period. But in 1983 he was transferred, and patients began dying

230

in unusually large numbers on the wards where he worked as a nurse's assistant. And other people outside the hospital who were associated with him and were aware of his fascination with death began to sicken, or suddenly die.

Nearly four years after becoming a morgue attendant, Harvey began a long-term love affair with a Cincinnati cosmetologist, Carl Hoeweler. But Harvey couldn't stay faithful for long, and sneaked away for frequent hit-and-run affairs with a series of lovers he met prowling gay bars, public parks, restrooms, and other popular homosexual hangouts. And he fretted and worried that Hoeweler was also cheating. They quarreled, and Harvey began slipping small doses of arsenic into the cosmetologist's food. He later explained that he didn't want to kill his lover, just give him enough poison to make him sick so that he would stay at home.

Unlike cyanide, arsenic is both odorless and colorless. And it takes longer to kill. Once known by the sardonic nickname, "inheritance powder" because of its frequent use to dispatch unwanted relatives, arsenic kills by dehydration. Victims become deathly sick with stomach pains, diarrhea, and sometimes vomiting. The ratio of salts to water in the body is critically unbalanced, and shock sets in. Centuries ago, in Italy, arsenic was favored by the mistress of poison, Lucretia Borgia and other members of her murderous family. Today it is favored by wives who prefer homicide to divorce for ridding themselves of unwanted husbands.

Small doses can be survived, however, and a tolerance can even be built up to the poison. Harvey's poisoned lover sickened and was treated for a variety of ailments while he was being systematically fed arsenic. Doctors treated him for heart disease, then for ulcers, and other apparent ailments. Although none of the doctors who treated him appeared to have had any suspicions that he was being slowly poisoned, the cosmetologist survived. Throughout the ordeal, Harvey posed as the compassionate Angel of Mercy who loyally stood by and nursed him back to health.

Helen Metzger, an insurance company employee and neighbor who rented an apartment from Hoeweler and quarreled

231

with him over utility bills and repairs, wasn't as fortunate. Harvey sprinkled arsenic into the whipped cream topping on a piece of pie he gave her, and she died a short time later at Jewish Hospital in Cincinnati. Harvey was one of the pallbearers at her funeral.

The more Harvey quarreled with Hoeweler and returned home unsatisfied from new sexual liaisons, the more disturbed and paranoid he became. He turned on Hoeweler's father, Henry. And on May 1, 1983, he doctored some pudding with a dose of arsenic at Providence Hospital where the elder Hoeweler was being treated. The eighty-two-year-old man died in terrible agony. Harvey later noted that he was fond of his lover's father, but decided that it would be better for him and the family if his suffering was ended.

Then Harvey began slipping small doses of the poison to Hoeweler's mother, Margaret. He resented her, and considered her to be a meddlesome snoop. For nearly two years, she was troubled with stomach pains and diarrhea as the slow poisoning continued. But like her son, she survived.

In January 1984, Harvey sneaked a lab specimen infected with hepatitis that he had stolen from the VA Medical Center into the iced tea of a woman who worked as a beautician for Hoeweler. She was a close friend, but he was jealous of her. Though she was hospitalized, she recovered from the incident.

Despite the constant friction, Harvey remained protective of his roommate, and when Hoeweler quarreled with an eighty-one-year-old neighbor about a utility bill, the homicidal orderly stepped in to permanently settle the matter. The old man, Edgar Wilson, lived in a second-floor apartment of a building owned by Hoeweler. When Wilson realized he was paying the hot-water bill for both apartments, he tangled with his landlord—who lived in the downstairs apartment with Harvey.

A few days later, Wilson mentioned to Harvey that he had a bad stomachache. Feigning concern, the nurse's aide gave his elderly neighbor a bottle of an over-the-counter liquid stomach medicine which he had laced with arsenic. Wilson became deathly sick. He vomited and suffered terribly from diarrhea, but he didn't die. So Harvey gave him a second bottle of medicine laced with arsenic, and Wilson was soon admitted to Providence Hospital in Cincinnati. He died shortly after. An autopsy at the hospital indicated that Wilson had succumbed to kidney failure, which could have been the result of natural causes. The presumed cause of death seemed believable, because he had previously suffered from kidney ailments.

After Wilson died, Harvey killed the old man's dog with another dose of arsenic.

More than a year later, Harvey fatally poisoned another acquaintance by doctoring his pudding with arsenic. The victim was a close friend, James Peluso, of Newport, Kentucky, who operated Peluso's Market, and whose brother was a former mayor of the Cincinnati suburb.

Hoeweler was not aware that Wilson had been murdered, but a few months after the old man's death, he was arrested and convicted on a charge unrelated to the homicide: public indecency. Hoeweler blamed Harvey for setting him up. Their association had come full circle from a deeply caring relationship to one of distrust and spite.

In July 1985, VA hospital police stopped Harvey on a loading dock as he was leaving work and searched a gym bag he was carrying. Inside they found a snub-nosed, .38-caliber revolver, VA textbooks, books on the occult, needles and syringes, a cocaine spoon, and slide-mounted samples of human tissue. Harvey was fined fifty dollars for introducing a firearm onto federal property. But Hospital officials declined to file more serious charges.

Harvey claimed much later that he suspected Hoeweler of planting the gun in his bag to get him fired. The claim wasn't taken seriously by authorities, but regardless, the relationship between the two men appeared to be irretrievably damaged. Harvey had lost his job, and his personal life seemed to be collapsing around him. He began avoiding old friends, drinking heavily, and stepped up his trolling of gay hangouts, picking up one one-night stand after another. He confided to an acquaintance that he hoped he would be infected with AIDS so that he could pass it on to Hoeweler.

By early 1986, after months of friction and agony, the tormented relationship ended for good. But in February, Harvey also found another job as a nurse's aide at one of Cincinnati's leading hospitals—Drake Memorial.

During his confession to Powell's murder, Harvey claimed that he killed the GE welder, who had lain helplessly in a coma for eight months, as an act of mercy. A few days later after conferring with an attorney, he entered a plea in court of not guilty by reason of insanity. And he informed court authorities that he had AIDS. He was tested for the disease, and the results were negative. But he remained depressed, and fretted that people would think he was a monster. His jailers put him under suicide watch.

Meanwhile, administrators at Drake, a 446 bed, county-owned hospital for chronically ill and long-term care patients confined to beds or wheelchairs, reacted with horror at the possibility that an employee was suspected of murdering someone in their care. Hospital spokesmen quickly assured law-enforcement authorities and the news media that the murder was an isolated case. But Harvey's apparent bad luck with patients hadn't gone unnoticed by other nurses at Drake Memorial, and even before the autopsy disclosed Powell's poisoning, they had begun to whisper that the young aide was a Death Angel. It seemed that Harvey was almost always around shortly before patients died. And they shuddered and recalled with near disbelief how they had shrugged off his tasteless jokes when patients died on his ward. Several times, he had left the rooms of patients found dead in their beds, grinned, and told other employees: "Well, I just took care of another one." In the double room occupied by Powell, six patients died within a few months. Patients in the room were assigned to Harvey during his shift.

The suspicious nurses approached their superiors and asked that some of the earlier deaths of Harvey's patients be investigated. The requests were refused. So the nurses took their suspicions to Pat Minarcin, news anchorman for WCPO-TV, Channel 9, the CBS outlet in Cincinnati. The employees had no eyewitnesses, but they had collected an impressive array of circumstantial evidence that was difficult for any seasoned journalist to ignore. The death rate on Harvey's ward had climbed

234

alarmingly; patients not considered critically ill had suddenly died; and the suspicious orderly was usually around shortly before the deaths were discovered, sometimes making the discovery himself as he had in the Powell case.

Minarcin was intrigued by the possibilities that the situation at Drake Memorial was indeed much worse than authorities there were willing to admit, and began digging into the story. The news anchor teamed up with Executive Producer Ed Wilson to launch an exhaustive in-depth investigation.

For more than two months, the determined news hounds tracked down leads, talked to Drake employees, families of patients who had died at the hospital, and to a glittering array of local and national experts on everything from serial murder to poison and suffocation. They collected bulging files of documents.

On June 23, Minarcin disclosed on the air in a special 6 P.M., half-hour news report that the investigation had turned up twenty-three mysterious or questionable deaths of patients at Drake Memorial while Harvey was employed there as a nurse's assistant. The startling broadcast was presented without interruptions from commercials, weather, or sports. And it landed on Cincinnati like a tornado, churning up an emotional mixture of outrage, fear, and embarrassment.

At last the story was out in the open, and residents learned that a remorseless serial killer had apparently been let loose to prey on helpless patients in at least one Cincinnati hospital, perhaps more. And there was no telling how many victims he might have claimed. Reaction was immediate. Within forty-eight-hours, Hamilton County Commissioners met with County Prosecutor Art Ney and asked for a special grand jury investigation of the Drake hospital deaths. Ney asked WCPO to share its information and sources with him. Station managers released a transcript of the broadcast.

A week after the report, Harvey's attorney, William P. Whalen, Jr., approached Ney and advised that the former hospital orderly might have information about additional deaths. Whalen hadn't asked his client about committing other murders at Drake until he was approached by Minarcin with questions.

235

On July 6, the special investigating grand jury was sworn in, and eventually listened to six weeks of testimony and watched hours of police video tapes detailing a shocking tale of serial murder. Law-enforcement officers, family members of suspected victims, and officials and nurses from Drake paraded grim-faced and silent past news reporters into the grand jury room. Two days after the jurors were sworn in, Ney, Whalen, and Harvey agreed to a deal: Harvey would confess and plead guilty to the murders he had committed at Drake in return for Ney's promise not to seek the death penalty. A few days later, law enforcement authorities began exhuming remains of the homicidal orderly's suspected victims.

Despite Harvey's ready admissions, in Ohio, confessions alone do not comprise sufficient evidence to qualify a killer for the death penalty. Corroborating evidence is required, and investigators had found the necessary backup in only a single case. Prosecutors wanted Harvey behind bars and out of circulation to stay, so they reluctantly agreed to the deal.

On August 19, barely four months after his arrest, he stood next to his attorney in a courtroom jammed with a standing-room-only crowd and calmly pleaded guilty to twenty-four murders in Hamilton county, including those of twenty-one patients at Drake Memorial. Moments before Harvey and his entourage entered the courtroom, a huge black bat fluttered along the outside corridors, alarming spectators and adding one more macabre touch to an already macabre case.

Inside the courtroom, while recommending the maximum sentences available, Ney told the court that Harvey wasn't a mercy killer, and he wasn't insane. "He killed because he liked to kill," the prosecutor declared. "This man is sane, competent, but is a compulsive killer . . . He builds up tension in his body, so he kills people." Harvey was a man with "a compulsion to kill like someone else might have a compulsion for malted milk or cold beer," Ney said. Hamilton County Common Pleas Judge William S. Mathews pronounced sentences of twenty years to life on each murder charge, with three of the sentences to run consecutively and the others concurrent. An additional seven to twenty-five-year term was ordered for the attempted murder charges, and an eight-to-fifteen-year sentence was ordered on a charge of felonious assault, all to be served concurrently. Harvey could conceivably have been sentenced to as many as 2,225 years in prison, but imposition of the consecutive life sentences meant that he would not become eligible for parole for sixty-years—when he was ninety-five.

"If I could have found one more body, I would have put him in the chair," the prosecutor told reporters after the sentencing.

Relatives of Harvey's victims were also frustrated at circumstances which forced acceptance of the plea bargain that spared the killer's life. And many of them were vocal about their bitterness and anger over the convoluted legal system that permitted him to thumb his nose at the death penalty.

"I think he deserves worse than the death penalty," said Betty Kissell, daughter of one of the poison victims. "I think every family member here today would like to see him injected with arsenic, rat poison, cleaning fluid, and everything and die a slow, painful death.

But Harvey's life had been spared, even though the dreadful list of slayings, recited during a grueling, sometimes rambling nine-and-a-half-hour videotaped confession disclosed that the killings were as methodically planned and executed as they were ruthless. The confessed serial killer's memory was spotty. He recalled a few names, but not others. And although his recollection of dates was poor, his memory improved when it came to recalling the method of killing his victims.

Details provided by the suspect, combined with hospital records and other information developed by investigators, were sufficient, however, to permit eventual identification of the murder victims and the manner in which they died. When law-enforcement authorities searched his trailer home in Middletown, Ohio, about midway between Cincinnati and Dayton, they found a chilling roster of the names of seventeen victims scribbled on a scrap of brown paper and secreted behind a picture frame—exactly where Harvey had told them it would be.

Harvey even told his attorney of another patient he had fingered for death but who escaped. The patient was Raphael Giron, who was paralyzed from the neck down after allegedly shooting to death his former girlfriend, then firing a bullet into his own head. Giron, who was yet to be put on trial, was on Harvey's ward, and the aide said he had planned to kill him but never got the right opportunity.

The sentencing hearing marked the first time that many of the relatives heard the true story of how their loved ones had died. But as the prosecutor used a large chart of names and a pointer to establish the chronology of Harvey's murder binge, the confessed serial killer sat unmoved at the defense table, alternately smiling, chuckling, and picking at imaginary lint on his brown, double-breasted suit. Harvey chose a white shirt and clean white tennis shoes to go with the outfit.

Survivors of the dead were less blasé about the horror that had stolen their family members, and sobbed or clutched at damp handkerchiefs as, one by one, Ney relentlessly recounted the names, dates and manner-of-death listed on the grim roster.

Leon Nelson died when Harvey pressed a plastic bag and wet towel over his mouth and nose; Virgil Weddle, after rat poison was sprinkled into his dessert; Edward Schreibeis, when arsenic or cyanide was added to his orange juice; Robert Crockett, when cyanide was injected into intravenous tube; and Donald Clifford Barney, after Harvey injected cyanide in water into a feeding tube and administered another dose injected directly into his buttocks.

Ernest Frey died when a mixture of cyanide or arsenic was placed in a gastric tube; James Woods, Milton Canter, Roger Evans, Mose Thompson, Odas Day, and Claborn L. Kendrick, each of a deadly mixture of cyanide and water administered through gastric tubes. William Collins, Cleo Fish, and Margaret Kuckro died when Harvey spiked their orange juice with cyanide. And Albert Buehlmann was killed when a mix of cyanide and water was put in his drink. Harvey held Buehlmann's head up to help him sip the deadly concoction.

Joseph Pike was given a fatal dose of a petroleum-based product used to clean tubes and colostomy bags in his orange juice; Hilda Leitz was killed the same way (after Harvey used all the cyanide he had to kill Powell); Leo Parker died after cyanide and water was slipped into his feeding bag; and Stella

238

Lemon died in another ward nearly a month after Harvey had dosed her with cyanide.

After the marathon confessions, Harvey was also named on four charges of attempted murder. The intended victims were named as Harold White, who was dosed with arsenic while a patient at Drake and later died at another hospital; John L. Oldenick, who was given arsenic on at least four occasions before he was transferred to a nursing home, then to Good Samaritan Hospital, where he died; Margaret Hoeweler; and the woman beautician.

Four days after sentencing for three of the homicides at Drake Memorial, Harvey pleaded guilty to the murder of a twenty-fifth victim. He admitted lacing Edgar Wilson's stomach medicine with fatal dosages of arsenic. It was okay for Harvey to quarrel with his lover, but he wouldn't stand for other people giving Hoeweller a hard time.

Assistant Hamilton County Prosecutor Joseph Deters responded to the latest admission by pointing out to the press that the Wilson slaying disproved Harvey's claims that he was a soft-hearted Death Angel who killed to end the suffering of the aged or critically ill.

"This should put the lie to Mr. Harvey's claim of being a mercy killer," the prosecutor charged. "What kind of mercy killing is it to kill someone over a dispute about hot water?"

Wilson's body was cremated shortly after his death, so authorities couldn't check it for traces of arsenic. But the second bottle of stomach medicine given to him by Harvey was found in a cabinet of the apartment still half full. An initial laboratory analysis failed to turn up any poison in the compound, but a second more sophisticated test found traces of arsenic.

Legal authorities had the evidence they needed to back up the confession and obtain another murder indictment from a Hamilton County Grand Jury. Justice Mathews ordered a new life sentence for the Wilson slaying, and stipulated that it be served concurrently with the earlier terms.

Responding to the criticism from relatives of the deal that spared Harvey's life, Ney pointed out that prosecutors might not have been able to obtain convictions if the cases went to trial because there was a lack of substantive evidence independent of the confessions tying him to the deaths. And there were no living witnesses.

Ney observed that the orderly's killing techniques made homicide difficult to detect during autopsies and nearly impossible after embalming. Exhumation of the bodies of ten of the suspected hospital victims yielded clues in only two instances. The prosecutor said the lack of backup evidence to follow up Harvey's confessions forced him to compromise his strong belief in the death penalty and accept the plea bargain in order to assure convictions.

Protected from the death penalty by his plea bargain, Harvey eventually confessed to committing fifty-seven hospital murders, the fatal poisoning of his friend's father, and the murders and attempted murders of other acquaintances over a sixteen-year period across two states. And during a shocking interview at the Hamilton County Justice Center with a reporter for the French magazine, *Paris Match,* he bragged that he would have continued killing if he hadn't been caught. But he added that he thought he would be able to control his urge to kill if he was released, and said he would like to begin a new career as a plumber because he enjoyed fixing things.

Harvey, with his attorney's concurrence, agreed to a jailhouse interview with Minarcin and claimed that all but two or three of the killings he was responsible for were crimes of compassion. Most of Harvey's victims were elderly or critically ill, and he said he felt sorry for them and wanted to end their misery. He boasted that many people believe in mercy killing, but unlike himself, don't have the nerve to act on their beliefs. "I thought I'd put them out of their misery, like I would hope someone would put me out of my misery," he said.

The prisoner also claimed that he studied case histories of his patients to help him select victims for the reputed mercy killings. But when the anchorman asked what exact criteria he used in determining if a patient was to live or die, he said he couldn't really explain. "It just had to be the right person, if they were close to dead," he stammered. "I can't really say why I picked them out. It just happened."

Harvey's dreadful litany of death had made him a much sought-after subject for interviews, and reporters from newspapers, television, and radio stations throughout the United States fought for access to the notorious serial killer. A major flap erupted in Cincinnati legal and media circles shortly after his arrest when a rumor circulated that the *New York Post* was preparing to put up two hundred thousand dollars bail for him in return for an exclusive jailhouse interview.

Assistant Prosecutor Deters approached Judge Mathews, and an unscheduled hearing was quickly convened. Deters asked that the bond established in the Powell case be immediately revoked. The judge complied. Harvey's attorney, Whalen, did not oppose the decision, and objected only to Deters' reference to his client as a danger to the community. As it turned out, the *Post* had never offered the bail/interview deal in the first place.

Harvey eventually did agree to another exclusive interview, however—with Bob MacKenzie of KTVU-TV, Channel 2 in San Francisco, a Fox Broadcasting Network affiliate. The confessed killer was familiar with the station from his days at Travis AFB and looked forward to appearing on the program. The wide-ranging interview was fleshed out with additional appearances by Harvey's mother, friends, relatives, and attorneys. The sixty-minute documentary was broadcast with the title, *Angel of Death*. Harvey listened attentively to the interviewers' questions before replying in calm, matter-of-fact detail, always taking care to paint himself as a compassionate mercy killer. He was pleased with the show.

Initially Harvey's unabashed recitation to law-enforcement authorities of his longterm blood spilling came in dribs and drabs. And he revealed that when he resumed killing after the murders at Marymount, he refined his homicidal techniques, generally abandoning suffocation for death by poison.

On August 20, Harvey admitted the murder of fifteen patients at the VA Medical Center. He told the Hamilton County Grand Jury about the VA slayings, but did not provide enough names or details to permit the return of indictments. A few weeks after his initial admission of killings at the VA center, Harvey remembered two additional slayings, hiking the total there to seventeen. The VA Medical Center is a U.S. government facility, and hospital authorities requested that a federal investigation be conducted. The FBI entered the case.

U.S. Air Force spokesmen confirmed that they were also looking into Harvey's possible activities at the Travis AFB Hospital in 1971 and 1972. Air Force officials became concerned after a job application he had completed surfaced in Kentucky. Harvey stated on the application that he had worked at the 185-bed David Grant Hospital, serving current and retired military personnel, while he was stationed at Travis.

But base spokesmen pointed out that they had no records placing Harvey on the hospital staff, and pinning down his claim on the application would be extremely difficult. Personnel records at the hospital are destroyed after three years, and because military personnel are transferred to new duty stations every year or two, it would be almost impossible to locate people who might have worked with him at the hospital there, the spokesman said.

Other inquiries about Harvey's whereabouts and activities were also received by investigators in Cincinnati and Kentucky, and from news organizations and law-enforcement agencies in Seattle and Chicago. Representatives of a police task force investigating a string of prostitute slayings in the Pacific Northwest known as the Green River killings that apparently began in 1982 and have claimed more than forty lives asked for information about Harvey. And police in Chicago investigating the deaths of seven people in the area from Tylenol pain medication laced with cyanide also expressed interested in Harvey's case.

There was no indication that Harvey was involved in either the baffling series of killings in Chicago or the Pacific Northwest. Most Ohio and Kentucky investigators indicated they believed Harvey was sincerely trying to remember and report all the killings he was responsible for. Lying could be fatal to him. His plea agreement called for him to be completely truthful in reporting all the deaths he was responsible for, not only in Cincinnati, but anywhere he killed. Accordingly, if police and prosecutors discovered a murder he hadn't confessed, he could

242

be tried for the crime and face the death penalty. The plea-bargain promise of no death penalty applied only to crimes he confessed to.

In a curious twist that provided new insight into the complexities of the serial killer's troubled mind, as well as his humble background, he disclosed another more surprising reason for sincerely attempting to dredge up the identities of all his victims. He appeared to be genuinely concerned that he might forget a name and thus be responsible for cheating survivors out of victims' compensation money they could claim from the state.

"He was quite upset, not about what happened today, but that the other names did not come out," Whalen said of his enigmatic client shortly after sentencing for the string of killings at Drake. Whalen noted that Harvey had fretted that some needy families of additional victims whose deaths he was responsible for might not be compensated.

The worst fears of authorities in Kentucky were realized when they were notified that the homicidal hospital worker had begun his killing ways at Marymount. In a statement given to Laurel County (Kentucky) Commonwealth Attorney Thomas Hardy at the Hamilton County Justice Center in Cincinnati, Harvey subsequently confessed to responsibility for thirteen deaths at the Catholic hospital owned by the Sisters of Charity of Nazareth. Journalists were told that two of the deaths may have been accidental.

Laurel county authorities and hospital officials had determined that seventy-two deaths occurred at Marymount while Harvey was working there. Prior to his confessions, none of them had been considered suspicious. But after his arrest and disclosure that he had begun killing while on staff at Marymount, medical records of all seventy-two deaths were forwarded to the Kentucky State Medical Examiner for review.

In chillingly frank remarks to journalists, Harvey's attorney added that the death toll in Kentucky might have been higher if his client hadn't failed in several attempted slayings.

Approximately two weeks later, Laurel County Commonwealth Attorney Thomas Handy accepted a plea bargain, and

243

Harvey pleaded guilty to eight counts of murder and one count of manslaughter in the deaths of nine patients at Marymount. Although he told prosecutors that he killed thirteen people at the Catholic hospital during 1970 and 1971, investigators could confirm only nine. Laurel Circuit Judge Lewis Hopper sentenced him to eight life sentences, plus twenty years. According to the agreement, his prison sentences in Kentucky would run concurrent with those in Ohio.

After the court proceedings, Harvey's mother, Goldy McKinney, spoke to reporters with tears in her eyes. "I'm sorry he did it. I'm sorry for the families . . . I love him, but if you commit a crime you've got to pay," she said.

"I wish I could unglue all this that has been done, but I can't."

Kentucky lawmen had hoped to dig up independent evidence to prove Harvey's guilt for the Marymount killings so that they could prosecute without a plea bargain. But although most of the people Harvey confessed to killing in Ohio were poisoned, he said he used less detectable methods on his earlier victims in Kentucky. So there appeared to be little to be gained by digging up suspected victims in the Bluegrass state to conduct toxicology tests. And Handy was blocked by psychiatrists and a judge in efforts to get a look at reports outlining Harvey's treatment at a mental health center in neighboring Knox County shortly after the Marymount deaths occurred. Psychiatrists complained that turning over the records would violate patient-doctor confidentiality. And the judge agreed.

Harvey got his plea bargain. And he insisted that the first killing at Marymount, as well as at least one other, was an accident caused by his inexperience. Speaking without apparent emotion, he calmly explained that he had been working at Marymount only a few weeks on June 22, 1970, when he mistakenly hooked a patient up to an oxygen tank that was nearly empty. When the oxygen ran out a few minutes later, the forty-two-year-old patient died. Instead of horrifying or depressing Harvey, however, the accident merely illustrated to him how easy it was for him to kill—and to cover up his tracks.

The orderly was fascinated, and exhilarated by the control he

244

had over the helpless men and women in his care. It was the power of life and death. And at least eight more times during the next approximate ten months he worked at Marymount, he chose death.

About three weeks after the first patient's death, Harvey slipped into the room of Eugene McQueen and pressed a pillow to his face until the helpless forty-three-year-old man suffocated.

Although he was seriously ill and flat on his back in a hospital bed, Ben H. Gilbert was a fighter. And as sick as he was, the feisty old man knew immediately that there was something wrong with the fidgety orderly assigned to help care for him. Gilbert didn't want the skinny mountain boy in his room, and they quarreled incessantly. The bad blood between them erupted in violence at one point when Gilbert angrily flung a bedpan in a roundhouse right that caught Harvey on the head and knocked him unconscious.

Harvey exacted a terrible revenge. He was deliberately rough with the old man, catheterized him frequently, and intentionally used tubes that were too large. Family members complained to hospital authorities once after Harvey inserted a catheter, causing Gilbert to scream in pain. A doctor confronted Harvey, and the frail, high-strung orderly became so upset that he deliberately broke a light bulb in the patient's room. But despite his bizarre behavior and pleas by Gilbert and members of his family to have Harvey replaced, the orderly was permitted to remain on the job. Harvey's outburst that led to the breaking of the lightbulb was unusual. The nasty, sadistic side of his personality usually surfaced only when he was alone with helpless patients. When doctors and other health-care professionals were around, the neatly attired young orderly was quiet, polite, and gave every indication of caring efficiency.

Late in July, Harvey was alone with Gilbert when he inserted a coat hanger through one of the catheter tubes and punctured the old man's bladder. The agonized patient hemorrhaged internally and died.

William Bowling was rushed to the emergency room at the hospital on August 3, barely able to breathe. He died after

245

Harvey hooked him to an oxygen tank and didn't turn it on. Sixty-four-year-old Maude Nichols was killed less than two weeks later when Harvey hooked her to an empty oxygen tank. Sixty-three-year-old Viola Wyan died the same way on November 4.

The holidays passed uneventfully at Marymount. Then on January 23, Harvey hooked Silas Butner to an empty oxygen tank. Minutes later, the sixty-two-year-old patient died struggling for breath. On January 25, the homicidal orderly suffocated eighty-four-year-old Maggie Rawlings with a pillow. The next day he cut off the oxygen supply of John Combs, and the sixty-eight-year-old patient died in agony soon after, unable to breathe.

The horrors disclosed at Marymount didn't go unnoticed in other Kentucky communities where Harvey had worked. But queries and more sophisticated investigations failed to turn up any evidence that he had killed in either Fort Thomas or in Lexington. Authorities at St. Lukes Hospital in Fort Thomas said his duties there did not involve patient contact, and that he had resigned voluntarily in 1975 after working about six months. In Lexington, officials at Cardinal Hill Hospital said he worked there for five to six months in 1974 and 1975, on a unit where handicapped students attending the University of Kentucky were treated. But a preliminary investigation by Lexington police and hospital authorities turned up no indications that he had murdered or attempted to injure anyone.

Shortly after his guilty pleas to the slayings at Marymount, Harvey acquiesced to pleas from Cincinnati *Enquirer* reporters and submitted to an interview in an office at the Laurel County Jail. He used the opportunity to repeat his defense that he was a highly motivated mercy killer who couldn't stand to see sick people suffer needlessly.

"Some of those might have lasted a few more hours or a few more days, but they were all going to die," he said. "I know you think I played God, and I did."

He conceded, however, that a few of his killings were inspired by more malevolent motivations, such as those of his two elderly neighbors when he was living with Hoeweler.

246

"They were threats to Carl. I did those out of love for Carl," he said.

The affable prisoner, who chatted animatedly while wolfing down a hot lunch of pork and beans, cabbage and beets, said he believed that his alleged rape by an older employee his first day on the job at Marymount might have triggered his crazed murder spree.

At times Harvey clearly enjoyed his notoriety and the attention he was getting from law-enforcement authorities and the press. He boasted and joked about his exploits. When a reporter recalled that his life sentences would keep him imprisoned until he was at least ninety-five, he smirked: "You never know. I might get out a few years early with good time. Maybe I'd only be seventy-five or eighty."

But his murder spree was no joke to law-enforcement authorities or to embarrassed hospital administrators. And shortly after Harvey's sentence was announced in Kentucky, Handy disclosed that at least one other individual was being investigated for crimes possibly committed in London while Harvey was working at the hospital there. Although Handy said the suspected crimes were not connected to the slayings, he admitted that the information was turned up as a result of the serial murder investigation. He declined to specify their nature.

The garrulous killer, however, had talked during interrogations and interviews of being raped at Marymount; of mysteriously missing drugs at the hospital; and of a homosexual love affair with a man who worked at a London funeral home and used corpses in lurid Satanic rituals.

Harvey was coyly evasive when he was asked if he himself had participated in satanic rites, replying only that he had been a Baptist, a Mormon, and a Catholic, and had a fascination with religions. He conceded that he had also been intrigued with the undertaking trade since he was a child. Funerals were important social events in the hills where he grew up, a time when family members and neighbors got together for eating, story-telling, and reminiscing, he pointed out.

Despite his demonstrated readiness to snuff out the lives of others, Harvey remained anxious to preserve his own, even if

247

his remaining years had to be spent behind bars. He seemed to be sincerely anxious not to neglect any of his victims. And in February 1988, a few weeks after a lengthy sit-down with investigators at the Southern Ohio Correctional Center in Lucasville where he was imprisoned, three more former patients were added to his previously acknowledged toll at Drake Memorial.

Harvey was indicted for killing Nathanial Watson by smothering him with a plastic bag and for the fatal cyanide poisoning of Henry Cody and Doris Nally. He was also indicted for the attempted murders of Willie Johnson and Anna Hood with arsenic, and of Lawrence Bernsden by repeatedly sprinkling rat poison in his food. Bernsden and Mrs. Hood died several months after they were poisoned by Harvey, and coroner's investigators were unable to establish definitely that he caused their deaths. Johnson's food was laced with arsenic several times over a six-week period, but each time he vomited up the poison and survived.

The former orderly used the term, "torture" in describing his diabolically cruel murder of Watson. The terminology was devilishly appropriate. He said he alternately pressed a plastic bag and a towel over the patient's mouth, allowing him to gasp desperately for breath before repeating the process. He kept the torture up until Watson no longer showed any remaining signs of life. Harvey later told Ney that he wanted the man to know that he was going to die. Prior to the confession, Watson's cause of death was listed as a pulmonary embolism.

The other two victims were killed with either arsenic or cyanide. Mrs. Nally's death certificate listed possible heart problems as the cause of her death, and recurrent pneumonia was blamed for the demise of Cody, a retired barber who had suffered a stroke.

When Mrs. Nally was killed, Harvey waited until her daughter left the hospital room, then slipped poison into his patient's apple juice. The woman died as soon as she took a first tentative sip of the deadly cocktail. Harvey also spiked apple juice with poison to kill Cody. He forced the concoction down the helpless man's feeding tube.

When Johnson learned that Harvey had attempted to kill him, he was shocked. "He used to take good care of me, and I thought he was good," he said.

Harvey pleaded guilty to the new charges and additional prison sentences were added to be served concurrently with the others.

Despite his admission of a string of eighteen or more murders at the VA Medical Center in Cincinnati, no charges were filed. Harvey talked with the federal investigators without the benefit of a plea-bargain agreement. Authorities pointed out that he was already in prison for life, and there was no federal death penalty that applied to his case, so he had nothing to fear. The investigation was kept open by the FBI, however.

Even though more than fifty murders were cleared with Harvey's admissions and it appears that he is safely behind bars for the rest of his life, disturbing questions were left unanswered. His perverse crimes left deep and lasting emotional scars on the communities of Cincinnati, London—even on his smalltown boyhood home in Island Springs—that may never heal.

Emotional wounds that had begun to close after the deaths of relatives were ripped open anew with the dreadful news that loves ones had been murdered in their beds, sometimes dying in horrible agony. Private grief became public, and took on a new dimension of torment. Anticipating the shock and renewed grieving, Ney enlisted the assistance of professional therapists to help break the news to survivors. Counseling sessions were set up, and in some cases continued long after Harvey's guilty pleas and sentencing.

Steve Sunderland, a professor of social work at the University of Cincinnati and a member of the board of Parents of Murdered Children, a nationally organized advocate for the families of crime victims, explained that some survivors were likely to be nagged with doubts and blame themselves for hospitalizing their loved ones.

"These people will all be thinking, 'My God! I put my father, or brother, or husband out there, and then this happened to him,'" he said.

Sunderland warned that the entire community was thrown

into shock as unthinkable questions were raised. "It tells us that this horror was possible at an institution that we trusted," he said.

The public's faith and confidence in hospitals where Harvey killed his victims was severely shaken and the reverberations of his crimes forever changed the lives of public officials and hospital employees, as well as relatives of the victims. Stunned survivors repeatedly expressed their shock and disbelief over his ability to continue killing for such a long time before his crimes were exposed. Unsurprisingly, official finger-pointing began almost immediately after the shocking revelations by the WCOP-TV news team alerted Cincinnatians that they had a serial killer in their midst.

One of the first questions asked was why Harvey had been permitted to resign from the VA without facing criminal charges after being caught with the loaded gun, stolen tissue sample, syringes, and other suspicious items. And why, tearful relatives of victims demanded to know, hadn't authorities at Drake Memorial investigated Harvey's background when he applied for his new job some seven months after his forced resignation from the VA Medical Center? VA spokesmen responded to the second query by remarking that federal privacy laws prohibited their passing on information about Harvey's troubles there to his new employers.

Some hospital employees angrily complained that after revelation of the murder spree, the administration was more concerned with protecting the institution's image than with the welfare of the patients. And many also struggled to deal with their own sense of guilt for not recognizing earlier what was going on and for not insisting on an inquiry into Harvey's activities.

Harvey's case and the lawsuits also touched off a nasty squabble at the VA Medical Center. The Government Accountability Project, GAP, charged that a terrible record of mismanagement at the VA facility had been exposed by the hospital murders. Tom Carpenter, an attorney for the GAP, an independent organization which functions as an advocate for the rights of federal employees who report misconduct, demanded a thorough investigation of what he claimed was "incompetence, brutality, and abuse of authority" at the VA.

The GAP was representing three former police officers who claimed they were fired after accusing the chief of security at the hospital of physical brutality toward patients and visitors.

One of the employees, former VA security officer John Berter, claimed that Harvey couldn't be charged because the hospital's police chief botched the case by conducting an illegal search of the autopsy assistant's gym bag. Berter also claimed that he was ordered by a superior to lie about the reason for confronting the suspect orderly the day before Harvey resigned.

A spokesman for the Vietnam Veterans of America also called on the U.S. Congress to investigate hiring and firing practices at the VA, as a result of the manner in which the Harvey case was handled at the medical center. A shower of civil lawsuits were filed against Harvey, Hamilton County, and hospital officials in both Ohio and Kentucky seeking nearly two hundred million dollars in damages in state and federal courts. A seventy-five-million-dollar action filed by the estate of one of the victims, claimed that there was such callous disregard for the welfare of patients that staff members frivolously placed bets on which one would be the next to die.

Early in 1989, just as it appeared Harvey was about to fade into obscurity, he announced that he might have remembered additional murders. Prosecutors hurried to the Southern Ohio Correctional Facility at Lucasville where he was imprisoned, but after a brief conference with his attorney, Harvey decided against talking about the other possible killings.

At a press conference shortly after the aborted inquiry, Ney said he thought that Harvey was simply bored and was making a play for media attention.

"Mr. Harvey has been up there for about a year now," Ney said. "He's a charming fellow who has not had any notoriety lately."

FOURTEEN

Nurses Who Kill in Europe

Gurgling in agony, her aged limbs flailing, the elderly woman lay helpless as four shadowy figures hovered over her bed.

The pathetic victim had no chance as her heftily built tormentors pinned her firmly to the mattress with their weight.

One of them grabbed her gray-haired head, holding it steady. Another pinched her nose firmly, wrenching the frail old lady's toothless mouth wide open and held her tongue as another calmly poured water into the victim's mouth.

The attackers giggled insanely among themselves as their victims convulsions grew weaker and weaker. Slowly, she drowned to death.

It could have been a scene in a torture room in a 1940's Nazi concentration camp.

But instead of jackbooted, sadistic killers, the torturers in this case were four highly regarded nurse's aides. It was the 1980's. And their victim was simply "a nuisance," another aged patient in a respectable hospital in Vienna, Austria, where the evil Angels of Death were accused of sadistically killing as many as three hundred elderly people over a six-year period.

The Vienna horror story—described as the worst-ever case of its kind in European history—rocked a nation trying to erase its wartime Nazi connections and its notoriety as the birthplace of Adolf Hitler.

Its cruelty and magnitude certainly eclipses any of the American cases discussed in preceding chapters. And it establishes without a doubt that hospital homicide is an international plague. The wings of the Angels of Death carry them to all parts of the globe.

No nation has a monopoly on murder—and there is no safe sanctuary as this horrifying look at international health-care homicides graphically illustrates.

VIENNA, AUSTRIA: "This one gets a ticket to God." These terrifying words signaled the death of as many as three hundred patients over a six-year period, ending in 1989 at the sedate, respected Lainz Hospital, the fourth largest hospital in the country's capital with a staff of two thousand strong.

The nightmare came to a halt after the murderous group of four were arrested and jailed when they confessed to murdering sixty-four of their elderly charges. But authorities placed the death toll much higher.

Leading an almost satanic double life was the ringleader, thirty-year-old Waltraud Wagner, a single woman considered by colleagues to be among the nicest nurses in the hospital.

She began the killing spree in 1983 when a seventy-seven-year-old dying woman patient asked Wagner to put her out of her misery. Wagner obliged with a double injection of morphine.

"The woman died, and at that point she felt like God, with the power of life and death," revealed a police investigator.

Wagner soon recruited three other aides as accomplices—Maria Gruber, 27, the unwed mother of a baby son; Irene Leidoff, 28, a married woman; and Stephanie Mayer, a 49-year-old divorced grandmother.

"Wagner awakened their sadistic instincts," said police. "Soon they were running a concentration camp, not a hospital ward. At the slightest sign of annoyance or complaint from a patient, they'd plan that patient's murder for the following night.

253

"For a patient who rang his night bell four times asking for help . . . for one who snored too loudly . . . for others who soiled their bed, Wagner would declare, 'This one gets a ticket to God.' "

As well as injections, the brutal nurses devised what they laughingly called "the water cure." This involved pinning vulnerable patients to the bed, holding their tongues and pinching their noses, and pouring glasses of water down their throats. Since many old people die of fluid in the lungs, the crime would go undetected. Observed Dr. Alois Stacher, head of Vienna's hospital services: "Though this is a painful death, it leaves absolutely no suspicious traces."

The wing of the hospital where the four worked is known as Pavilion Five, but is cryptically nicknamed "the Death Pavilion." The doctor in charge of Pavilion Five, Dr. Franz Pesendorfer, was suspended from duty shortly after the nurse's aides were arrested.

Wagner told police: "Of course the patients resisted, but we were stronger! We could decide whether these old fogies lived or died. Their ticket to God was long overdue in any case."

Wagner also admitted administering a heavy dose of narcotics to another trusting patient. "To her amusement, he went delirious. She watched him go totally out of his mind—then climb out of a window and leap to his death," reported Austrian crime reporter Pieter Grotter.

"The nurses used to meet after work for coffee and beer. They would sit around and joke about their murders, toast their victims, and trade killing techniques," reported *Bunte*, West Germany's largest news magazine. The four accused were all from rural villages in and around Vienna. They were considered to be poorly paid. All were Austrian, with the exception of Mayer, who came to the country from Yugoslavia two years earlier.

"Not since the Holocaust has Europe seen such horror . . . these cruel killings are beyond the imagination," said a police spokesman.

The barbaric nature of the case prompted a horrified outcry at the highest level of government.

"This has to be the most brutal and gruesome crime in Austria's history," Chancellor Franz Vranitzky told his cabinet.

"The death angels of Lainz remind me of the death angels of Auschwitz," said Vienna Mayor Helmit Zilk on television.

Many Austrians, just as outraged by the killings as the mayor, winced at his reference to Nazi atrocities. Austria has spent forty years trying to bury its wartime past. Austria's ties to the Nazis were spotlighted a short time before when, despite allegations he was a Nazi war criminal, the country elected Kurt Waldheim its president.

Investigators revealed that there had been rumors of murders in the accused's wing of the hospital for some time. But doctors and nurses refused to take the murder gossip seriously. But the four women were heard to laugh and joke about their deeds in wine bars. In fact, the overheard whispers in a bar by a doctor finally triggered the crucial investigation that ended six years of bizarre killings.

Orkdal, NORWAY: It took five years before the ostensibly kind medical supervisor of an old folks home in this peaceful little town was unmasked as the worst mass murderer in the history of Scandinavia.

"I am able to decide over life and death," former Salvation Army officer, Dr. Arnfinn Nesset, a forty-four-year-old father of two, told detectives when they arrested him for murdering as many as 138 patients during a five-year spree.

"I was doing God's bidding when I killed."

Dr. Nesset disposed of his victims with an injection of Curacit, a form of the exotic South American dart poison, curare. Then for five agonizing minutes he prayed with his victims for deliverance, as the poison paralyzed their breathing muscles.

Dr. Per Broch, the medical official investigating the case, said: "He had twelve thousand milligrams in stock, enough to kill more than three hundred people. Thank God, he was discovered before he killed more."

Dr. Nesset's undoing came following the death of a lively eighty-nine-year-old woman. A nurse found unexplained needle marks on the patient's arm. "I did the only thing I could," the nurse testified. "I went to Dr. Nesset and told him what I had found. He tried to tell me he had taken blood samples. But blood tests were not listed in her medical file. I knew I had to ask why. That's when he broke down and told me what he had been doing these past five years."

Dr. Nesset often held hands with dying patients and comforted them about their "reward in heaven."

"Life will be happier for you there," he admitted telling them. "There you will be reunited with your departed loved ones. You will find release, far from the pain and sorrow of this world."

Then he would administer the curare, which he had purchased from an unsuspecting druggist by claiming he needed it to put his dog to sleep.

At police headquarters, Dr. Nesset excused his actions, saying: "It may seem cruel, but I am sure I have been kind. I could not just stand by and watch those old people die slowly, painfully, as they certainly would have. I helped them through the abyss of death's darkness to their own salvation on the other side. They prayed for me to help them. I only did what I could, the only way I knew how."

At his trial, Nesset's defense proved confusing. At one stage, he said he murdered the old people because he was "investigating the line between life and death." Another time, he claimed: "I was only the unwilling instrument of voices from beyond."

A psychiatrist witness testified that, in his opinion, Dr. Nesset got a depraved kind of sexual charge every time he murdered one of his unfortunate clients.

But a jury in Trondheim, Norway, convicted Nesset of murder, rejecting pleas he was insane or a sexual deviant. He was jailed for twenty-one years.

Malmo, SWEDEN: A seventeen-year-old hospital worker confessed to poisoning one of his twenty-three victims in a hospital geriatric ward here because the patient was "harassing" him.

256

Anders Hansson, a nurse's aide, was charged in what was called Sweden's worst serial murder after being arrested for feeding an old woman a deadly brew composed of a disinfectant mixed with fruit juice. Police said he was caught redhanded.

He told police he began his bizarre serial "mercy killings" shortly after he began work because he felt the patients' lives at the geriatric ward "had no meaning."

But at his arraignment he told police he poisoned one of his twenty-three victims because the patient "harassed him and other personnel," police said.

Two days later, the young aide told police he poisoned his patients because, "I could not stand to see them suffer."

"He shows no remorse," District Attorney Sten Rumerheim said of the hospital worker. "He seems to have a mental block protecting him from seeing the gravity of his deed."

The rising death rate at the hospital had been a cause for concern two months after Hansson started work.

Several nurses reported their patients died in great pain, but police initially believed they were the victims of massive infections.

The matter remained a mystery until a nurse heard screams from a ninety-four-year-old woman patient who was being given poison by the young killer.

"The moment I smelled that acid, memories of strange events from the last months fell into place," nurse Gun-Britt Nilsson said. "I remembered all the swollen tongues and lips – the burns in dead patients' throats." The ninety-four-year-old woman survived, along with four other patients the youth had tried to poison on his last day at work.

There was a bizarre postscript to the Hansson case. In 1985, two years after the young aide died in prison under mysterious circumstances at the age of twenty-one, a former senior physician at the Eastern Mental Hospital in Malmo, Dr. Jorgen Svenonious, came forward and made a startling allegation.

Dr. Svenonious caused a sensation when he called a press conference and alleged the Swedish government was behind the killings in the hospital's geriatric ward six years earlier. The youth Hansson, he claimed, was merely a scapegoat framed by the government.

The doctor said the government was responsible for the cold-blooded murder of more than two hundred elderly bed-ridden patients in state-controlled hospitals. He alleged it was all part of a secret conspiracy to cut costs in Sweden's socialized medicine system.

Dr. Svenonious, who said he feared for his own life, claimed: "Hansson had the intelligence of a bright five-year-old. Before he even came to work at the hospital, patients were disappearing. I started my own investigation when I saw a sharp rise in deaths."

The doctor refused to elaborate on his bizarre claims. He said that documents substantiating his allegation were on file with his lawyers and were to be made public should anything happen to him. There, the mystery rests.

Liverpool, ENGLAND: Pensioner Abraham Rosenfield thought he'd found a friend in caring nurse Ruth Thomas. Her kind words and bright smile brought a little ray of sunshine into the sixty-seven-year-old's life.

Mr. Rosenfield met his new friend when he arrived at the Sharon Jewish Rest Home in the seaside vacation town of Southport for a two-week holiday. He was impressed by her charm, and confided his secrets to her.

Yet, within days of his arrival, the "kindly" state-registered nurse repaid the old man's trust in a way later described to Liverpool Crown Court as "merciless, cold-blooded, and inhumane."

As the retired tailor relaxed in the holiday home, thirty-seven-year-old Thomas dispatched her boyfriend to plunder his life savings of thirty thousand dollars, then battered her elderly charge senseless with a bottle and left him for dead in a pool of blood.

But she never reckoned on the old man's will to live. He survived and helped police expose Thomas as an Angel of Death with a history of preying on trusting people.

258

Thomas was jailed for ten years after admitting attempted murder. Today, from her prison cell, Ruth Thomas blames tranquilizer addiction and heavy drinking for her diabolical activities. "I feel physically sick when I think of what's happened," she says.

The divorced mother of two began preying on vulnerable people in 1989, while working at another Southport home. She overdosed the seventy-year-old owner with sedatives and stole two thousand dollars from her while she recovered in the hospital.

"It was her first venture into crime and it must have seemed easy," says Detective Inspector Philip Walker, who investigated the case. "There was only one motive—greed."

Thomas shared the cash with twenty-five-year-old health-care assistant Sara Wrighton, who was to become her partner in crime.

Wrighton was with her when she persuaded old Mr. Rosenfield to tell the evil pair where he had stashed the thirty thousand dollars. Thomas then sent her boyfriend, Rab Burns, to Mr. Rosenfield's home in Manchester to steal his nest egg.

Knowing the old man would soon discover the theft, Thomas decided to make it appear he'd committed suicide. She told card-loving Mr. Rosenfield that she was planning a late-night poker party for him.

In June, Thomas and Wrighton arrived at the unsuspecting pensioner's room with a party surprise—a bottle of whiskey spiked with a deadly cocktail of the drugs Temazepam and Chlorohydrate. They plied him with the cocktail until he slumped into unconsciousness. Then nurse Thomas proceeded to batter him with the bottle.

Calmly, the two women wiped their fingerprints from the bottle and placed it near their victim. While Abraham Rosenfield lay bleeding, naked, and unconscious, the two nurses coolly ate their supper.

But Mr. Rosenfield refused to die. Next morning, when Thomas returned to his room, she was shocked to find him still alive. Unabashed, the calculating nurse telephoned the police.

"Mr. Rosenfield has a drink problem," the callous nurse lied to ambulancemen. "He's hurt himself." As Mr. Rosenfield remembered nothing, no one suspected the truth.

But, after three days in Southport General Infirmary, he went home to find his life savings gone. That's when he called the police and when luck ran out for Thomas and her partners-in-crime.

Thomas and Wrighton were arrested the next day after police found some of Mr. Rosenfield's money at their homes.

Thomas, Wrighton, and Burns, the boyfriend, appeared in court together. Thomas admitted drugging the rest-home owner and attempting to murder Mr. Rosenfield, helping Burns commit the thirty-thousand-dollar burglary, and an additional charge of robbing the old man of seven hundred dollars in cash.

Sara Wrighton admitted drugging Rosenfield and to two charges of handling stolen goods, while Rab Burns admitted stealing the thirty thousand dollars.

Mr. Justice Sanderson Temple said the nurses' behavior was almost beyond belief. Thomas hung her head as he told them: "The facts are horrific. The conduct of you two women was revolting and abominable."

He jailed Thomas for ten years and Wrighton for four and a half, putting Burns on probation.

Meanwhile, Mr. Rosenfield survives on state benefits. Police recovered only fourteen thousand dollars of his savings—all of which went on medical bills. He is suing the Sharon Rest Home for failing to protect him.

Ruhr, WEST GERMANY: Is a nurse who gave lethal injections to her critically ill patients a victim of her own compassion or a cruel, callous thrill-killer? That is the question which has divided West Germans attending the bizarre trial of Michaela Roeder.

Roeder was jokingly called the Angel of Death by her colleagues in a Ruhr intensive care clinic because so many patients died while she was on duty, and the German press has subsequently dubbed her the Mistress of Life and Death.

"I just wanted to put an end to the agony these people were suffering," Roeder said after confessing to police to murdering nine patients between 1984 and 1986.

Yet many of her victims were on the road to recovery and some were looking forward to leaving the ICU.

After her confession, police ordered autopsies on all patients who had died in her care and discovered that seventeen had been given Clonidine, a drug that lowers blood pressure and can cause the heart to stop beating—without a doctor's order.

In several cases, Clonidine had been combined with a cardiac-paralyzing drug called Chloride of Kalium.

Roeder set herself up as a "goddess of life and death," said prosecutor Karl-Herman Majorowsky. "These murders were coldly executed for somber motives."

Prior to her arrest, no one at Ruhr's St. Petrus Hospital suspected that the thirty-year-old nurse was anything but hardworking and dedicated to her job. She was so dedicated, a court heard, that she quickly killed seventy-seven-year-old Gertrud Horch so she could sit down and watch a televised soccer match between West Germany and Italy.

"I did it out of compassion," she told police after her arrest.

Another of her victims was feeling so good he asked his relatives to bring him a book to read. But he didn't get as far as the first page.

At first, the hospital staff joked about Roeder's "run of bad luck." They were accustomed to seeing death in the intensive care ward, but started to wonder when seventeen patients died in Roeder's care.

Then male nurse Stefan Judick saw her blatantly giving a cancer patient a lethal dose of potassium chloride. The game was up.

"I couldn't bear to see these people suffer anymore," Roeder told the police. "All my life I wanted to help people in need."

But the public prosecutor described her as a cold-blooded murderess who didn't care who she killed.

"She killed for satisfaction, and as an exhibition of her power," said Majorowsky. "She enjoyed making decisions about who was to live and who wasn't. She considered herself the master over life and death."

In her diary police discovered details of the deaths of some patients, including that of a ninety-four-year-old man who had a broken leg. Her treatment of him, she wrote, "worked splendidly."

Another entry spoke about a woman being transferred to the mortuary "according to her own wishes."

Majorowsky said Roeder showed no mercy in her scribbling, only "cynicism and brutality."

PINNACLE'S HORROW SHOW

BLOOD BEAST   (17-096, $3.95)
by Don D'Ammassa
No one knew where the gargoyle had come from. It was just an
ugly stone creature high up on the walls of the old Sheffield Library. Little Jimmy Nicholson liked to go and stare at the gargoyle. It seemed to look straight at him, as if it knew his most
secret desires. And he knew that it would give him everything he'd
ever wanted. But first he had to do its bidding, no matter how
evil.

LIFE BLOOD   (17-110, $3.95)
by Lee Duigon
Millboro, New Jersey was just the kind of place Dr. Winslow
Emerson had in mind. A small township of Yuppie couples who
spent little time at home. Children shuttled between an overbur-
dened school system and every kind of after-school activity. A
town ripe for the kind of evil Dr. Emerson specialized in. For
Emerson was no ordinary doctor, and no ordinary mortal. He
was a creature of ancient legend of mankind's darkest nightmare.
And for the citizens of Millboro, he had arrived where they least
expected it: in their own backyards.

DARK ADVENT   (17-088, $3.95)
by Brian Hodge
A plague of unknown origin swept through modern civilization
almost overnight, destroying good and evil alike. Leaving only a
handful of survivors to make their way through an empty land-
scape, and face the unknown horrors that lay hidden in a savage
new world. In a deserted midwestern department store, a few
people banded together for survival. Beyond their temporary haven, an evil was stirring. Soon all that would stand between the
world and a reign of insanity was this unlikely fortress of human-
ity, armed with what could be found on a department store shelf
and what courage they could muster to battle a monstrous, merciless scourge.

*Available wherever paperbacks are sold, or order direct from the
Publisher. Send cover price plus 50¢ per copy for mailing and
handling to Pinnacle Books, Dept. 17-449, 475 Park Avenue
South, New York, N.Y. 10016. Residents of New York, New Jer-
sey and Pennsylvania must include sales tax. DO NOT SEND
CASH.*